BY DR. HUME

TRANSLATION OF
The Thirteen Principal Upanishads
FROM THE SANSKRIT

EDITOR AND COMPILER OF
Treasure-House of The Living Religions

THE WORLD'S
LIVING RELIGIONS

THE WORLD'S LIVING RELIGIONS

WITH SPECIAL REFERENCE
TO THEIR SACRED SCRIPTURES
AND IN COMPARISON
WITH
CHRISTIANITY

An Historical Sketch
by
ROBERT ERNEST HUME, Ph.D., D.Théol.

formerly Professor
of the History of Religions,
Union Theological Seminary, New York

COMPLETELY REVISED

CHARLES SCRIBNER'S SONS
New York

Printed in the United States of America
Library of Congress Catalog Card Number 58-12515

ISBN 0-684-15611-3

PREFACE
TO THE REVISED EDITION

1959

WHEN the publishers wrote and asked that I read this book, which has for so many years been a familiar title to persons concerned with the religions of the world, and advise them as to whether or not it ought to be revised or rewritten, I agreed to do so. I was already familiar with the book, having used it on many occasions and assigned parts of it to be read by students from time to time. But this time I read it with special care, having in mind that I must pass judgment upon it and possibly condemn it to pass out of print or give it a new lease on life by my report.

My considered judgment was that it merited revision. It is a very useful book in many respects. I do not know any other book quite like it. It is a simplified treatment—sometimes, perhaps over-simplified. It bases itself squarely on the sacred writings of the various faiths. No other book of its size cites so much original scripture. There are no frills about it. It is clearly and sharply outlined. One can get from it the salient facts concerning the religions about as easily as from any book ever written. But it could hardly be rewritten. If it were to be, it would probably be so different that it would be no longer Hume's book, and could hardly bear his name properly. Because I think there is value in Dr. Hume's name, I said the book ought simply to be revised at points required by new discoveries, or where the varying fortunes of races and cultures have brought about changes in the religions which must be reported. In other words, that revision ought to be chiefly a matter of bringing the book up to date.

When I was then asked to do the revising, I said that I would do so only on condition that it be done in this way. I would be quite willing to undertake to make the necessary changes to bring it into line with the present status of our knowledge of the religions of the world today, but I would not assume responsibility for changing any of the many value judgments expressed in the book, especially in the listing of the elements of strength and weakness in each faith, or in the comparison between religions. In many of these I do not concur. Indeed, I disagree sharply with some of them. But in Hume's book, published under his name, they have a right to stand. In one or two cases I did omit a judgment which seemed harsher than the present temper of even conservative Christian scholarship —and Hume was not of that group—would be likely to express in view of the increased sensitivity of representatives of other cultures to criticism from the Christian West. And I have added a footnote here and there noting exceptions to some of the more general statements of Dr. Hume concerning a given religion.

So the book continues, as in the past, to be Hume's *The World's Living Religions*. It is not the wholly objective approach which some may prefer. But many persons want guidance as to how to evaluate the religions as they come to them, perhaps for the first time, knowing nothing about any of them except Christianity. They need not accept Dr. Hume's judgments uncritically. Indeed, in a class these offer a point of departure for discussion which may prove highly fruitful because they provoke dissent from some members of the group. At any rate, a scholar and writer has the right to set forth his own ideas, and if people find his treatment useful, they have an equal right to accept it in whole or in part as they see fit. Evidently, many people have found it useful over the period of more than a generation. This revision extends the life of the book, and Dr. Hume continues to make his contribution to the understanding of the religions of the world as he knew them.

CHARLES S. BRADEN

Dallas, Texas
September 1958

PREFACE
TO THE FOURTEENTH PRINTING

THIS volume aims to furnish a concise survey of the origin, the sacred scriptures, the historical career, and the chief values of the organized religions of culture which have lived for more than a century. There are eleven such, only two of them being younger than Christianity.

Besides, there are in existence a few recent cults, more or less independent and active, which have arisen both in the Orient and in the Occident; and some of these have already become international. There is also animism, a long-lived form of religion, which still holds sway among primitive peoples; but it has not contributed, and is not likely to contribute, much to the civilization of the world. All the various systems of religion which have arisen and then which have ceased, are more numerous than the ones which are functioning now. The scope of this volume includes only those movements in mankind's religious life which have maintained continuous social organization, art and literature, as well as worship, through a succession of centuries.

In this large, but definite, field of the world's living religions there is an enormous bulk of complicated material which needs to be grasped and analyzed comprehensively and accurately. In every group of religionists there are operative, of course, various kinds of forces—climatic, economic, sociologic, nationalistic, etc. But the main differentiating characteristics are the ethical and religious ideals concerning man and the Divine which are continuously taught and accepted as sacred. Accordingly, the most important single systematic source of information among the historic religions is their canonical scriptures. The author has found very rewarding the results of learning to handle in their original languages the sacred texts of most of the religions of the Near East, the Middle East and the Far East. And a special feature of this presentation is the method of presenting the main historical facts and the teachings of each religion by means of citations from its own sacred documents.

This short volume is the concentrated result of a long course of gathering material and of testing it. There were several years of vital personal contacts with the adherents of the religions of India, conversing and writing in one of the chief vernaculars of that country. Further field observations have been conducted on repeated journeys to several countries and on a journey around the world. Studying in three language-areas of Europe, lecturing at six of the colleges and universities of India, and teaching for many years in the United States have helped to an understanding of the interests of students and teachers as well as of the methods of gaining and presenting knowledge. Delightful friendships and professional interchange with leaders of many of the world's living religions have added much valuable information and insight.

Every religion is itself an attempt to compare and to conserve the higher values in human life through connection with the Supreme. Accordingly, after ascertaining the important historical facts, a thorough-going study of various religions properly proceeds to the making of careful scientific and evaluating comparisons. In concluding the study of each religion and in concluding the book as a whole, the author has attempted what every broad-minded student of religion attempts to make, namely, a comparative estimate which should be intelligent, friendly and fair.

A number of improvements have been made since the book was first published, fifty-four such being introduced in the fourteenth printing. And further improvements will be added as further knowledge is gained. The book has been translated and published in a foreign language.

The author hopes that the reader will find here the main historical facts presented with scholarly exactitude and also with a discerning appreciation of the essential features and the essential differences of the different religions. Surely there is ample incentive for further investigations and further evaluations of the religious faith of human beings in their relation with the Divine Power of the world.

R.E.H.

CONTENTS

RELIGIONS ORIGINATING
IN WEST ASIA
(PALESTINE, PERSIA, ARABIA)

ABBREVIATIONS USED

BT   *Buddhism in Translations,* by H. C. Warren, in Harvard Oriental Series. (Cambridge, Mass., 1909, 1923.)

ERE   *Encyclopædia of Religion and Ethics,* edited by James Hastings, 13 volumes. (Edinburgh, T. & T. Clark, and New York, Scribners, 1913–1922.)

EZ   *Early Zoroastrianism* by J. H. Moulton, in Hibbert Lectures, Second Series. (London, Williams & Norgate, 1913.)

SARJ   "Shinto, the Ancient Religion of Japan," by W. G. Aston, in *Religions Ancient and Modern* (London, Constable, 1910.)

SBE   *Sacred Books of the East,* edited by F. Max Müller, 50 volumes. (Oxford, 1879–1910.)

SWG   *Shinto, the Way of the Gods,* by W. G. Aston. (Longmans, Green, 1905.)

TASJ   *Transactions of the Asiatic Society of Japan.* (London, Trübner; Tokyo, Maruzen; Shanghai, Kelly & Walsh.)

TPU   *Thirteen Principal Upanishads,* by R. E. Hume. (Oxford, 1921; second edition, revised and enlarged, 1931.)

Trumpp   *The Adi Granth, or The Holy Scripture of the Sikhs, Translated from the Original,* by Ernest Trumpp. (London, Trübner, 1877.)

TTK   *Tao-Teh-King,* the chief sacred scripture of Taoism. See page 287.

A CONSPECTUS OF THE ELEVEN LIVING RELIGIONS OF THE WORLD

ARRANGED IN THE CHRONOLOGICAL ORDER OF THEIR ORIGIN

NAME	DATE OR BIRTH OF FOUNDER	FOUNDER	DEITY	PRESENT LOCATION	SCRIPTURES	NUMBER [1] IN MILLIONS OF ADHERENTS
Hinduism	1500 B. C.	None	Brahma, or various	India	Vedas	322
Judaism	1200 B. C.	Moses	Jehovah	Scattered; nearly half in N. America	Old Testament	12
Shinto	Nominally 660 B. C.	None	Nature-gods	Japan	Ko-ji-ki and Nihon-gi	79
Zoroastrianism, Parsi Religion	660 B. C.	Zoroaster	Ahura Mazda	Persia and India	Avesta	.14
Taoism	604 B. C.	Lao-tze	The Tao	China	Tao-Teh-King	50
Jainism	599 B. C.	Vardhamana, Mahavira	Originally none; now founder	India	Angas	1.6
Buddhism	560 B. C.	Gautama, Buddha	Originally none; now founder	The East	Tripitaka	150–275
Confucianism	551 B. C.	Confucius	Heaven, or founder	China	Classics	300
Christianity	4 (P) B. C.	Jesus Christ	Father-God	World	Bible	835
Islam	570 A. D.	Mohammed	Allah	Muslim countries	Koran (Qur'an)	420
Sikhism	1469 A. D.	Nanak	True Name	India	Granth	6.2

[1] These are only rough estimates in most cases.

I

RELIGION AND THE RELIGIONS

1. RELIGION UNIVERSAL TO MAN

Religion is the chief differentiating characteristic of man. Some animals may surpass some men in certain abilities, such as keenness of sense-perception, practical constructiveness, companionability, and economic productiveness, but no animal has to human knowledge displayed any evidences of religious life, nor has any animal ever done anything which might be interpreted as a preparation for a life beyond death. Certain human individuals do seem to be lacking in religious interest, just as they are lacking in the higher mental and moral interests, yet mankind as a whole is universally religious.

In the history of mankind there never has been a tribe of men without some form of religion. Even the bushmen of Central Australia and the Indians of Patagonia, who represent the lowest forms of existent human life, cherish some belief in the spirit world and engage in some kind of worship. In the oldest monuments of civilized man, as shown in the pyramids of Egypt and the early Vedic scriptures of India, religious convictions, aspirations, and practices are in evidence.

Religion has been one of the most powerful factors in human history. Other aspects of human life have indeed been important, yet the pre-eminently noble characteristic of man throughout his entire history has been his religion. He is convinced that he stands in certain superhuman relations, and is satisfied that he has received needed superhuman help.

2. THE FUNCTION OF RELIGION

Religion gives to a person what he can obtain from no other source—a confidence in the outcome of life's struggles through a personal connection with the superior Power or powers in the world. Every religion does many things for the religious individual and also usually for society. For example, it assists in providing the individual with added power and satisfaction; it helps him to bear the troubles of life uncomplainingly; it offers a solution of the problem of evil; it improves the quality of this present life; it offers the hope of a better life in the future; it outlines an ideal society; it sets a working plan of salvation.

The distinguishing function of religion, in contrast with that of philosophy or ethics, or any of the idealizing or cultural activities, is to give to a human being the supreme satisfaction of his life through vital relationship with what he recognizes as the superhuman Power, or powers, in the world.

3. AN ANALYSIS OF RELIGION

Religion is so simple that any intelligent child, as well as an adult, may have a real religious experience. Religion is also so inclusive and complex that it needs to be analyzed so as to be completely understood and fully enjoyed. It may be defined in simple terms as that aspect of a person's experience, including his thoughts, feelings, and actions, whereby he endeavors to live in relationship with what he deems to be the Divine, *i. e.,* the supremely worthful Power controlling in the world.

From a psychological point of view, religion is partly intellectual, partly emotional, and partly an act of the will. But religion involves more than merely a subjective experience. It always has some reference to an object of faith and of worship. What constitutes a person's religion is his belief in some God, or gods, and his experience of that God, or gods.[1]

[1] Not all scholars define religion in this way. Some prefer to define it from the standpoint of the motives which underlie the behavior which is called religious. For example, one defines it as "the cooperative quest for a completely satisfying life." According to this definition, persons could be considered religious though their behavior might not seem to be religious according to the definition given here. Such persons might conceivably neither believe in nor worship a divine being or beings and still be considered religious by the proponents of this newer type of definition. Some modern humanists certainly consider themselves religious while denying that there is any divine aid available to man. If this be accepted as religion, it becomes

What differentiates one particular religion from another is the kind of deity in which its adherents believe and the kind of human experience which appropriately follows from that belief.

4. THE ESSENTIAL CHARACTERISTICS OF A DEITY

Whatever has become an object of supreme religious belief, worship, and experience will be found to possess at least five characteristics:

(1) It is superhuman in character and in power, even though in some respects a deity is like unto a human being; (2) it is supersensuous or invisible, even though in certain aspects the deity may be represented in material ways; (3) it is controlling; that is, a deity is believed to exercise some rule over the natural world and over human welfare and destiny; (4) it is responsive to the efforts of the human being who acts religiously; (5) it is worshipful or adorable, arousing in the human religionist such emotions and actions as awe, reverence, trust, obedience, co-operation, or submission.

Every deity is complex in character, just as every worshipper is complex. But every human being who is truly religious must have had experience with a deity which is believed to possess these five foregoing characteristics.

5. SOME ALTERNATIVES IN THE CONCEPTION OF DEITY

A deity of some kind is an indispensable feature of religion. Nevertheless, a person's actual conception of deity, even with those five characteristics, varies greatly. For example:

(1) As to number, there are some polytheistic religions with many deities, and there are four monotheistic religions which recognize only one deity.

---

desirable to distinguish those religions which involve a divine being or beings as theistic; the others as humanistic religions. Thus, if Communism be regarded as a religion, as it is by many, it must be classified as humanistic rather than theistic. Most of the religion of the world is, of course, theistic.

(2) As to personality, there are two religions, viz., philosophic Hinduism and Taoism, which teach that the supreme deity is an impersonal metaphysical being or abstract principle, while popular Hinduism and popular Taoism, and all the other religions teach that deity is personal.

(3) As to power, Islam teaches that the one supreme personal deity is unlimitedly omnipotent; Zoroastrianism teaches that the one personal deity's power is limited from outside himself by an opposing cosmic power; Christianity teaches that the one deity's power is limited by moral responsibility to himself, and by moral responsibility to human personalities.

(4) As to moral responsibility, Islam regards the one supreme personal deity as an arbitrary, irresponsible personality; Confucianism and Christianity insist that the supreme deity is consistently responsible.

(5) As to the chief virtue of deity, Zoroastrianism and Confucianism regard deity as supremely just; Christianity regards deity as supremely loving.

A fair comparison of Christianity with the other religions of the world may be based upon these important contrasts. Christianity is not unique as regards the first four of these five possible contrasts. Yet at each possible alternative Christianity selects the more difficult and the higher characteristic.

The peculiarly unique feature in the Christian conception of God is that His power, while not metaphysically limited by any other power outside Himself, is qualified by the divine characteristic of regard for moral personality. A Christian normally thinks of God as cherishing redemptive love toward men.

6. VARYING EMPHASES IN THE CONCEPTION OF RELIGION

Religion is so rich and comprehensive that different aspects of it, quite properly, seem important to different temperaments. For example:

(1) The intellectual emphasis has been expressed by Max Müller:

Religion is a mental faculty or disposition, which independent of, nay in spite of, sense and reason, enables man to apprehend the Infinite under different names and under varying guises. *Introduction to the Science of Religion*, 1882, 13.)

(2) The moral emphasis has been expressed in two famous historic definitions of religion by Immanuel Kant and Matthew Arnold:

Religion is the recognition of all duties as divine commands. (*Critique of Practical Reason*, translated by Abbott, 226.)

Religion is morality touched by emotion. (*Literature and Dogma*, 46.)

(3) The emotional emphasis has been expressed by the great theologian, Schleiermacher:

The essence of religion is the feeling of absolute dependence. (*Discourses on Religion*, chap. 2.)

(4) The emphasis on worship has been made by Allan Menzies:

Religion is the worship of higher powers from the sense of need. (*History of Religion*, 13.)

(5) An emphasis on self-advantage has been expressed by Albert Réville, one of the early modern historians of religion:

Religion rests, above all, upon the need of man to realize an harmonious synthesis between his own destiny and the opposing influences he meets in the world. (*Religions of Non-Civilized Peoples*, 1. 120.)

(6) A very favorite modern emphasis is the social emphasis, defined thus by Professor Edward Scribner Ames:

Religion is the consciousness of the highest social values. (*Psychology of Religious Experience*, vii.)

(7) Another emphasis, quite different, is the individual emphasis which has been stated with extreme precision in a well-known volume by Professor William James:

Religion, therefore, as I now ask you arbitrarily to take it, shall mean for us the feelings, acts and experiences of individual men in their solitude, so far as they apprehend themselves to stand in relation to whatever they may consider the divine. (*Varieties of Religious Experience*, 31.)

(8) Religion as the supreme idealizing process is the point of view presented by Professor G. W. Stratton:

Religion is the appreciation of an unseen world, usually an unseen company; and religion is also whatever seems clearly to be moving toward such an appreciation, or to be returning from it. Or perhaps, it might better be described as man's whole bearing toward what seems to him the Best or Greatest. (*Psychology of the Religious Life,* 343.)

(9) An emphasis which attempts to include all the others is finely expressed by Professor William Adams Brown:

By religion is meant the life of man in his superhuman relations; that is, his relation to the power on which he feels himself dependent, the authority to which he deems himself responsible, and the unseen being with whom he is capable of communing. In the ideal of religion dependence, responsibility and communion belong together. (*Christian Theology in Outline,* 29.) [1]

7. DIFFERENT APPROACHES TO THE STUDY OF RELIGION

Religion is so vast a subject that it cannot be exhausted by any single kind of investigation. It must be studied from many points of view. For example:

(1) One important approach is the historical. Along with the economic, geographical, political, cultural, and other factors which have influenced human history, religion, too, must be studied, particularly because of its tendency to organize communities of people around a religious faith in a superhuman Power or powers.

(2) A favorite new approach is psychological, which studies religion as a characteristic of man, involving his entire equipment of thinking, feeling, and willing.

(3) Religion must also be studied philosophically, as part of the human quest for a knowledge of supreme reality. It is

---

[1] See "A Symposium—The Definition of Religion," *Journal of Religion,* Vol. 7, pp. 113–135, and "Trends in the Re-definition of Religion," *Journal of Religion,* Vol. 8, pp. 434–453, for an extended discussion of the definition of religion.

differentiated from philosophy, because religion is an attempt, not merely to know about, but also to live in vital relation with, the Supreme.

(4) Religion may also be studied as one of man's many social activities, yet only as he endeavors through religion to produce an ideal social order by means of a vital relationship with the Supreme Orderer or orderers operating the world.

(5) An especially rich approach is found in literature—in all those writings where man has endeavored to express in words his ideals and feelings, often seemingly beyond words, concerning the Supreme Being. Moreover, religion may be studied most advantageously in the sacred scriptures of each organized religion.

(6) The æsthetic approach must not be neglected. Religion has been one of man's many methods of appreciating, expressing, and creating beauty, not only through literature, but also through music, sculpture, architecture, and all the other arts. This is because the Supreme has been regarded specifically as the supremely beautiful.

(7) By an ethical approach religion may be viewed as man's effort to attain unto the supremely good kind of life for himself by a vital connection with what he deems the supremely good Power in control of the affairs of men.

(8) The most intimate approach is the personal. Every religion offers some specific method whereby a person may attain unto salvation through proper personal relation with the Being or beings in supreme control of human life.

(9) A comparative study of religion, now made thoroughly available by scholarly research, should not be overlooked. It is very surprising and very profitable to see the similarities and the differences in the beliefs which human beings still hold concerning the Supreme Being or beings, and the results of such beliefs in the life of the individual and of society.

It is clear that the study of religion deserves all the foregoing approaches, and every possible approach, if its abundant significance is fully to be understood.

8. SACRED SCRIPTURES AS A SPECIAL APPARATUS FOR STUDYING RELIGIONS

The most important advance in the understanding of religions in recent years has been made through the direct study of the sacred scriptures of the various organized religions. Most, though not all, of these important documents are now available in English translation. These render indispensable aid in solving the important problem of deciding what was the true form of any one of the eleven living religions in the world. For example, in the case of Christianity, how shall a person determine whether Greek Christianity or Roman Christianity or Protestant Christianity is the proper expression of that religion?

The teachings of the founder should in each case furnish an authoritative norm for all his followers. In the course of subsequent history these original principles have of course been elaborated and applied. Yet it is possible and necessary to go back to them by means of recent historical and linguistic research.

The sacred scriptures furnish the only uniform basis for reporting the various religions. In every one of the eleven living religions of the world the supreme seat of authority is located in, or connected with, their respective sacred scriptures. These always contain the teachings attributed to the original founder, in case there was one.

The difficulty of an accurate understanding of the scriptures will always remain a problem in the historical and comparative study of religions. To interpret worthily one's own religion is a task requiring much linguistic and historical knowledge. To secure a reliable knowledge of the eleven different religions, through their sacred scriptures, written in sixteen different languages, is a task formidable enough to baffle almost any student.

9. DIFFERENT STANDPOINTS IN COMPARING RELIGIONS

Every student of religion necessarily comes to it from some point of view. Sometimes he maintains this unconsciously; sometimes inconsistently. But it affects his interpretation.

(1) One standpoint is to condemn all religions whatsoever as being without exception the outcome of superstition, bigotry, heredity, or ignorance. This position of general depreciation is taken by some persons who have studied the different religions widely:

As there are a great many religions, so there are a great many limitations. And I propose to define religion as "A sum of scruples which impede the free exercise of our faculties." (Reinach, *Orpheus: A General History of Religions*, 3.)

(2) Another standpoint almost as uncritical condemns all non-Christian religions. This position is taken by some advocates of Christianity, even by those who have studied other religions considerably.

The Christian religion is altogether good. The false systems cannot be regarded as progressive steps toward the true. Christianity is the absolute religion; that is, it is wholly free from error. (Burrell, *Religions of the World*, 4.)

(3) A third standpoint, slightly more historical, condemns all non-biblical religions. It recognizes that Christianity is, historically and inextricably, connected with Judaism, and that the Christian Bible as a whole records one continuous course of religious development.

All the religions, save Christianity and the religion of Israel, belong to the natural stage. Biblical religion is the only purely moral religion. (*Non-Biblical Systems of Religion: A Symposium*, 199–200.)

(4) Another common standpoint is to condemn all other religions besides one's own, whichever that may be. This is the usual point of view of a person who has studied neither the history of other religions nor the history of his own faith. This attitude is just as common among Hindus as among Christians.

(5) A standpoint somewhat more charitable, but undiscriminating, premises that all religions contain some good, perhaps equally, at least enough good for their own followers. This position is typical of Theosophists, and also of those individuals who do not believe in any propaganda in religion.

Each religion has its own mission in the world, is suited to the nations to whom it is given, and to the type of civilization it is to permeate. (Besant, *Four Great Religions*, 7.)

(6) A last standpoint is that all religions contain some good, but unequally; yet the world needs to choose the very best. This view is held by an increasing number of intelligent, active, progressive Christians, who stand enthusiastically for the great missionary movement of the churches. It is also being adopted by a few recent advocates of several of the non-Christian religions. A striking illustration may be cited from an active Hindu writer of to-day:

In studying Western civilization I have felt that there is something wanting. This something India has. If we want to avert all future wars, even the possibility of war, we must humbly sit on a prayer-rug, instead of always rushing about in motor-cars. (Harendranath Maitra, *Hinduism, the World Ideal*, vii–viii.)

10. UNSCIENTIFIC CLASSIFICATIONS OF RELIGIONS

It has been quite common to classify religions in ways which are neither scientific nor truly helpful.

(1) Religions have been classified as true and false. This method uses no objective, scientific, or social test. It is an individualistic classification, which is usually based chiefly upon a person's ignorance or on his sympathies. A religion should be classified in accordance with an intelligent estimate of its worth.

(2) A traditional classification of religions is into natural and revealed. But these terms are correlative, not exclusive. Every religion is partly natural and partly revealed. The gaining of truth is a natural and normal process, conditioned by

the capacity of the individual to appropriate truth. It may also be viewed as a process of revelation, whereby God gives to the individual increasingly clear glimpses of truth.

(3) A very natural classification is along the line of personal choice. Every human being should indeed demand from his religion the fullest satisfaction for himself. Yet the person who is most fully religious will set up a social as well as an individual test for the religion of his choice. The complete test of religion should be from a twofold point of view. It should be good for others as well as good for himself. A person should ask himself and others: "Will this religion satisfy all mankind as it satisfies me?"

11. VARIOUS MATTER-OF-FACT
CLASSIFICATIONS

In passing from the unscientific classifications just noted it will be interesting to consider a number of purely objective classifications which, though valuable, do not all rest upon elements of real worth.

(1) Religions as dead or living. A dozen or more well-developed religions have passed off the scene, though most of them have left their mark on some one or more of the religions which have survived them: the religions of ancient Egypt in Africa; the religions of ancient Mexico and Peru in the Americas; the ancient religions of Babylonia and Assyria, of the Phoenicians and Hittites, Mithraism and Manichaeism in Asia Minor; the religions of ancient Greece and Rome, and those of the Celtic and Teutonic peoples of Europe.

The living religions are eleven, if Sikhism and Jainism, which grew out of Hinduism, are counted as separate religions. Some of these have only a very small present-day following and are limited to a relatively small area geographically. Two of them, Jainism and Zoroastrianism, have fewer followers than some of the sects of the great religions. Indeed, the followers of one of the offshoots of Islam in the modern period, the Bahai faith, are much more numerous than these, and much more widely scattered over the world. They definitely consider Bahai as one of the world religions. Taoism in China seems to be in eclipse, and Confucianism under the impact of the modern world and, in more recent years, of Communism, has suffered seriously. It is difficult to discover just what is happening in China at present. Buddhism is dormant in some countries, but very active in others. Hinduism is certainly alive. Some marked new tendencies are observable within it. Judaism suffered terrific losses in the European purge of the Jews just before and during the Second World War, but it is an active force in the post-war world. Both Christianity and Islam are intensely active on many fronts. All of the eleven are thus alive, though the future of some of them, especially Taoism, appears uncertain.

(2) Religions according to their geographical origin. Asia was the birthplace of every one of the world's living religions. They may be grouped, however, as follows: Hinduism, Jainism, Buddhism, and Sikhism originated in Southern Asia; Confucianism, Taoism, and Shinto originated in Eastern Asia; Judaism, Zoroastrianism, Islam, and Christianity originated in Western Asia.

(3) Religions arranged chronologically, according to the date of their founder. For the two religions which had no personal founder, the date assigned is the approximate or traditional date of origin.

Hinduism	2000–1500 B. C. (Aryan invasion of India).
Judaism	1500–1200 B. C. (approximate date of Moses).
Shinto	660 B. C. (first Japanese emperor).
Zoroastrianism	660 B. C. (latest possible date for Zoroaster).
Taoism	604 B. C. (nominal founder, Lao-tze).
Jainism	599 B. C. (nominal founder, Mahavira).
Buddhism	560 B. C. (Buddha's approximate birth-date).
Confucianism	551 B. C. (Confucius's approximate birth-date).
Christianity	4 B. C. (Jesus Christ's approximate birth-date).
Islam	570 A. D. (Mohammed's exact birth-date).
Sikhism	1469 A. D. (Guru Nanak's exact birth-date).

It is interesting to note that about the sixth century before Christ there was a period of unusual religious creativeness when six of the world's living religions originated. That same century was a period of great importance to Judaism.

(4) Religions according to the number of their adherents. Statistics, of course, are difficult to obtain and difficult to interpret correctly. Numbers do not count as the most vital factor in any religion. However, they do serve to indicate a certain general trend. In two countries, China and Japan, where three non-Christian religions are inextricably intermingled not only in the country at large, but even in the same individual, the figures assigned to the different religions are only approximate. However, the best available figures, compiled from many sources, are given below, expressed in round numbers:

Christianity	835 millions.
Confucianism	300 millions.
Islam	420 millions.
Hinduism	322 millions.
Buddhism	150–275 millions.
Taoism	50 millions.
Shinto	79 millions.[1]
Judaism	12 millions.
Sikhism	6.2 millions.
Jainism	1.6 million.
Zoroastrianism	.14 million.

Christianity has the largest nominal following of any of the living religions, indeed almost twice as many as any other. However, it must be remembered that there exists no method by which those who are truly Christians can be enumerated. For example, South America is classified as a Christian country, yet its population contains large numbers of genuine pagans.

(5) Religions according to their scope. There exist only three religions which aim to be truly universal; these, mentioned chronologically, are Buddhism, Christianity, and Islam. The other eight are hereditary or national, being satisfied with their own following.

[1] This figure is given in the 1956 *Religions Year Book of Japan*, but the sum of those counted as Buddhist and as Shintoists is much larger than the total Japanese population.

(6) Religions according to the conception of deity with which they started. Six were clearly theistic in origin: Sikhism, Taoism, Judaism, Zoroastrianism, Christianity, and Islam. Two, Jainism and Buddhism, started without emphasis on deity. The other three, Hinduism, Confucianism, and Shinto, grew out of a polytheistic nature-worship.

(7) Religions according to the number of deities recognized at present. Some of the world's living religions have passed through markedly different theological phases during the course of their history. For example, Judaism reached its belief in one sole God of the universe through its absolute loyalty to its own righteous God Jehovah, without denying the right of other nations to be loyal to their deities. Hinduism likewise, passed from a polytheistic nature-worship through various phases into a popular polytheistic idolatry, even while retaining the philosophic theory of one Supreme Being.

The situation may fairly be summarized as follows: Four religions, Sikhism, Judaism, Christianity, and Islam, are strictly monotheistic. One, Zoroastrianism, is approximately monotheistic, even though its metaphysics is dualistic, and its sacred scripture recognizes the worship of many demons. The remaining six religions are practically polytheistic.

(8) Religions according to the personality of their founders. There are three different ways in which the founders of religions have been significant: as originators, as types, and as teachers. Three religions carry the personal name of their founder: Confucianism, Islam,[1] and Zoroastrianism. Three religions are named from an honorific title of their founder. Jainism is so named from Mahavira, having been regarded as the "Jina," the "Conqueror." Buddhism is so named because Gautama, its founder, is regarded as "the Buddha," "the Enlightened One." Christianity is so named because Jesus is regarded as "the Christ," "the Anointed One." Four religions

---

[1] The followers of the Prophet do not like to be called Mohammedans, since it is Allah, not the Prophet, whom they worship. The name of their faith, as explained below, is Islam, and they call themselves Muslims (sometimes spelled Moslems).

are named from a principal teaching of the founder: Taoism, which means "The (Divine) Way"; Shinto, literally "The Way of the Gods"; Mohammedanism, also commonly known as "Islam," or "Submission"; and Sikhism, the religion of "The Disciples."

12. A CLASSIFICATION ACCORDING TO VALUE AND OUTLOOK

The best possible classification of religions is according to the extent of the opportunity and responsibility which each provides for the individual, and also for human society at large.

Each of the eleven living religions in the world does make an estimate of the worth of the individual, and also of the worth of society.

Most non-Christian religions are concerned chiefly for the salvation of the individual, even while they place relatively little value on human personality as such. Islam might seem to be an exception, in that it does have a vigorous missionary program; but that is for the sake of social domination, not for the sake of a comprehensive social betterment through co-operative service.

Christianity is the only religion in the world which regards each human individual as a child of God the Father. And Christianity is the only religion which seeks a salvation, both individual and social, by means of co-operative service.

13. PREREQUISITES FOR THE STUDY AND COMPARISON OF RELIGIONS

All the general methods which have been proven useful in other fields are also needed for the study of religions. The student of the religions of the world needs to use a certain unusual combination of abilities, which may be enumerated as follows:

(1) Scientific accuracy is needed in order to know the vast range of facts. The sacred scriptures of each religion deserve

to be studied with care. Generalizations with regard to any religion are peculiarly difficult but they need to be made with exactness.

(2) Sympathetic appreciation is indispensable for an understanding of the satisfactions which each particular religion gives to its followers.

(3) Judicial discriminations must be exercised upon the different values which the different religions assign to the varying experiences and ideals of life.

(4) Constructive inclusiveness will help to gather up all the values which may be found among the religions of the world into a harmonious unity.

(5) Fearless trust in spiritual worth, wherever found, will serve to enhance students' reverence for the universal God of truth and also their respect for the religious aspirations of humanity.

(6) A universal point of view is epecially needed in the field of religion. In Hinduism's most widely known sacred scripture there stands the frequently overlooked injunction:

"Thou oughtest indeed to act, looking comprehensively to the welfare of the world." (*Bhagavad Gita* 3 : 20; also similarly in three other verses—*Bhagavad Gita* 3 : 25; 5 : 25; 12 : 4.)

Followers of the Christian religion are enjoined in the New Testament to observe constructively this universal point of view:

"Prove all things. Hold fast that which is good" (I Thessalonians 5 : 21).

Justin Martyr's remark still holds true:

Whatsoever things have been rightly said by all men, are the property of us Christians. (2 *Apology*, 13 : 4.)

A study and comparison of the world's living religions will prove beneficial to the Christian's own life and thought. It should also benefit every person who undertakes it conscientiously.

II

HINDUISM

The Religion of Divine Immanence
and An Hereditary Graded Social Structure

1. INTRODUCTION: AMONG THE WORLD'S LIVING RELIGIONS

Hinduism, dating from perhaps 1500 B.C., is the oldest living organized religion in the world. It is also one of the largest, numbering 303,200,000 adherents in India according to the 1951 census. From 1931 to 1951 the reported increase was over sixty-four million, or more than three million per year. On this basis the present figure (1958) would be in excess of 325,000,000. Hinduism has been largely confined to India, except as Hindus have migrated to other areas. Two other missionary religions, Christianity and Islam, have been winning an increasing number of converts in that land. Eventually the large proportion of Muslims in certain areas led to the partition of India and the formation of Pakistan, a new Muslim state. Even so, there remain some forty million Muslims in India proper. In 1931 the percentage of Hindus in the total population was 67.7; in 1941 it was 65.5. Thus, Hinduism seemed during that decade to be decreasing in proportion to the total population. Comparable percentage figures are no longer possible since the partition.

Hinduism is unique among the religions of the world for its system of caste. There are four main historic castes, whose members must follow their hereditary occupation, and must refrain from marrying and even from eating with members of other castes. Arranged in successively subordinate position, they are: Brahmans, the priestly and intellectual class; Kshatriyas, the rulers and warriors; Vaisyas, the common agriculturists and artisans; and the low-caste Sudras. The process of subdivision has continued until fifty-eight castes now number more than 1,000,000 members. Altogether there are over 2,000 mutually exclusive subcastes in the Hindu system. There are in addition some fifty million or more who are variously called "outcastes," "Harijans," Mr. Gandhi's term for them, "Untouchables," or legally, the "scheduled classes." But under the impact of the modern world, caste is rapidly breaking down, and "untouchability" is specifically outlawed in India's constitution.

Hinduism is remarkable among the religions of the world for the devotion of adherents characterized by so great a variety and vagueness of their religious beliefs.

In this country no one has any objection to stating his religion. And if all the creeds were clear and definite and mutually exclusive, there would be no difficulty whatever in the way of obtaining an accurate return. . . . No one is interested in what his neighbor believes, but he is very much interested in knowing whether he can eat with him or take water from his hands. (*General Report of the Census of India, 1911,* 113.)

Hinduism's main theological belief is in one omnipresent Divine Being named Brahma. Yet this pantheism is not to be found in the four *Vedas* and the *Brahmanas,* which are the two earliest groups among Hinduism's sacred scriptures, although clear indications of a tendency in this direction are to be found, especially in the tenth book of the *Rig Veda* and in the *Atharva Veda* which are comparatively late. (See below, p. 25.) As a matter of fact, orthodox Hindus have believed in every kind of theism, polytheism and pantheism. They have worshipped any object which they prefer, or virtually none. They have followed any standard of morality, or almost none. Yet they have been recognized as Hindus in good and regular standing so long as they have not flagrantly violated the rules of caste and for that offense been outcasted.

Hinduism is the complex gradual growth of a very religiously minded people with many different temperaments. It has been diversified, yet unified, by its theoretical belief in one immanent, all-inclusive, all-sanctifying World Soul, and by its practical social control through caste. Hinduism has developed at least six different types of religion, which have been embodied in successive sets of documents. These together constitute the sacred scriptures of Hinduism. They are all written in the Sanskrit language, which is the grandmother of most of the modern Indo-European languages. Hinduism may be known comprehensively and authoritatively from a survey of its historic documentary sources.

But long before the coming of the Aryans who were largely responsible for the religion reflected in the *Vedas,* there was a relatively advanced culture, at least in the valley of the Indus river, and a well-developed religion which it now seems has contributed not a little to the Hinduism which we know today. This ancient civilization, uncovered mostly since the First World War by the archeologists, had large well-built cities as long ago as 3000 B. C., thus making it contemporary with ancient Egypt and Babylon. It had a pictographic system of writing, not yet deciphered, and the artefacts and images found in the ruins indicate clearly the presence of certain ideas which we now consider as Hindu, but which were not held by the Aryans on the basis of our knowledge of them from the *Vedas.* These, it should be said, were not written down, but were preserved for centuries in the memories of living men. The discovery of the Indus civilization has made it much easier to explain the development of some non-Vedic ideas in later Hinduism such as transmigration, and the strong emphasis on the mother goddess. These may well have been ideas held by the pre-Vedic inhabitants of India, but suppressed by the conquerors, only to appear again in time among the people as the Aryans intermarried with the indigenous people and gradually took over some of their folk beliefs and practices. It has happened thus not infrequently in history. The story of the recovery of this ancient culture is not yet complete. The discovery of still other cities has been reported quite recently. The excavation of these may reveal yet more clearly the nature of the religion of these ancient people. (See the Bibliography on Hinduism in the Appendix for titles of books reporting and interpreting the materials which have been unearthed.)

2. EARLY NATURE-WORSHIP: THE FOUR *VEDAS* (BEFORE 1000 B. C.)

The name for all the sacred scriptures of Hinduism inclusively is the *Vedas*, meaning "(Books of) Knowledge." Different schools in Hinduism have their special *Vedas*. The four earliest are: "The Veda of Verses, or Psalms," *Rig Veda;* "The Veda of Sacred Formulas," *Yajur Veda;* "The Veda of Chants," *Sama Veda;* and "The Veda of Charms," *Atharva Veda.* The first of these four is the most important. Indeed, the *Rig Veda* is the oldest document among the world's living religions. Later sacred scriptures and the usual orthodox theory in Hinduism represent the *Rig Veda* as having been created before the world. The dates assigned by European scholars vary from 2,000 B. C. to 1,000 B. C. The *Rig Veda* is a collection of 1,028 lyrics, about five times as long as the Hebrew Psalter. The Hindus think that the *Rig Veda* is verbally and unerringly authoritative. And they have succeeded in transmitting the Sanskrit text so that it now has fewer variant readings than exist in the present Hebrew text of the *Old Testament* and the Greek text of the *New Testament.* One of the verses in the *Rig Veda,* the famous Gayatri, which is at least a thousand years older than Christianity, is still used by orthodox high-caste Hindus as a daily morning prayer to the sun:

> Let us meditate upon the adorable
> Glory of the Divine Vivifier!
> And may He direct our thoughts!
> (*Rig Veda,* 3 : 62. 10.)

The type of religion which is found in these earliest documents of Hinduism is mostly nature-worship. The *Rig Veda* contains prayers and praises addressed to some seventy-six different objects, mostly personalized objects or powers in nature; for example, sun, moon, sky, wind, rain, dawn, earth, air, fire, etc. The most important of the Vedic deities is Indra, regent of the atmosphere and the rain. The desires expressed in the prayers to these early Hindu deities are mostly for long life, sons, cattle, good crops, freedom from disease, success over enemies, and general worldly prosperity. Yet those early documents of India, more than a thousand years before Christ, contain also some noble ethical ideas. One of the two sky-gods is designated Dyaus Pitar, meaning "Heaven-Father."

> Heaven is my Father, Progenitor!
> There is my origin. (*Rig Veda*, 1 : 164. 33.)

Yet the idea of fatherhood connected with Dyaus Pitar is almost that of physical paternity, this male deity being coupled regularly with a female deity, Prithivi Matar, "Earth-Mother."

The most highly ethical of the various Vedic deities is Varuna, the encompassing "Heaven." Perhaps the most beautiful hymn in all the four Vedas is a psalm on the omnipresence and omniscience of Heaven (*Atharva Veda*, 4 : 16). It contains a remarkable parallel to Psalm 139 : 7–10, yet it ends with an imprecation on an enemy. Varuna and practically all of the Vedic deities have passed away in later Hinduism, yet the primitive worship and dread of the powers in nature still continues in Hinduism.

There is one, and only one, mention in the *Rig Veda* of the four castes of Hinduism. In this earliest document of Hinduism, perhaps 3,000 years old, the four main groups in human society represent the successively lower organs, or functions, of the primeval person:

> His mouth became the Brahman.
> His arms became the Kshatriya.
> His thighs are the Vaisya.
> The Sudra was produced from his feet.
> (*Rig Veda*, 10 : 90. 12.)

The chief method of salvation in the *Rig Veda* is prayer.

3. PRIESTLY HINDUISM: THE *BRAHMANAS*
(1000–800 B. C.)

The first great war of the Hindus at the original invasion into India had been accompanied by much prayer and personal sacrifice. The continuance of these processes was stressed, but in a formal perfunctory manner. The particular interpretation which was put upon the early military and religious success resulted in a distinct hardening of religion. The relatively simple Vedic religion was transformed in this period of Hinduism into a system of strict domination, elaborate ceremonies, various material offerings, and even bloody animal sacrifices, all under the control of the Brahman priests.

A new type of literature as well as religion arose. The *Brahmanas,* meaning "Priestlies," are a group of extensive prose treatises on religion. They contain chiefly directions for various prescribed sacrifices and some religious legends. In the literature of the world these Hindu *Brahmanas* are the earliest Indo-European prose writings now extant.

The special emphasis in the *Brahmanas* is on the sacrifices.

Assuredly the sun would not rise, if the priest did not make sacrifice. (*Satapatha Brahmana* 2. 3. 1. 5; *SBE,* 12 : 328.)

The most important and elaborate is the Asva-medha (horse-sacrifice), which requires a whole year for its completion. Its mere beginning involves the slaying of 609 animals in a certain prescribed succession (*SBE,* 44 : 311). The mere performance has unlimited saving efficacy.

Whosoever performs the Asva-medha sacrifice, obtains all his desires, and attains all attainments. (*SBE,* 44 : 347.)
This is the atonement for everything, the remedy for everything. He who performs the Asva-medha, redeems all sin. (*SBE,* 44 : 328.)

As the sacrifice performed by hired priests was considered the most important act in religion, so the old Vedic deities became less important. They were declared to have been mortal, and to have attained immortality through sacrifices (*SBE,* 43 : 356–357). Indeed, the Brahman priests, who knew the ritual, were elevated to a position on a level with the deities. No other sacred scriptures of the world can parallel the claim made in these "Priestlies" of Hinduism, that a person's salvation depends upon paying fees to officiating priests.

Certain innovations also were made in the *Brahmanas* which have continued into all subsequent Hinduism. In stressing Hinduism's graded caste system with its topmost layer of priests, the low-caste Sudra is still further demeaned. Neither gods nor Brahmans now speak to that caste (*SBE*, 26 : 4). For the first time in Hinduism restrictions are placed on eating beef (*SBE*, 26 : 11), and on a wife's eating along with her husband (*SBE*, 12 : 259; 43 : 369–370). And the idea of reincarnation is first clearly stated in the *Brahmanas* (*SBE*, 26 : 11; 43 : 358).

However, the special type of religion which was developed in the *Brahmanas* was sacerdotalism. And that type has held a permanent place in Hinduism during all its subsequent 2,700 years. Salvation, according to the *Brahmanas*, is to be obtained chiefly through sacrifice performed by the Brahman priests.

4. PHILOSOPHIC HINDUISM: THE *UPANISHADS*
(800–600 B. C.)

Fondness for philosophic speculation has always been a characteristic of the Hindus. This trait began to manifest itself in some remarkable speculations about the origin of the universe, even in the early documents (*Rig Veda*, 10 : 72; 10 : 81; 10 : 121; 10 : 129; *Atharva Veda*, 10 : 2; 10 : 7). But it became dominant in the third set of sacred scriptures, the *Upanishads*, "Séances," where youths and even women display interest in philosophic discussion.

The *Upanishads* represent almost a new type of religion, which centers in the concept "Brahma." In the *Vedas* and *Brahmanas* that word had meant "prayer," "sacred utterance," or "sacred knowledge." But in the *Upanishads* the word is used to designate the one Supreme Being. The Vedic deities are frankly represented as having been unaware of Brahma (Hume, *Thirteen Principal Upanishads*, 337–339). The course of philosophic thought in the *Upanishads* themselves passed through phases, which may be briefly formulated and illustrated.

All the Vedic deities, indeed all things and all events, are to be regarded as manifestations of one Power at the heart of the world. In the language of traditional religion, that "It" may be called the power of prayer (*brahma*). But philosophically Brahma is to be interpreted as the absolute, infinite, eternal, omnipresent, impersonal, indescribable, neuter Being. It may also be designated as spirit (*atman*), a world soul, into which the individual human spirit is also to be merged. The most frequently quoted single sentence from the *Upanishads* is:

That Soul! That art thou! (Nine times repeated in the *Chandogya Upanishad;* Hume, *TPU,* 246–250; *SBE,* 1 : 101–108.)

This knowledge is frankly presented as superseding the Vedic polytheism.

Whoever thus knows "I am Brahma!" becomes this All. Even the gods have not power to prevent his becoming thus, for he becomes their soul (self, *atman*). (Hume, *TPU,* 83–84; *SBE,* 15 : 88.)

In contrast with the one infinite abiding Reality the manifold world with all its changing finite phenomena must be regarded as a dream or an illusion (*maya*).

Theoretically, then, salvation is simply a quiet unstriving realization of one's real self as free from all changes, even from transmigration, and as completely absorbed in Brahma-Atman.

Practically, however, the way of knowledge may be supplemented by the Yoga method of inducing trance-consciousness or trans-consciousness. Quiet suppression of all sense activity, even of breathing, may be made to promote breathless contemplation on the ineffable, eternal, absolutely inactive, indescribably blissful Brahma, which is already immanent within one's own heart.

Since Brahma, the World Soul or Ultimate Reality, transcends all distinctions of good or evil, of right or wrong, one who has, through the proper disciplines, attained to complete oneness with that serene, supernatural, incomprehensible, impersonal Supreme Being may also be regarded as having likewise transcended all ethical distinctions. (Hume, *TPU*, 136, 143–144, 169, 276–277, 299–300.) Thus:

Such a one, verily, the thought does not torment: "Why have I not done the good?" "Why have I done the evil?" He who knows this, saves himself from both these thoughts. For truly, from both of these he saves himself,—he who knows this.
This is the Upanishad mystic doctrine.
(Hume, *TPU*, 289; *SBE*, 15 : 63.)

But since this experience may presumably be attained while an individual is still alive, this doctrine has at times led to what is known as antinomianism.

It must not be thought that all Hindus think exactly alike in respect to their religion. As a matter of fact, six orthodox schools of interpretation of philosophic Hinduism are recognized, and these differ substantially both as to theory and practice. In the bibliography will be found titles of books by both Eastern and Western scholars which deal with these various schools. Nor have many thoughtful Hindus been lacking in concern for moral values, even when they have regarded them as of secondary importance. While morality is not in itself sufficient to win salvation, which properly comes, they think, through knowledge, there is a clear indication in some of the schools of Yoga, for example, that one cannot even enter on the way of self-realization until he has attained a high standard of morality. That is, morality takes its place not as the means whereby salvation may be won, but as only one of the stepping-stones on the way to its achievement. Thus, for example, in the *Aruneya Upanishad*, 3 ff., the *yogin* is enjoined to renounce passion, wrath, greed, confusion, deceit, pride, envy, egotism, selfishness and untruthfulness, and to practice chastity, non-injury, truthfulness, and to be without worldly possessions. (See further, E. W. Hopkins, *Ethics of India*, chap. 4.)

Hinduism in the *Upanishads* still retains the fourfold caste system as aboriginally created, though now from Brahma (Hume, *TPU*, 84–85). But salvation according to the *Upani-*

shads is to be obtained chiefly through one's own philosophic speculation upon a pantheistic Supreme Being.

5. LEGALISTIC HINDUISM: THE *LAWS OF MANU* (ABOUT 250 B. C.)

Hinduism had been presented attractively to three different human temperaments by the *Rig Veda*, the *Brahmanas*, and the *Upanishads*. These three successive sets of documents had interpreted religion as being chiefly an affair of prayer, of sacrifices, and of philosophic speculation respectively. But Hinduism has continued to be an effective force in the lives of its followers because about 2,100 years ago it was elaborated as a compulsory social institution, with some detailed commandments and prohibitions for daily living through all the stages of life.

The *Law-Book of Manu* is the most highly revered and influential among several codes of Hindu law. It has been estimated by a former professor of Sanskrit at Oxford University as "one of the most remarkable books that the literature of the whole world can offer, and some of its moral precepts are worthy of Christianity itself" (Monier-Williams, *Hinduism*, 54; *Indian Wisdom*, 204). Its twelve chapters do contain some wise maxims; for example, respectful obedience to parents and teachers (2 : 225–229); repentance and confession (11 : 228–231); fulfilling troth (9 : 99); reverential eating (2 : 54–56); unresentful, patient endurance of evil:

Let him patiently bear hard words. Let him not insult anybody. Against an angry man let him not in return show anger. Let him bless when he is cursed. (6 : 47–48.)

However, as a whole, *Manu* is unmistakably a Hindu document. It teaches the sacredness and saving efficacy of the *Vedas* (2 : 14–15, 107–113, 156; 11 : 246, 257, 262–264; 12 : 94–107), the performance of Hindu sacrifices (3 : 69–81; 4 : 25–28; 11 : 261), the sanctioning of war (7 : 87–201), Upanishadic knowledge of Brahma-Atman (6 : 29, 79; 11 : 263; 12 : 123–125), and final release from transmigration (2 : 249).

The fourfold caste system has been presented in *Manu* with great elaboration. With their respective occupations they were a primeval divine creation "for the prosperity of the world" (1 : 31, 87–93; 10 : 45; 11 : 236). The Brahman by the mere fact of his birth as the supreme incarnation of deity has been placed in a position of permanent paramountcy (1 : 93–100; 9 : 317–319; 11 : 35). The low-caste has been placed in a corresponding position of permanent, even economic, inferiority (2 : 39, 103; 4 : 61, 79–81; 8 : 413–417; 9 : 334–335; 10 : 51–56, 121–125, 129; 11 : 13).

Some noticeable innovations in Hinduism were made in *Manu*, particularly the mapping out of four stages (*asramas*) in the life of the perfect religionist: a youthful student (2 : 69–246), a married householder (3 : 1–5, 169), a retired hermit (6 : 1–32), and finally a religious mendicant (6 : 33–97). Temples and temple priests are first mentioned in the sacred scriptures of Hinduism in this document (3 : 152, 180; 8 : 248; 9 : 280, 285). Idols are first clearly referred to in *Manu* (9 : 285) along with some other vaguer but probable allusions (4 : 39, 130, 153; 7 : 54; 8 : 87). Allowed and forbidden foods are listed (5 : 11, 17). Offenses and penances are first put into graded lists (11 : 49–266). Wife-beating is allowed under certain limitations (8 : 299–300). All modern innovations contrary to the *Vedas* are condemned as false and worthless (12 : 95–95).

Salvation in *Manu* is to be obtained chiefly through obedience to law, particularly the law of caste.

6. DEVOTIONAL HINDUISM: THE *BHAGAVAD GITA* (ABOUT 1 A. D.)

Among the many sacred scriptures of Hinduism the one which has been most highly esteemed by Hindus themselves, and also by outsiders, is the *Bhagavad Gita*. It was the first one to be translated into English in 1785 by Charles Wilkins, one of the earliest English Sanskritists, with an introduction by Warren Hastings. The translation by Sir Edwin Arnold, under the title "The Song Celestial," was made "because English

literature would be the poorer without it"; this has been included in the Harvard classics. This favorite Hindu sacred
scripture has been rendered into English by more than two-
score translators.

The *Bhagavad Gita* is a dramatic poem which starts with a
stirring scene at the beginning of a battle. A Hindu knight,
Arjuna, for the first time in the recorded history of Hinduism,
raises the question of the propriety of killing people in war
(1 : 28–45; 2 : 4–8). His charioteer allays his conscientious com-
punctions by a remarkable discourse on the immortality and
irresponsibility of the soul, which proceeds with a quotation
from the *Katha Upanishad* (2 : 18–19).

It slays not, and it is not slain. It is never born, and it never dies.
Weapons cleave it not, nor does the fire burn it. The waters wet it
not, nor do the winds dry it up. Wherefore, knowing it to be such,
thou oughtest not to grieve for it. (2 : 19–25.)

Thus the practical duty of the knight as a member of the
second caste remains unchanged.

To a Kshatriya warrior nothing is better than a lawful fight. If thou
wilt not undertake this lawful fight, then by abandoning thy proper
duty and thy honor, thou wilt be guilty of a crime. (2 : 31, 33.)

The chief speaker in the *Bhagavad Gita* proves to be the
deity Krishna in the form of the charioteer. Hinduism here has
undergone another very remarkable transformation when it
represents the supreme deity in the form of one particular
man. Krishna declares that he became incarnate.

for the protection of good men, for the destruction of evildoers, for
the re-establishment of piety. (4 : 8.)

Whoever worships Krishna with utter devotion (*bhakti*)

dwells in Me, whatever be his course of life. (6 : 31.)
They who worship Me devoutly, are in Me; and I also am in them.
Be well assured that he who worships Me, does not perish.

(9 : 29, 31.)

Very remarkable in Hinduism is the offer in the *Bhagavad
Gita* of universal salvation to sinners (4 : 36; 9 : 30), even to
women and low-caste Sudras (9 : 32). However, the *Bhagavad*

Gita reaffirms this main feature of historic and orthodox Hinduism when it describes the inherent, unchangeable nature and function of the four castes almost in the words of *Manu:*

The office of a Kshatriya, born of his proper nature, is heroism, energy, firmness, skill, resolution in battle, liberality, and a ruler's bearing. The office of a Vaisya, born of his proper nature, is agriculture, tending of cattle, and commerce. The essential office of a Sudra, born of his proper nature, is servitude. (18 : 43–44.)

Indeed, the new deity of the *Bhagavad Gita*, Krishna, declares:

The four castes were created by me. (4 : 13.)

Other continuities of Hinduism in the *Bhagavad Gita* are reverence for the *Vedas* (2 : 4), and the termination of reincarnation or transmigration as being the greatly desired goal (4 : 9).

The main feature of the *Bhagavad Gita* is the new formulation of religion in terms of devotion. This supplements, rather than supplants, traditional Hinduism. The practical message of the *Bhagavad Gita* may be paraphrased in simple language: "Do your caste duty, and trust your God for the rest for your salvation."

Salvation, according to the *Bhagavad Gita*, is to be obtained chiefly through personal devotion to a personal deity.

7. POPULAR HINDUISM:
THE *EPICS* AND *PURANAS* (1–250 A. D.)

The main structure of Hinduism seems to have been completed before the time of Christ, although the popularizing of Hinduism has continued, and although certain new sects have arisen within the Christian era. The final literary product among the sacred scriptures of Hinduism, and also the most effective literary agency for the popularizing of Hinduism were the two great epics, the *Mahabharata*, or "The Great Bharata War," and the *Ramayana*, or "The Career of the God Rama," and also eighteen *Puranas*, or collections of religious stories, literally "Ancient Tales."

Popular Hinduism is a vast conglomerate of all the features which have been enumerated in the sacred scriptures; it contains also other features, among which the following are important.

Caste rules prevent a Hindu from eating, marrying, and all intimate dealings with persons who belong to the other main castes, or even to other subcastes of his own main caste, though it should be said that the twentieth century has witnessed a progressive breakdown of caste in India.

Sects are numerous in Hinduism. The chief two worship the deities Vishnu, the Creator, and Siva, the Destroyer. There are at least fifty-nine subsects or denominations, representing widely different religious types, both philosophical and practical. But they all worship some personal deity. Their characteristics differ from salvation by faith among the Bhakti schools to sensual and cruel practices among the Vallabhacharyas and the worshippers of Kali, the black goddess of death.

Idolatry is abundantly manifest throughout Hindu India. It is directed toward all kinds of human and animal representations, and even to images of the male and female sexual organs.   —

Popular Hinduism has innumerable temples and shrines, large and small, for the worship of local as well as general deities. The devotions here are chiefly individual, often with offerings made to the images of the deity and to the attendant priests. Worship of the idol often includes circumambulation, always keeping it to the right.

Sacred places, seasons, and festivals are prominent in popular Hinduism. Devotees in large numbers make pilgrimages to various holy rivers, mountains, cities and temples all over India. They observe holy days, feasts, and gala celebrations in the lunar and solar cycles. The sowing of seed and the harvesting of crops and other activities in agriculture are connected with religious ceremonies.

Popular Hinduism has been brought intimately into home life through prescribed observances for meals, birth, marriage, death, funeral, and recurring offerings for the dead. There are numerous ceremonial bathings and purifications. Every adolescent boy in the three upper castes is invested sacramentally with a three-ply sacred thread, which is never removed from his body.

Popular Hinduism connects itself closely with eating and drinking. A strict vegetarian and non-intoxicating menu is prescribed for the higher castes. Water must not be taken from the defiling hands of any low-caste person.

The lowest caste Hindus or outcastes are regarded as "untouchables." They were formerly excluded from the regular temples and from all social intercourse except menial servitude. Their religion is practically animism.[1]

Many animistic traits prevail in popular Hinduism, even among the higher castes, such as the fear of evil spirits and of eclipses, a belief in astrology, in horoscopes, curses, the evil eye, and charms.

8. THE ESSENTIALS OF HINDUISM

Amid the unequalled variety of religious belief and practice which has prevailed in Hinduism, caste is the only feature which has been present through all its historical phases and successive scriptures.[2] Yet some modern Hindu reformers are attempting to reject caste, or at least to reform it.

Reverence for the *Vedas* is another important feature which has prevailed throughout Hinduism subsequent to the first Vedic period. Yet very few Hindus possess personal acquaintance with their revered scriptures.

The fundamental theological belief is in one immanent, all-inclusive Being or Spirit, Brahma. Yet this belief was not present in Hinduism's first two stages and sets of sacred scriptures.

Karma and transmigration are two other beliefs which probably all Hindus believe. Yet these were not taught in the beginning of Hinduism, and are quite independent of the theological belief in Brahma.

[1] See Henry Whitehead, *The Village Gods of Southern India* (London, Oxford University Press, 1916) for a description of this type of Hinduism.
[2] It does not seem to have been present in pre-Vedic India, and does not appear in the *Vedas* save in the late tenth book.

⅁. ATTEMPTED REFORMS OF HINDUISM
(557 B. C.–1917 A. D.)

During more than half of its entire history Hinduism has had conscious protests and endeavors for improvement. But for the most part these have been ineffective.

Mahavira, the son of a Hindu rajah, in 557 B. C. started a movement against the following features of Hinduism: the domineering exclusiveness of the Brahman priests; the claimed authority of the Sanskrit *Vedas;* the cruel system of bloody animal sacrifices; and the absolute monism of the current *Upanishad* philosophy. But the immediate result of Mahavira's effort was the starting of another religion, Jainism.

Gautama Buddha, another Hindu prince, in 525 B. C., started a movement which protested against the following features of Hinduism: the whole unethical system of fixed hereditary castes; dependence for salvation upon paid priests or bribable deities; excessive speculativeness, ceremonialism, and emotionalism; and the sacred scriptures in an unintelligible ancient language. This movement resulted in the establishment of the second personally founded religion in India, Buddhism.

Tiruvalluvar, a low-caste Hindu, some time after 800, preached a salvation which is available only by the grace of God. His *Sacred Kurral* is one of the most influential poems in the Tamil language of south India. "The Jains claim him as their own" (Pope, *The Sacred Kurral,* 189).

Manikka-Vasagar, another low-caste Hindu of south India, in the eleventh century, taught: one supreme personal God; His incarnation in Siva; salvation as a gracious divine gift; and a conscious immortality after death. His *Tiruvasagam* ("Sacred Utterances") is generally regarded as the most beautiful Hindu poem in the Tamil language.

Ramanuja, a Brahman of the Chingleput District in the Madras Presidency, about the beginning of the twelfth century, started the "Qualified Non-duality School," Visishtadvaita. He was an extensive commentator on the *Upanishads,* the *Bhagavad Gita,* and later Hindu philosophic works. But he was also a remarkable popular preacher, who taught that the Supreme Being must be personal. He preached to all classes of people freely, organized a missionary propaganda, endeavored to overcome caste exclusiveness, and strove for the uplift of women. The Principal of the Serampore Christian College ventures to predict:

When an Indian Christian theologian will seek to give an adequate expression to the philosophy of the Christian religion from an Indian point of view, he will receive much inspiration and derive considerable help from the religious philosophy of the mystic Ramanuja. (Howells, *Soul of India,* 368.)

Madhava, or Anandatirtha (1119–1199), a Brahman from the Kanara District in southwest India, was the founder of the "Duality School," Dvaita. He was a travelling preacher of theism, protesting against bloody animal sacrifices. He taught salvation through a moral knowledge of the divine excellence, which developed a separate sect.

The pretended identity of God and the soul, contained in the famous words, "That art thou," he calls mere babbling from ignorance. However, in most respects the sect has relapsed into the ordinary corruptions of the orthodox Hinduism around them. (Howells, *Soul of India,* 370–372.)

Ramananda, in the fourteenth and fifteenth centuries, emphasized that salvation comes primarily through divine grace (*prasada*), even as had been intimated in the *Upanishads* (Hume, *TPU,* 350, 402, 411). His motto was: "Let no one ask a man's caste or sect. Whoever adores God, he is God's alone."

He preached the gospel of Rama's boundless love for men of every race, order or creed. The sect is still numerous in northern India, chiefly among the poorer classes. Caste has reasserted its power over them, but the ideal remains. (Howells, *Soul of India,* 374.)

There has been sharp controversy between the worshippers of the Hindu deity Rama. The North School (*Vada-galais*) teaches the cat doctrine, that divine grace is irresistible, even as a mother cat of her own will carries a little kitten away from danger. The South School (*Ten-galais*) teaches the monkey doctrine, that the human will must co-operate with divine grace, even as a little monkey must hold onto its mother in order to be carried safely out of danger. (Hopkins, *Religions of India*, 500–501; Macnicol, *Indian Theism*, 110; Howells, *Soul of India*, 368).

Nanak (1469–1538), a second-caste Hindu in the Punjab, under the influence of Islam, preached one God for both Hindus and Muslims. But the result was the starting of a third altogether separate religion in India, Sikhism, treated in Chapter V.

Chaitanya (1485–1527), a worshipper of Vishnu, was a musical revivalist in Bengal, who preached the equality of all castes before deity, salvation by singing and emotional devotion, and relaxation of the Hindu restriction against widow remarriage. But sensual excesses have appeared among his followers.

Kabir (1488–1512) was a Hindu poet of a kindly theism. Some of his poems have been incorporated in the sacred scriptures of Sikhism. But the immediate result was the addition of another Hindu sect, the Kabir Panth.

Tulsi Das (1532–1632), the greatest poet of mediæval India, popularized the Sanskrit *Ramayana* in the Hindi vernacular. He was a distinct theist, who taught that "by abandoning himself to utter loving faith in Rama's power to save him from its thraldom, a man can escape from the weary round of perpetual transmigration." (Hastings, *ERE*, 12 : 472.)

Dadu (about 1600), a cotton-spinner, preached theism and incarnation. But the result was the formation of another sect, which now worships him.

Ram Mohun Roy, a Bengal Brahman, was the first Hindu to translate some of the *Upanishads* into English. He also published a collection of quotations from the New Testament under the title *The Precepts of Jesus, the Guide to Peace and Happiness*. In 1828 A. D. he started the Brahma Samaj as a protest against the following features of Hinduism: idolatry and polytheism; widow-burning, enforced widowhood, and polygamy; the strictness of the caste system; national and religious isolation; restrictions on the common people. The Brahma Samaj is notable as the first attempt to reform Hinduism as the result of a knowledge of Christianity, but it has become internally divided and feeble.

Doctor Atmaram Pandurang, in 1867 A. D., started in Bombay the Prarthana Samaj, "Prayer Congregation," for a more personal religious life and for some social reform. It has had some notable subsequent leaders, but it has remained small and select. Dayanand Saraswati, in 1875, started the Arya Samaj (Congregation of the Noble), as a protest against idolatry. Otherwise it has stressed the importance and infallibility of the *Vedas*. Harendranath Maitra, in 1916, published *Hinduism, the World Ideal*. G. B. Vaidya, in 1917, in Bombay, started the Hindu Missionary Society as an avowed repudiation of traditional Hindu exclusiveness, and in conscious imitation of successful Christian propaganda. Its slogan was: "To make the whole world Hindu." But it has remained a small movement, especially since the death of the founder.

The Arya Samaj was much more aggressive than the Brahma-Samaj and ultimately attained a following of more than a half million, whereas the latter never had more than some six thousand at any one time. The Arya Samaj was strongly nationalistic in its outlook and became actively anti-missionary. One of its chief preoccupations in later years was the reconversion of Hindus who had become either Muslims or Christians. It suffered heavily from the partition of India and seems to have lost much of its vitality.

Quite the most influential of modern reform movements in Hinduism is the Ramakrishna Movement which had as its founder Sri Ramakrishna, born in 1836. Utterly unlettered, Ramakrishna was one of the great mystics of India. He was himself a devotee of Kali, but made the startling discovery that he could arrive at the same profound experience of *Samadhi* whether he came by the way of Christianity, of Islam, of Buddhism, or of Hinduism. This led to his central conviction and teaching that all religions lead to God if duly followed, and it has been a principal emphasis in the teaching of his followers. It was a young Brahman who was early attracted, as were many educated people, to the following of the master, one Vivevananda, who gave institutional form to the movement and made of it an essentially missionary faith. He himself established centers in Europe and America, now manned by members of the Math or order which has its headquarters on the banks of the sacred Ganges River not far out of Calcutta. Here the chief temple enshrines an image of Sri Ramakrishna and is a center for his worship. He is regarded as the consummation of all the previous incarnations of deity. "He who was Krishna, Rama, Christ, Buddha, Chaitanya, has now become Ramakrishna," he is reported to have said. And this his followers believe.

To the eclectic teaching of the movement and its strong emphasis on mystical experience is joined a pronounced activist and practical interest in social betterment manifested in schools, orphanages, hospitals, clinics, etc. There are some 900 Ramakrishna centers scattered over India and in its foreign outreach it touches Europe, North and South America as well as other countries in Asia.[1]

The modern age has had a vast influence upon India's religious, social, political and economic life. The coming of industrialism; the increased ease of communication; the greater mobility of the population through improved means of travel; the modern movies; the radio, and increasingly also television, opening up a world unknown before; the world-wide spread of Communism, have done much to modify her faith and practice. Among other things, the institution of caste is rapidly breaking down, the old family system is being modified; India's women are asserting their right to freedom from the older restrictions under which they lived, and are taking their place alongside men in public life. A secularism not unlike that of the western world constitutes a growing threat to India's boasted spir-

[1] For a number of books dealing with the various reform movements in India, see Bibliography.

ituality. Great figures such as the poet-educator-philosopher, Rabindrinath Tagore; Mahatma Gandhi, saint, astute politician, and apostle of non-violence, who led India to independence without resort to violent warfare; and statesman Jawarhalal Nehru, western-educated Brahmin, who has directed the new Republic during its early formative years—these and many others, themselves products, in part, of the new age, have been enormously influential both in holding on to proven values in India's rich heritage, and in mediating the changes necessary to fit India for an increasingly important role in the life of the modern world.[1]

10. A COMPARISON BETWEEN HINDUISM AND CHRISTIANITY

There has been so much variation in Hinduism that only its most important teaching can be taken at each point. The teachings of Jesus must be taken in general to represent Christianity.

God

In Hinduism the Supreme Being is the impersonal Brahma, a philosophical Absolute, serenely blissful, beyond all hamperings either ethical or metaphysical. In Christianity the Supreme Being is supreme personality, perfect in character, creatively purposeful, ethically controlling, lovingly serviceful, co-operatively redemptive.

Man

In Hinduism the human individual is an emanation or temporary manifestation of the impersonal Supreme, is not inherently or permanently worthful, is not responsible before God, is not permitted to be brotherly with all fellow human

[1] For the forces that have operated to affect India's religion and life, see, Charles S. Braden, *Modern Tendencies in World Religions*, New York: The Macmillan Company, 1933, Chapter 2. A much later book *India Changes*, by Tanya Zinkin, New York: The Oxford University Press, 1958, shows, particularly, the social, political and economic changes that are taking place, with some reference to religion, though this is the least satisfying part of the book.

beings. In Christianity the human individual, a child of the heavenly Father, shares in the moral character of God, though capable of tragic selfishness, disobedience, and degeneration; he is responsible before God for loving service to fellow men, and is designed for abundant personal life with God and fellow men, both here and hereafter.

The World

In Hinduism the world is a temporary, worthless illusion (Maya). In Christianity the world is a substantial manifestation of the divine plan, wisdom, and power. It is to be progressively understood and enjoyed as a subordinate means of moral and spiritual life.

Sin

In Hinduism there is no real sin. Lamentable philosophic ignorance (*avidya*) and practical violation of caste rules are defects which will entail continued reincarnation. However, all apparent evils are overcome by immersion of oneself in the non-moral Brahma and by compliance with hereditary social conventions. In Christianity sin is real and is against God, against fellow men, and against self. The struggle against it is the contest into which all Christians are called.

Salvation

In Hinduism a person may follow any of three optional methods: the intellectual way of knowledge (*jnana-marga*) concerning pantheism, the emotional way of devotion (*bhakti-marga*) to any favorite deity, and the practical way of works (*karma-marga*) in prescribed ceremonial law. In Christianity salvation is obtained through whole-souled devotion to the love and law of the Father-God; and Jesus Christ more than any other person helps to transform the character of his follower into the full likeness of a child of God.

Human Society

In Hinduism the people who have been born in the fourfold caste system constitute a divinely arranged structure of superimposed, mutually exclusive strata, to be accepted unquestioningly. In Christianity mankind constitutes a family, all its members designed for varied mutual service, to be improved progressively.

Karma and *Grace*

In Hinduism there is acknowledged to exist, quite apart from Brahma or any deity, a cosmic power of justice named Karma. This is an impersonal "law of the deed," which administers due retribution to every person for his deeds by assigning to him in his next reincarnation a higher or a lower social status. However, by abstaining from all efforts and desires a Hindu may succeed in overcoming the consequences of all his previous deeds, and thus escape altogether into a superior state of impersonality. In Christianity the righteous God does indeed administer just rewards and punishments, but not in the form of reincarnation. The supreme principle operative in the world is that the gracious personality of God and of the godlike Jesus, and of every godlike human being, is able winsomely to attract a sinner into godlikeness.

11. ELEMENTS OF STRENGTH IN HINDUISM

Belief in one supreme, omnipresent, non-material spiritual Reality underlying all phenomena.

Belief in a knowledge of, and union with, the Divine as life's goal.

Belief in a sure future life, with appropriate retributions for deeds done.

Belief in the solidarity of the society into which one is born, something divinely instituted, and superior to the individual.

Ability to make religion thoroughly permeate the life of its followers.

Ability to hold together so many groups, for so many centuries, within a social unity, by means of a common religious faith.

12. ELEMENTS OF WEAKNESS IN HINDUISM

No personal character or moral responsibility in the Supreme Being.

No permanent worth or moral ideal for the human individual.

No universal moral standard, except social distinctions.

No possible improvement in a person's social status, except after death.

No possible improvement in the general arrangements of society, except in the teachings of a few unheeded reformers.

The excessive general ceremonialism of worship, or else the extreme of empty meditation.

The gross idolatry, theoretically justifiable by pantheism, and only slightly repudiated by Hinduism's leaders.

Caste, with its inertia and divisiveness.

The generally low position of womanhood, to be found even in all the sacred scriptures except the *Bhagavad Gita*.

No outlook for the rest of the world outside its own national group, except by a few modern reformers.

No outstanding admirable historic figure recorded in Hinduism's scriptures.

The sacred scriptures of this religion not even yet generally available to its own adherents.

III

JAINISM

The Religion of Asceticism

1. INTRODUCTION: AMONG THE WORLD'S LIVING RELIGIONS

Jainism is one of the Oriental religions which is little known. Yet it holds a certain notable place among the religious systems and philosophies of its native land, and even of the whole world.

(1) *In Relation to the History of India*

Jainism is the oldest personally founded religion in India. It was the first organized effort in several centuries of a powerful leader to bring about a conscious improvement of Hinduism, which has been India's earliest spontaneous religion. Thirty-two years later Buddhism arose as another reform movement. Both of these offshoots have exercised a certain kindly and democratic influence in India over against the animal sacrifices and the caste divisions of Hinduism. However, the main result of these protests was the formation of two separate religions rather than the reformation of Hinduism.

Jainism holds an important place in the architecture and archæology of India. The Jain *stupa* (memorial mound) at Mathura bears an inscription which dates from near the beginning of the Christian era, and which states that its antiquity was so great that it had actually been "built by the gods." This religious structure, which is built of brick, is "probably the oldest known building in India" [1] (*Archæological Survey of India, New Imperial Series*, 20 : 12–13). The Jain temples

---

[1] There are, of course, ruins of older buildings dating from the ancient Harappan culture in the valley of the Indus River.

at Ahmedabad, Ellora, Ajmere, and Mount Abu in west India, and the exquisite monolithic Jain temple at Kaligamalai in south India, are among the architectural treasures of the land. They are visited profitably by travellers around the world.

Jainism was the earlier of two almost simultaneous reform movements, but it has been the lesser in subsequent history. It has never extended itself outside of India, as did Buddhism. Even within India the Jains are found in limited areas, mostly in the southern and western districts. However, with shrewd business ability the Jains, who are mostly merchants, have acquired wealth and social importance far beyond their numbers. Yet the fact remains that the percentage of this rather self-centered religious community to the total population of India has been gradually decreasing.

In the census of 1881 the Jains formed a little less than one half of one per cent of the total population, 0.49 per cent to be exact. A decade later the per cent increased to 0.51 per cent. But in successive census reports it decreased to 0.47 per cent, 0.41 per cent, 0.39 per cent, 0.37 per cent, then held at 0.37 per cent in 1941. The total number of Jains in 1941 was 1,449,286. In 1951 it had increased to 1,618,406. This represented a smaller numerical gain than in the previous decade, but it should be pointed out that this does not include the Jains which may now be in Pakistan. How many of these there are is not disclosed in available census reports from Pakistan. Nor would a percentage of the present-day Jains of India to the total population be comparable with the figures given above, since the partition of India removed something like a sixth of India's population. Thus Jainism's position in India is important historically, but minor and probably diminishing.

(2) In Relation to Other Religions and Philosophies

The founder of Jainism did his work during a period of creative importance in several countries of the world. Besides Buddha, Mahavira was a near contemporary of three other founders among the world's living religions: Confucius and Lao-tze in China, and Zoroaster in Persia, according to the latter's latest date. Israel's epochal Babylonian period, with the great prophets Jeremiah, Ezekiel, and Isaiah of the Exile, fell within the lifetime of the founder of Jainism. The lives of the six earliest Greek philosophers, viz., Thales, Anaximander, Anaximenes, Xenophanes, Pythagoras, and Heraclitus, overlapped on the life of Mahavira. But none of those pioneers of thought in a land famed for philosophy and beauty have left living personal memorials of themselves. On the contrary, in India Mahavira is revered at the present time by more than a million and a half people who actually idolize him, even with images for worship. Their most frequent designation for him is a title, Mahavira, meaning "Great Hero." And they call themselves "Jaina," meaning "Followers of the Jina," which latter is another honorific name for their adored "Victor" or "Conqueror."

(3) *In Relation to Christianity*

Jainism may be brought into two striking comparisons with Christianity. The Jains claim to have known the religious significance of the fateful conflict between a person's flesh and spirit centuries before Paul described it with illuminating explanations in the seventh and eighth chapters of his Epistle to the Romans. And the idea of an active universal religion, which is a prime characteristic of Christianity, seems to have been anticipated by Jainism. Three passages in two of the canonical documents report that Mahavira, more than 500 years before Christ, received divine encouragement to propagate a religion that should be supreme in benefit to all the world. (See page 47.) Yet this noble start toward religious universality has been largely lost by Jainism.[1]

[1] There is at the present time a vocal minority within Jainism which is attempting a revival of Jainism. They are active in seeking to win converts to the faith in the West. They publish a magazine, *Ahimsa*, in the English language and have circulated a number of tracts and books setting forth the teachings of Jainism. Some of their scholars assert that Jainism is really much older than Hinduism.

2. THE LIFE OF THE FOUNDER, MAHAVIRA
(599–527 B. C.)

No attempt at a biography of the founder of this religion is contained in its sacred scriptures. Some biographical material may be found, however, in three of the canonical documents which are available in English (*SBE*, 22 : 79–87; 22 : 217–270; 45 : 287–292). The longest of the three sections was composed about 1,000 years after Mahavira, and is occupied chiefly with marvellous events in connection with his birth; for example, the fourteen marvellous dreams of his mother interpreted as prophecies of a wonderful son to be born; the family's sudden prosperity, and many favorable circumstances at his birth. The simple historic fact was that he was born the second son of a petty rajah in northeast India, in the town of Vesali.

(1) *Palace Life* (1–30 *years*)

He was reared in luxurious surroundings.

Mahavira was attended by five nurses: a wet-nurse, a nurse to keep him clean, one to dress him, one to play with him, one to carry him, being transferred from the lap of one nurse to that of another. (*SBE*, 22 : 192–193.)

He married into another princely family, and had one daughter. He spent a glorious youth as a prince.

(2) *The Great Renunciation* (*at* 30)

Upon the death of his parents Mahavira determined to become a religious ascetic in accordance with one of Hinduism's recognized methods of obtaining salvation.

I shall for twelve years neglect my body. (*SBE*, 22 : 200.)

This plan is reported as having been a prenatal resolution, which in great filial considerateness for his parents he did not perform during their lifetime. Then he cast aside his fine clothes, gave away all his property, plucked out his hair in five handfuls, and vowed absolute holiness. This action caused a great stir among the gods of Hinduism, who thereupon acclaimed this Hindu of the second caste as a devotee of a religion which should become a universal blessing.

Blessed One (*arhat*)! Propagate the religion which is a blessing to all creatures in the world. (*SBE*, 22 : 195.)
Luck to thee, best bull of the Kshatriyas! Awake, reverend Lord of the world! Establish the religion of the law which benefits all living beings in the whole universe! It will bring supreme benefit to all living beings in all the world! (*SBE*, 22 : 256.)
Victory, victory to thee, gladdener of the world! . . . O Hero, in the arena of the three worlds gain the supreme best knowledge, called Absolute (*kevala*). (*SBE*, 22 : 258.)

(3) Seeking Salvation through Asceticism (30–42)

For the first year and a month he continued to wear clothes, but thereafter he was a naked ascetic (*SBE*, 22 : 79; 22 : 259–260). He wandered about receiving injuries from men and beasts, and undergoing strange self-imposed bodily sufferings (*SBE*, 22:79–87).

He was indifferent alike to the smell of filth and of sandalwood, to straw and to jewels, to dirt and to gold, to pleasure and to pain, attached neither to this world nor to that beyond, desiring neither life nor death. (*SBE*, 22 : 262.)
With supreme knowledge mildness, patience, control, contentment, . . . the Venerable One meditated on himself for twelve years. (*SBE*, 22 : 263.)
During the thirteenth year, in a squatting position . . . exposing himself to the heat of the sun . . . with the knees high and the head low, in deep meditation, in the midst of abstract meditation, he reached Nirvana, the complete and full, the unobstructed, infinite Absolute (*kevala*). (*SBE*, 22 : 201.)

(4) Preaching the New Religion of Asceticism (42–72)

After he felt that he had gained complete self-control over his body and over the world, Mahavira changed from being a solitary ascetic to a leader and teacher of many monks. He won large numbers of converts and disciples. Legends report that he visited, preached to, and gained favor from four kings. He continued preaching to the end of his life.

Reciting the fifty-five lectures which detail the results of Karma,
when he had just explained the chief lecture, he died, freed from
all pains. (*SBE*, 22 : 269.)
In that night in which the Venerable Ascetic Mahavira died . . .
a great confusion and noise was originated by many descending and
ascending gods. (*SBE*, 22 : 265.)

3. THE VENERATION OF MAHAVIRA

According to the teaching of Mahavira himself there exists
no object to be worshipped. He himself lived what he taught
—a life quiet and unperturbed, self-denying and harmless
and prayerless—yet his followers pray to Mahavira. The
sacred scriptures represent him as possessing divine attributes.
He is revered as sinless.

Having wisdom, Mahavira committed no sin himself. . . . He
meditated, free from sin and desire. (*SBE*, 22 : 86–87.)
The great sage does not commit any wrong. (*SBE*, 45 : 291.)
Knowing the current of worldliness, the current of sinfulness . . .
practising the sinless abstinence from killing . . . whatever is
sinful, the Venerable One left that undone. (*SBE*, 22 : 81.)

He is revered as omniscient.

He knew the thoughts of all sentient beings. (*SBE*, 22 : 200.)
He possessed supreme, unlimited, unimpeded knowledge and in-
tuition. (*SBE*, 22 : 257.)
This wise and clever great sage possessed infinite knowledge and
infinite faith. (*SBE*, 45 : 287.)
Omniscient, he shines forth. . . . The Omniscient sage has pro-
claimed the Law. . . . The Omniscient is the most famous . . .
He, the Omniscient. (*SBE*, 45 : 288–291.)

He is declared in the sacred scriptures of Jainism to have
been pre-existent and planfully incarnate.

He descended from heaven . . . the Venerable Ascetic Mahavira
descended from the great Vimana (palace of the gods). . . . Here
in the continent of Jambudvipa (India), in the southern part of
Bharata-varsha (north India), he took the form of an embryo in
the womb of Devananda. (*SBE*, 22 : 189–190; 22 : 217–228.)

Along with this doctrinal deification, Mahavira has actually been worshipped idolatrously. Indeed, the two main sects among the Jains differ from each other on the question whether their idols of Mahavira, like their own bodies, should be clothed or naked. Mahavira has been venerated as a veritable savior of men, and the sacred scriptures report him as the last of a series of twenty-four such saviors (*SBE*, 22 : 218, 280).

4. THE SACRED SCRIPTURES

The inclusive name for the sacred scriptures of Jainism is *Agamas* (precepts), or *Siddhantas* (treatises). The first section of the canon is acknowledged to consist of twelve Angas (bodies), but the twelfth has been lost.

None of them can be dated earlier than 200 years after the founder. The thirty-seventh in the present list, which contains the most extensive biographical sketch of Mahavira, states twice that the founder had died 980 years previously.

The authority of the extant scriptures is a point of difference between the sects of Jainism. The Sthanakvasi sect recognizes only thirty-three documents as canonical, while the Svetambara sect recognizes forty-five. Some Jains claim a longer list of eighty-four. The foremost European authority on this religion reports that the sacred scriptures are little used by the Jains.

They do not seem much to study the sacred texts themselves, but usually content themselves with quoting lists of the names of their books. (Mrs. Stevenson, *Heart of Jainism*, 13.)

The language of the Jain scriptures is one of the Prakrit vernaculars which was current in north-central India at the time of Mahavira. The early important commentaries on the Prakrit canon and much of the later religious literature of Jainism were written in Sanskrit. Neither language is known to the bulk of the Jains now living. The sacred scriptures in the original are read or chanted in the temple regularly, and even pious laymen do recite from the texts daily. But most Jains are quite ignorant of their own sacred scriptures. A few have been translated into the present vernaculars. Four have been translated in two volumes of the *Sacred Books of the East*. Three others have been translated by European scholars.

Thus only a small fraction of the sacred scriptures of Jainism have become available in English.

5. THE CONCEPTION OF SUPREME BEING

Jainism started by denying any Supreme Being in the world. Mahavira rejected the whole current Hindu polytheistic belief in various natural and supernatural powers as quite superfluous. He condemned the practice of praying to or even talking about any deity.

A monk or a nun should not say, "The god of the sky!" "The god of the thunderstorm!" "The god who begins to rain!" "May rain fall!" "May the crops grow!" "May the king conquer!" They should not use such speech. But, knowing the nature of things, he should say, "The air." "A cloud is gathered, or come down." "The cloud has rained." This is the whole duty. (*SBE*, 22 : 152.)

The sturdy Mahavira scorned the plea that any person needs the help of a friend on high.

Man! Thou art thy own friend! Why wishest thou for a friend beyond thyself? (*SBE*, 22 : 33.)

The usual cosmological argument for a Creator God is denounced in the scriptures as an indication of sheer ignorance.

Those who on arguments of their own maintain that the world has been created do not know the truth. (*SBE*, 45 : 245.)

However, a reaction subsequently took place. Mahavira himself became apotheosized, and many other saviors, perfect ones, and victors were believed in, despite the founder's denial of any kind of theistic belief.

There is a strange mystery in Jainism; for though it acknowledges no personal God, knowing Him neither as Creator, Father, or Friend, yet it will never allow itself to be called an atheistic system. Indeed, there is no more deadly insult that one could level at a Jain than to call him a *nastika* or atheist. (Mrs. Stevenson, *Heart of Jainism*, 298.)

Mahavira did teach the doctrine of Karma (the law of the deed), which administers moral retribution in a future life.

This is an impersonal cosmic power which is active, knowable, and inescapable. Jainism's conception of the Supreme Being is quite different from Hinduism's doctrine of the Supreme Being, Brahma, which is unknowable, non-moral, and merely metaphysical.

But if, indeed, there is no supreme personal divinity, there are beings which, while not technically gods, have come to take the place of divinities among the Jains, certainly at the popular level. These are the Tirthankaras, or Ford-finders, twenty-four in number, of whom Mahavira was the last, who have succeeded in achieving final release or *Moksha.* They are not able to help anyone else. Each person must win salvation by his own efforts, as Mahavira taught. But the Jains have built innumerable temples all over India, some of the most elaborate to be found, where they come and do *puja* or worship before the Tirthankaras. The instructed say that while the Tirthankaras cannot know what the worshippers say, and are incapable of response, there is nevertheless great subjective value in such worship.[1] The very existence of the Tirthankaras is proof that man can win *Moksha,* and men are thus encouraged in their efforts. One suspects that the ordinary layman makes no such distinction, and seeks help from them as men everywhere do from their gods.

6. THE ETHICS OF JAINISM

The perfect Jain is an ascetic, humble, inoffensive, and unvindictive.

Learn from me the noble Law of the Jains as it is. . . . Deceit, greed, anger and pride: a wise man should abstain from these. . . . Shoes, umbrella, dice, working for another, helping each other: from all this a wise man should abstain. . . . If beaten, he should not be angry; if abused, he should not fly into a passion; with a placid mind he should bear everything, and not make a great noise. (*SBE*, 45 : 301–305.)

[1] For an extremely useful distinction between subjective and objective worship, see J. B. Pratt, *The Religious Consciousness* (New York, Macmillan, 1926). See also his *India and Its Faiths* (New York, Houghton Mifflin, 1915), chap. 13, especially 270–272.

A monk should not be angry, if beaten; nor should he entertain sinful thoughts. Knowing patience to be the highest good, a monk should meditate on the law. (SBE, 45 : 12.)

Love, as well as hate, must be abandoned, because both are forms of attachment.

A monk who loves not even those who love him, will be freed from sin and hatred. (SBE, 45 : 32.)
By conquering love, hate, and wrong belief he will cut off the fetters of Karma. (SBE, 45 : 172.)
By the teaching of true knowledge, by the avoidance of ignorance and delusion, and by the destruction of love and hatred, one arrives at final deliverance. (SBE, 45 : 184.)

The chief virtues of Jainism are mendicant asceticism and non-injury (ahimsa).

Alone, living on allowed food, he should wander about. . . . He should beg food. A wise man should not care whether he gets alms or not. (SBE, 45 : 12–13.)
Dish-water, barley-pap, cold sour gruel, water in which barley has been washed: such loathsome food and drink he should not despise, but call at the lowliest houses for alms. Then he is a true monk. (SBE, 45 : 72.)
This is the quintessence of wisdom; not to kill anything. (SBE, 45 : 247.)

Though this principle of ahimsa is to be found also in Hinduism and Buddhism, nowhere has it been so rigorously practiced as among the Jain monks who are forbidden to take life at any level, even the very lowest. This has, of course, led to the practice of a rigid vegetarianism, and has led even the laymen, of whom not so strict a practice has been required, to refrain from any means of livelihood which might cause the direct destruction of life. Thus, there are few Jain farmers, since it is next to impossible to avoid killing insects, worms, etc., when tilling the soil. They are more often found in commerce or banking or the professions. It was this principle of ahimsa which furnished the basis for Mr. Gandhi's non-violent method of seeking India's independence from Great Britain.

Mahavira enjoined upon his followers "Five Great Vows," which prohibit killing, lying, stealing, all sexual pleasures, and attachments. (*SBE*, 22 : 202–210.)

7. OTHER IMPORTANT FEATURES OF JAINISM

The cause of all misery is the connection of the vile material body with the pure eternal spirit of man. This theory is philosophically known as dualism. Matter and human spirit are two absolutely different kinds of being.

The practical application of this theory is that every Jain should suppress his body for the sake of liberating his soul, even as did the "Great Victor" Mahavira. The goal of salvation is Moksha or Nirvana. This is a state of blessedness in which the individual soul is released from all bodily encumbrance or attachment, and also from all previous "karma" or deeds.

The complete method of salvation has been formulated in "The Three Jewels" of Jainism.

Knowledge, faith and right conduct are the true causes of final liberation. (*SBE*, 45 : 123.)

One of the clearest differentiations of Jainism from Hinduism is that Mahavira condemned the fourfold hereditary caste system. In place thereof he brought all of his devotees into a voluntarily entered monastic order, the "Sangha," literally "congregation." Yet, for lack of a constructive principle of social organization, Jainism has not succeeded in freeing itself from the idea of caste, which has been so strong in the life of India. Even the gods, who subsequently were reinstated in Jainism, have been arranged in social ranks.

As on earth, or rather as in India, there are sweepers who act as scavengers for men, and live apart from them, so in the heavens there are gods who do menial service for the other gods, and live apart from them. Altogether there are in heaven and hell ninety-nine kinds of gods who are regarded as menial because they serve. (Mrs. Stevenson, *Heart of Jainism*, 270.)

Karma, the moral law of retribution for deeds done, is another important feature of Jainism. The exact application of the law of Karma is in the transmigration of souls, which causes rebirth in this same miserable world or into one of the several hells or heavens which they carried over from Hinduism according to the deeds of a previous existence.

I shall now explain in due order the eight kinds of Karma, bound by which the soul turns round and round in the circle of births. (*SBE*, 45 : 192.)

By hurting these beings, men do harm to their own souls, and will again and again be born as one of them. (*SBE*, 45 : 292.)

Womankind is utterly condemned in the scriptures of Jainism.

He, Mahavira, to whom women were known as the causes of all sinful acts, he saw the true state of the world. (*SBE*, 22 : 81.)

Women are the greatest temptation in the world. This has been declared by the sage. He should not speak of women, nor look at them, nor converse with them, nor claim them as his own, nor do their work. (*SBE*, 22 : 48.)

And yet women were admitted as nuns into a separate monastic order.

8. SECTS IN JAINISM

The main division in the Jain community has been between the "White-clad" Svetambara sect and the "Sky-clad" Digambara sect. About the year 310 B. C., when the mendicant community was suffering from a great famine in north India, a party of perhaps 12,000 Jains, under the leadership of Bhadrabahu, emigrated to Mysore, in south India. In that warmer region, where less clothes are needed, a stricter asceticism has been observed than by the Jains in the north. The two sections split definitely about the year 82 A. D., on the troublesome question of wearing clothes. Ever since that date most of the Jains who live in the cooler regions north of the Vindhya Mountains have belonged to the white-clad Svetambara sect, while the Jains in the southern half of India have belonged to the naked Digambara sect. But Islamic invaders have compelled the Digambara Jains to wear at least a loin-cloth.

These two main sects differ also on the propriety of garbing their idols. Among the Svetambara Jains idols as well as human beings are clad in simple white. The idols of the Digambara Jains are unclad, like their worshippers.

Another marked difference is in the treatment of women. Recognized nuns are found, naturally, only among the Svetambara sect. The Digambara sect does not allow the possibility of religious salvation to a woman until by reason of a good life she becomes reborn as a man.

The third chief group among the Jains is the non-idolatrous Sthanakvasi sect, founded by a Svetambara reformer who in 1474 A. D. discovered that certain of the Jain scriptures make no reference to idols. The Sthanakvasi Jains themselves have divided into eleven subsects, and the Svetambara Jains into at least eighty-four subsects.

9. THE HISTORY OF JAINISM

During their twenty-five centuries of existence the Jains have sometimes been active, and have won the favor of kings in India. They have produced some notable religious literature and architecture. However, on the whole they have remained an hereditary, self-centered, self-divided community. They have suffered from internal divisions of their own as well as some persecutions from Hindus and Muslims. In their long history there are a few outstanding events.

B. C.

513   The first schism took place fourteen years after the death of the Founder.

400   An image of Mahavira was first set up for worship in a Jain temple, though the date may possibly have been later. (Mrs. Stevenson, *Heart of Jainism,* 69.)

300   The first two main groups in the sacred scriptures were reputed to have been settled at the Council of Patna.

250   The great Buddhist monarch, Asoka, donated five caves to the Jains "for so long as the sun and moon do endure."

232   Samprali, grandson and successor of Asoka, established Jain temples and monasteries.

A. D.

100   Jain literature arose in the Tamil language in south
       India.

200   Jain literature arose in the vernaculars of Gujarat,
       western India.

514   Jainism's canon of sacred scripture was reputed to
       have been closed at the Council of Valabhi.

550   Jainism became popular in southern Maratha country
       in western India.

640   The famous Chinese Buddhist pilgrim, Hiuen Tsang,
       found many Jain temples and adherents at Con-
       jeevaram and elsewhere in south India. He also
       found in north India the nude and white-robed
       ascetics, who showed him "the spot where the
       original teacher arrived at the knowledge of the
       principles he sought, and where he first preached
       the law. (Beal's translation, *Buddhist Records of
       the Western World,* 1 : 144–145.)

650   The Hindu king, Kuna, persecuted the Jains at Arcot,
       south India, impaling 8,000. (Vincent Smith, *Early
       History of India,* 3d ed., 455.)

8th century.   The *Naladiyar,* a collection of gnomic quatrains which
       stands second highest in the literature of the Tamil
       people in south India, sprang from a nameless,
       though unmistakably, Jain source.

800   Tiruvalluvar's *Sacred Kurral,* perhaps the most
       famous poem in Tamil, used some technical terms
       of Jainism, and has been claimed as the work of a
       Jain.

815–880   Jainism in north India under the leadership of Jina-
       sena and Gunabhadra made notable progress in the
       reign of King Amoghavarsha.

1125–1159   The most eminent Jain scholar and author, Hema-
       chandra, converted a Hindu king in Gujarat, Ku-
       marapala, who thereupon built thirty-two Jain
       temples, and made his province the permanent
       stronghold of Jainism.

1174–1176   A later Hindu king of Gujarat, Ajayadeva, "began
       his reign by a merciless persecution of the Jains,
       torturing their leader to death," and destroying

                      Jain temples. (Vincent Smith, *Early History of India*, 3d ed., 203.)

1297–1298   The Islamic conqueror of Gujarat, Ala-ud-din, wrought a great devastation upon Jains.

1542–1605   The Grand Moghul Islamic emperor of India, Akbar, was favorably disposed to the Jains; he abolished the poll-tax in Gujarat, acknowledged their claim to certain holy pilgrimage places, and in deference to Jainism's teaching of kindness to animals, proclaimed a half-yearly abstinence from the slaughter of animals throughout India.

10. A COMPARISON OF JAINISM AND HINDUISM

Important points of original similarity and of original dissimilarity and then of growing resemblance may be noted between the first personally founded religion in India and the older spontaneous chief religion of the land.

(1) *Points of Original Similarity*

Mahavira was born and brought up, lived and died, in the Hindu faith. He did not reject Hinduism. And he was not rejected by the Hindus, as Jesus was rejected by the majority of his hereditary co-religionists, the Jews. Even after he had started at the age of thirty on a religious movement, which developed into an independent system, Mahavira continued to hold two firm Hindu beliefs: Karma, an impersonal cosmic law of moral retribution, and transmigration, or reincarnation of souls after death.

(2) *Points of Original Dissimilarity*

Jainism started with many more points of disagreement than of agreement.

Jainism protested against Hinduism's belief in deity, whether the many deities of the *Vedas* and the *Brahmanas*, or the one metaphysical Absolute of the *Upanishads*. Instead, Mahavira advocated no deity at all.

Jainism protested against Hinduism's monistic philosophy, which interprets the individual soul and all matter as a phase of the world soul. Indeed, Mahavira advocated a dualistic philosophy, which denies the theory of a world soul, and which affirms the reality of the individual soul and all matter.

Jainism protested against Hinduism's animal sacrifices, as reported both in the *Vedas* and in the *Brahmanas*. Instead, Mahavira advocated ascetic self-sacrifice and kindness to animals.

Jainism protested against Hinduism's social system of four graded castes. Instead, Mahavira advocated the equality of all men who practise religious asceticism.

Jainism protested against Hinduism's method of salvation by prayers and ceremonies with the help of priests and deities. Instead, Mahavira advocated a strictly self-saving scheme.

Jainism protested against Hinduism's sacred scriptures, the *Vedas,* written in the archaic Sanskrit language. Instead, Mahavira taught in the vernacular of his time, and all the sacred scriptures of Jainism were composed subsequently in that Prakrit vernacular.

Jainism protested against Hinduism's exclusive interest in one's own caste and in one's own country. Instead, Mahavira is reported to have received divine command to establish a religion which should prove beneficial to all people and to all the world.

(3) *Points of Subsequent Resemblance*

During the long course of their history these two religions have dwelt together in the land of India, and nowhere else. Accordingly, the younger, smaller religion has become assimilated to the older, larger religion at certain distinct points.

Both Jainism and Hinduism now have the belief in personal deity, Jainism chiefly in the person of its apotheosized founder, and Hinduism chiefly in the person of its incarnations, Krishna, Rama, Vishnu, and Siva.

Both Jainism and Hinduism now have polytheism, Jainism proceeding subsequently to evolve numerous deities, even as Hinduism did both before and after the origin of Jainism.

Both Jainism and Hinduism now have idolatry, although it was not present in Hinduism before the time of Mahavira, and although the anti-idolatrous Sthanakvasi sect in Jainism has arisen to protest against it.

Both Jainism and Hinduism now have temples, although previously temples were unknown in both religions, and now they resemble one another closely.

Both Jainism and Hinduism now have Brahman priests officiating in their temple-worship, although only individual members of the Hindu sacerdotal class are admitted into the Jain temples for this purpose occasionally.

Both Jainism and Hinduism now have the caste principle, which was rejected theoretically by Mahavira, but which was not supplanted by any other constructive principle of co-operation in human society, and which has subsequently been admitted even into the hierarchy of the deities in popular Jainism.

At the present time the Jains are feeling less and less of the differences which have separated them from the great environing body of Hindus in India, and are variously coming under the remarkable assimilative power of Hinduism, with its slight demand on belief, conscience, or conduct.

11. ELEMENTS OF STRENGTH IN JAINISM

A certain noble earnestness in the example of its self-sacrificing founder, who was utterly devoted to the highest religious ideal as he at last found it.

A certain noble insistence upon self-renunciation by every person at all personal cost in loyalty to the highest religious ideal as taught by the founder.

Its insistence upon the reality of the human soul, and also of the body, both being involved in a program of salvation.

Its subordination of all material things in the world for the sake of the religious values of the soul.

Its reverence for life, even though undiscriminating and imperfectly realized in practice.

A certain positive kindliness, viz., to animals.

Its theoretical condemnation of the principle of caste, even though not successful in rising wholly above caste.

Its "congregation," oldest among the voluntarily entered religious organizations in the world.

12. ELEMENTS OF WEAKNESS IN JAINISM

Its lack of a supreme personal deity, even though Mahavira is venerated.

Its lack of any divine help available for a human being, even though worship has been recovered in this originally atheistic system.

The essentially self-centered interest prescribed for each individual in a narrow self-saving scheme.

Its false analysis of the cause of evil as located primarily in the body.

Its excessive emphasis on external asceticism.

Its general negative method of repression.

Its inconsistence in advocating kindness to animals, while advocating harshness to oneself.

Its lack of discrimination between different values to be included in an abundant and harmonious life.

Its general indifference to joy, beauty and the world.

Its low estimate of the value of human life.

Its condemnation of woman and the family.

Its lack of any constructive principle of social organization or of social amelioration.

Its total loss of a certain former universal outlook.

Its historic lapse into idolatry and caste.

IV

BUDDHISM

The Religion of Peaceful,
Ethical Self-Culture

1. INTRODUCTION: AMONG THE WORLD'S LIVING RELIGIONS

Buddhism was the first religion in the world to become international. Yet theoretically Buddhism has often been denied the designation of being a religion.

Though for historical purposes we may class it as a religion, . . . it comes short of the notion of a religion, and is not properly entitled to that name. (Menzies, *History of Religion,* 353; similarly, 380, 424.)

The original Buddhism of Buddha might more precisely be thus disqualified, as by one of the foremost authorities on the subject.

Buddhism, at least in its earliest and truest form, is no religion at all, but a mere system of morality and philosophy founded on a pessimistic theory of life. (Monier-Williams, *Buddhism,* 537; similarly, 539.)

Doubtless the founder did not set out to found a new religion. His main emphasis was on saving oneself from a world which is thoroughly infected with misery. IIe did not teach a personal deity, worship, or prayer. Yet he taught a moral law in the universe which was ethically superior to the metaphysical Supreme Being taught in the Hinduism from which he reacted. Subsequently Buddha himself was deified; numerous other deities have been believed in by the majority of Buddhists; and there have been developed worship and prayer and an ecclesiastical organization which, next to that of Jainism, is the oldest voluntarily entered religious organization in the world.

Only two others of the eleven world religions today claim to be universal. The world-wide outlook of Christianity started more than 500 years later, and that of Islam more than 1,100 years later than Buddhism. There are distinguished modern Hindus who believe that Hinduism is one which in a sense embraces all religions and might well become the religion of humanity as a whole, but Hindus have not generally acted logically upon the basis of this belief. That is, they have not sought actively to propagate their faith in other lands, except in the case of the Ramakrishna Movement, and to a lesser degree the Arya Samaj, and that only very recently.

Nobody knows how many Buddhists there are in the world. Estimates vary widely. A generation ago T. W. Rhys Davids, one of the great authorities on Buddhism, placed the number at five hundred million, though on the very next page he qualified it considerably:

Not one of the 500,000,000 who offers flowers now and then on Buddhist shrines, who are more or less moulded by Buddhist teachings, is only or altogether a Buddhist.

The fact that both in China and Japan one may be a Buddhist and at the same time follow also some form of the religions native to these countries makes it quite impossible to say with any exactness what proportion of these populous lands should be considered as Buddhist. An estimate as low as 150,000,000 is sometimes made.

At the present time Buddhism has virtually died out in India. According to the 1951 census, only 180,767 Buddhists were enumerated. Pakistan which was once a part of India reported 319,000. Thus, there was a total of just under one half million Buddhists in a combined population of over 432,000,000. This is only a little more than one tenth of one per cent. There are now Buddhist missionaries working in India, the land of the Buddha's birth.

Once an active and powerful missionary religion, Buddhism

was until comparatively recently quiescent. But that is no longer true. There are many evidences of an awakening within widely separated sectors of world-wide Buddhism. This has been notable in Japan, in Ceylon, and most recently in Burma. A new sense of world solidarity of Buddhists, not wholly unlike the ecumenical movement within non-Roman Catholic Christianity, is bringing together the widely different Northern and Southern schools of Buddhism. Successive World Conferences of Buddhists have been held in recent years, the most noteworthy being that held in Rangoon, Burma, in 1956 in celebration of the 2500th anniversary of Buddha's birth. This conference, initiated by Burmese Buddhists and paid for in considerable part by the Burmese government, was signalized not simply by the bringing together of delegates from Buddhist lands, but by the co-operation of scholars from all over the world in the translation and publication of Buddhist scriptures, the revision of earlier translations, the creation of new periodicals, the publication of learned studies of Buddhism, and in Burma itself, the revival of the study of Pali, the language of the scriptures, the establishment of numerous schools for this purpose, and the founding of a new Buddhist university in Burma to be housed in the buildings erected for the housing of the world conference. Something of the earlier missionary urge of Buddhism seems once again to be stirring.

2. THE LIFE OF THE FOUNDER, BUDDHA
(560–480 B. C.)

Some biographical material is to be found in the canonical scriptures, but no attempt at a complete biography. Later stories and poems contain many wonderful accounts; for example, his mother's dream of a non-human conception, and his supernatural birth from a queen mother when she was forty-five years old (Warren, *Buddhism in Translations*, 42–48).

Her son was born for the welfare of the world, without pain and without illness. Thus was his birth miraculous. (*SBE*, 49 : part 1, pp. 5–6.)

Many marvels accompanied his advent. A Hindu saint prophesied the future greatness of the infant (Warren, *BT*, 45–47; *SBE*, 19 : 16–18).

Doubts concerning the historicity of the founder of Buddhism were settled when in December, 1896 Doctor Fuhrer, of the British Archæological Survey, unearthed the inscription on the stone pillar which the famous Buddhist convert, King Asoka, had erected at Kapilavastu, the birthplace of Buddha, about 250 B. C.[1]

(1) *A Palace Prince* (*Age* 1–29)

His own name was Gautama in Sanskrit, or Gotama in Pali. He was born the only son and heir presumptive of the rich Hindu rajah of the Sakya clan at the town of Kapilavastu, about a hundred miles north of Benares. He was reared in luxurious circumstances.

And the king procured nurses for the future Buddha, women of fine figure, and free from all blemish. And so the future Buddha began to grow, surrounded by an immense retinue, and in great splendor. (Warren, *BT*, 53.)

At sixteen his father built three palaces for the young prince.

And in the enjoyment of great magnificence he lived, as the seasons changed, in each of these three palaces. (Warren, *BT*, 55.)

At nineteen he was married to a neighboring princess, but he had no son for ten years.

(2) *The Great Renunciation* (*Age* 29)

While out pleasure driving Prince Gautama was deeply impressed by four passing sights, viz., a decrepit old man, a loathsomely sick man, a corpse, and a calm religious ascetic unperturbed by any suffering. He became distressed at the thought that he himself and all mankind were liable to the miseries of oncoming old age, sickness, and death. And he became convinced that only resolute self-sacrifice and search would win triumphant peace. Therefore, despite a fierce temptation, he renounced his wife, a new-born son, and the

[1] *Archæological Survey of North India*, vol. VI, 27–28, 1897.

inheritance of his father's throne. Cutting off his hair, he assumed the garb of a monk (*SBE*, 19 : 31–58; 49 : 1. 27–61; Warren, *BT*, 56–67).

(3) *Seeking Salvation* (*Age* 29–35)

He started to solve the problem of wide-spread suffering by following Hinduism's most approved method of salvation, viz., philosophic speculation concerning the interrelationship of the human individual with the Supreme Being.

Yet even so he came not out of the mire. (*SBE*, 19 : 142.)

Thereupon he tried bodily asceticism, the method which Jainism advocates for salvation.

Living on one sesamum seed, or on one grain of rice, a day. Now, the six years which the Great Being thus spent in austerities were like time spent in endeavoring to tie the air into knots.

(*Warren, BT*, 70–71.)

(4) *The Great Enlightenment* (*Age* 35)

Alone in quiet meditation one night, while sitting cross-legged under a *bo*-tree, he analyzed out a simple psychological solution of the cause and cure of evil. The fundamental universal "Four Noble Truths" of Buddhism may be summarized thus:

All existence involves suffering.
All suffering is caused by indulging in inherently insatiable desires. Therefore all suffering will cease upon the suppressing of these desires.
And the way leading to the cessation of suffering is the Middle-Path, or the Noble Eight-fold Path, that is, right views, right aims, right speech, right action, right livelihood, right effort, right mindfulness, right contemplation. (*SBE*, 10 : 1. 52; 11 : 148–152; 13 : 95–102; 17 : 104–105.)

The Four Noble Truths and the Eight-fold Path formed the heart of Buddha's own teaching and have continued to be the core of the teaching of the Southern School of Buddhism or Hinayana, though the Northern School, or Mahayana, has developed ideas which seem to differ appreciably from the relatively simple, rather austere outlook of the founder.

The word which seems most completely to have characterized this critical spiritual experience was "buddha," the past participle of the Sanskrit verb "to become enlightened," or "wise." And "Buddha" has been his special appellation or title ever since.

As soon as my knowledge and insight were quite clear regarding each of these four noble truths, then did I become certain that I had attained to the full insight of that wisdom which is unsurpassed in the heavens or on the earth. Immovable is the emancipation of my heart. This is my last existence. There will be no rebirth for me. (*SBE*, 11 : 152–153.)

His sense of relief in being freed from the dread of transmigration is recorded in several of the canonical documents as an integral part of his "enlightenment" (*SBE*, 10 : 1. 42–43; 11 : 153; 13 : 97; Warren, *BT*, 338).

(5) *Public Ministry* (*Age* 35–80)

Straightway he went forth throughout his native country of Magadha, in north India, and preached his new-found gospel of salvation by psychological, self-disciplinary, ethical culture, saying that an earnest person needs only to exercise a wise manipulation of his own states of consciousness, without any of the conventional appliances of religion, such as deity, worship, ceremony, dogma, priesthood, or supernatural connections. Buddha inveighed particularly against the current Hindu conceptions of an alleged metaphysical supreme being and the value of prayer and the sacredness of the Vedic scriptures.

Who has ever seen Brahma face to face?
Would the further bank of the river Akirvati by reason of that man's invoking and praying, hope and praising come over to this side?
The talk then of these Brahmans, versed in the Vedas, turns out to be ridiculous, mere words, a vain and empty thing! (*SBE*, 11 : 172, 174, 180.)

When he had gained sixty disciples, he sent them also to carry abroad his simple message of a salvation more urgently needed, and more freely available than Hinduism had announced.

Go ye now out of compassion for the world, for the welfare of gods and men. Let not two of you go the same way. Preach the doctrine which is glorious. Proclaim a consummate, perfect and pure life of holiness. (*SBE*, 13 : 112–113; similarly, 11 : 60.)

Buddha was an effective preacher and personal worker, who wrought many conversions. Some of his parables are similar to those of Jesus, yet are remarkably different, such as the parable of a Sower (*SBE*, 10 : 2. 11–15), of a Prodigal Son (*SBE*, 21 : 99–106), of the Mustard Seed (Rhys Davids, *Buddhism, a Sketch*, 133–134). A large number of parables are collected in E. W. Burlingame, *Buddhist Parables*.

By hundreds of arguments and illustrations have I, in one way or another, gladdened all creatures. (*SBE*, 21 : 44.)

Buddha died at the age of eighty, very decrepit in body, but invincible in spirit, in a little "wattel-and-daub town, in a branch village," where he happened to be at the time in his task of itinerant preaching, surrounded by a group of 500 disciples.

In this whole assembly of the brethren there is not one brother who has any doubt or misgiving as to the Buddha, or the truth, or the path, or the way. . . . Then the Blessed One addressed the brethren, and said: "Behold now, brethren, decay is inherent in all component things! Work out your own salvation with diligence!" This was the last word of the Blessed One. (*SBE*, 11 : 114; 19 : 307; Warren, *BT*, 109.)

3. THE VENERATION OF BUDDHA

One of the striking facts in the history of religions is the way in which Buddha, who taught no divine object of worship, but who labored self-sacrificingly for the saving of the world, has himself been loved and worshipped.

(1) *Evidence for the Humanity of Buddha*

The earlier and simpler narratives in the canonical scriptures report various incidents which show that Buddha was subject to common human weaknesses, even after his "enlightenment."

The Blessed One was troubled with wind on his stomach.

(SBE, 17 : 68.)

Now, when the Blessed One had eaten the food prepared by Kunda, the worker in metal, there fell upon him a dire sickness, the disease of dysentery; and a sharp pain came upon him, even unto death. (SBE, 11 : 72.)

(2) His Disciples' Unbounded Admiration of Buddha

His devoted, loving disciples had no condemnation to make of him who might easily have ruled as a king, but who voluntarily relinquished his royal inheritance for religion's sake, and who then for well-nigh half a century made himself as one of the common folk for the salvation of the world.

No fault in the perfectly enlightened, thoughtful Buddha.

(SBE, 10 : 2. 29.)

So unequalled in the world, so mild, so kind! And held before him aims so high and endeavors so grand! (SBE, 35 : 178.)

A king of universal kings, a conqueror. (SBE, 10 : 2. 102.)

Emotional admiration of Buddha as perfect grew into formal adoration of him as superior even to the gods of Hinduism.

The noblest of men, like Indra himself. (SBE, 49 : 1. 56.)

The heavenly beings with Brahma at their head, went to the city and worshipped him, propitiating his favor. (SBE, 49 : 1. 190.)

Gods and men will worship him as "The Great One that hath transcended time." Nor is there in the world with its gods any one Thy equal.

(J. H. Moore, Iti-vuttaka, the Sayings of Buddha, 132–133.)

(3) Evidence for the Divinity of Buddha

He appeared and taught in an assembly marvellously, and disappeared, leaving the people to wonder:

Who may this be, who has thus vanished away? a man, or a god? (SBE, 11 : 49.)

His birth was accompanied by thirty-two prognostications, which included the following items:

The blind recovered their sight, as if from desire to see this his glory. The deaf received their hearing. The dumb talked. The hunchbacked became straight of body. The lame recovered the power to walk. All those in bonds were freed from their bonds and chains. (Warren, *BT*, 44.)

His "enlightenment" was accompanied by similar attestations:

The blind from birth received their sight; the deaf from birth their hearing; the cripples from birth the use of their limbs; and the bonds and fetters of captives broke, and fell off. (Warren, *BT*, 83.)

(4) Buddha, the Object of Theological Speculation

There have been two main branches in Buddhism. The followers of the "Lesser Vehicle," Hinayana Buddhism, in southern Asia, have sought to remain true to his own teaching, viz., that he was only a teacher of a way of escape from misery, and that speculative questions are profitless for religion.

Misery have I elucidated. The origin of misery have I elucidated. The cessation of misery have I elucidated. And the path leading to the cessation of misery have I elucidated . . . because this has to do with the fundamentals of religion, and tends to aversion, absence of passion, cessation, quiescence, knowledge, supreme wisdom, Nirvana. (Warren, *BT*, 122.)

The northern branch, which has carried Buddhism so extensively to China and Japan, has developed certain theological doctrines which constitute the Mahayana, "Greater Vehicle." It sees in Buddha not simply a teacher who passed into Nirvana at his death, but a veritable divine savior:

Pre-existent, planfully incarnate, supernaturally conceived, miraculously born. (Warren, *BT*, 42–46.)
Sinless, yet suffering inexplicably. (*SBE*, 35 : 178.)
Entered the world with a redemptive purpose. (*SBE*, 21 : 40, 46.)
All-knowing and all-seeing. (*SBE*, 21 : 44, 118, 121.)
Saviour of gods and men. (*SBE*, 21 : 120.)
He is everlasting. (*SBE*, 21 : 302.)

Not only has Buddha been deified, but he has been made a member of a Buddhist Trinity.

Differences in the interpretation both of the Buddha and his teachings early developed within Buddhism. Thought of at first as unique, in time the belief grew up that there was not one and one only Buddha, but that others existed also. Even Southern or Hinayana Buddhism now makes room for multiple Buddhas, while in the Northern school the number of Buddhas is infinite.

How this came about it is not difficult to see. Buddhism began by repudiating all the gods, at least any dependence on them, though the Buddha often referred to the gods as though they existed. Then Buddha himself began to be deified. But the medium in which Buddhism developed was polytheistic. There were gods almost without number. Why not also plural Buddhas? Hinduism was beginning its reabsorption of its daughter faith. One of the suggested reasons for the virtual disappearance of Buddhism from India is that it thus lost its distinctiveness and hence its reason to exist separately.

Not only did Buddhahood become a plural concept, but the very ideal and aim was eventually changed from that of seeking release from the wheel of life in Nirvana to that of becoming a Buddha. Buddhahood thus became the goal of their striving, the definition of salvation or Moksha for Northern Buddhists.

How could Buddhahood be won? At first by a long slow disciplined process which eventually distinguished ten stages through which the individual must pass. He must take the vow to become a Buddha, then subject himself to the disciplines appropriate to the various stages. Many, many existences might be required before reaching the coveted state of Buddhahood, which, defined, did not seem to differ greatly from the state of Nirvana. One who had set himself on the way to Buddhahood came to be called a Bodhisattva. At first only a human individual, eventually the belief arose that after passing through the seventh stage there could be no turning back, and the Bodhisattva then became a cosmic being.

Probably under the influence of the idea of *Bhakti* that had
developed in Hinduism, and the belief that a god or gods in
whom one had the requisite faith might enable one to achieve
Moksha or salvation, these Bodhisattvas came to be regarded
as cosmic helpers, or saviors, who could aid others on the
way. If, from the standpoint of the original Buddhism which
believed that salvation must be won without the help of anyone outside the self, this seems a far cry from the Buddha's
teaching, it nevertheless made a great popular appeal, and
millions of Buddhists in China and Japan who believe thus
think of themselves as true Buddhists today.

One Bodhisattva, called in India "Amitabha," in China
"Omito-fu," and in Japan "Amida," is said to have taken a vow
not to enter finally into the state of Buddhahood without the
assurance that all who might call upon his name would be
saved. Thus, he is considered the saviour by great numbers
of Buddhists of the so-called Pure Pand Sects. They believe
that it is through him that they win entrance into the Western
Paradise. This is a type of devotional religion somewhat like
that associated with Krishna in Hinduism and with Jesus in
some Christian sects.

Among the non-popular Mahayana sects of China and Japan
may be found some whose philosophical outlook bears the
mark of the metaphysical influence of India. It is difficult to
distinguish sharply, for instance, between the Dharmakaya
of Mahayana Buddhism and the Hindu Brahman. And the
relation of the various Buddhas and Bodhisattvas to the
Dharmakaya seems strangely similar to the relationship between the lesser gods of India and Brahman, the metaphysical
world ground of Hinduism.

(5) *Buddha Idolized*

It is one of the ironies of history that he whose main message and very last words before dying were a call to a self-
reliant, ethical life as over against dependence upon any kind
of a Divine Being, should himself be subsequently worshipped
with larger and perhaps more numerous images than exist of

any other person in the history of the world. (*SBE*, 11 : 114; Warren, *BT*, 109.)

4. THE ETHICS OF BUDDHISM

The practical message of Buddha is in marked contrast with the dreamy speculations of philosophic Hinduism concerning an ineffiable Supreme Being, and, too, in marked contrast with the paid priests, the ritual sacrifices, and the many religious ceremonies of sacerdotal Hinduism. One short Buddhist document, the *Dhamma-pada,* contains more than a score of passages which enjoin self-control, self-conquest, self-purification, the need for unceasing alertness, and personal responsibility for personal salvation.

It is good to tame the mind, which is difficult to hold in and flighty. A tamed mind brings happiness. (*SBE*, 10 : 1. 12.) [1]

Not even a God, a Gandharva [*i. e.*, spirit], not Mara [*i. e.*, demon], with Brahma could change into defeat the victory of a man who has vanquished himself, and always lives under restraint.

(*SBE*, 10 : 1. 31–32.)

Buddha had the daring of a truly remarkable reformer in his denunciation and reinterpretation of the Hindu caste system. Five hundred years before Christ and with some of the same words Buddha told the proud rapacious sinners of his day that the really admirable high-class man and the really despicable low-down man must be judged in terms of moral character, not primarily in terms of heredity or status or according to the externals of conventional religion.

A man does not become a Brahman by his family or by birth. In whom there is truth and righteousness,—he is blessed; he is a Brahman. O fool, within thee there is ravening, but the outside thou makest clean! (*SBE*, 10 : 1. 91; similarly, 10 : 1. 38–39, 90–96; 10 : 2. 88, 111–115; 13 : 79–80.)
The man who is angry and bears hatred, who harms living beings, who speaks falsely, who exalts himself and despises others,—let one know him as an outcast. (*SBE*, 10 : 2. 21–22.)

[1] The references to vol. 10 in the *Sacred Books of the East* are to its second edition.

All the four Hindu castes are dropped on entering the Buddhist Order (*SBE*, 20 : 304).

Five prohibitions are enjoined by Buddha upon all lay Buddhists:

Do not kill, steal, commit adultery, lie, or drink intoxicants.
(*Sutta-Nipata*, 392–398; *SBE*, 10 : 2. 63–66.)

Ten prohibitions are enjoined upon the higher grade of monastics.

In addition to the previous five, the five following abstinences: from eating at forbidden times; from dancing, singing, music, and seeing spectacles; from garlands, scents, unguents, ornaments, and finery; from high or broad beds; from accepting gold or silver. (*SBE*, 13 : 211.)

The main trend in Buddhist ethics is negative, repressive, quietistic, individualistic, non-social.

Forsake children, wealth and kin. (*Theri-gatha*, 301; Mrs. Rhys Davids, *Psalms of the Sisters*, 133.)
Let him wander alone like a rhinoceros. (*SBE*, 10 : 2. 6–11.)
If a disciple should desire to become converted, to be no longer liable to be reborn in a state of suffering, and to be assured of final salvation,—then let him fulfil all righteousness; let him be devoted to that quietude of heart which springs from within; let him not drive back the ecstasy of contemplation; let him look through all things; let him be much alone. (*SBE*, 11 : 213.)

But at the same time it must also be said that this is not the whole story. In the *Dhamma-pada* one finds sayings like these which are certainly not negative:

For hatred does not cease by hatred at any time; hatred ceases by love. (I.5)

Let a man overcome anger by love, let him overcome evil by good; let him overcome the greedy by liberality, the liar by the truth. (XVII. 3)

And in his famous Sermon on Abuse, the Buddha said:

If a man foolishly does me wrong, I will return to him the protection of my ungrudging love; the more evil comes from him, the more good shall go from me.

It is told of the Buddha that he once found one of his monks sick and unattended, lying in his own vomit. The Buddha ministered to him, leaving him clean and refreshed. Later he rebuked the other monks who acknowledged that they had seen him in his illness but had done nothing to relieve him. Preoccupation with even monastic duties must not render his followers indifferent to human need. It is not accidental that in the Buddhist world there exists a widespread gentleness and kindliness which is not always found in peoples of the West. Nor that in the history of the spread of Buddhism violence has played no role. It is true that certain Buddhist monks at one time in Japan carried swords, and violence has attended the struggle between sects in Tibet, but in general, Buddhism is freer from the element of violence than either Christianity or Islam.

The acme of the Buddhist ethical ideal is reached in a state of perfection which is beyond the realm of ethics, even by him who

Has ceased to think of good or evil. (*SBE*, 10 : 1. 13.)
Has risen above both good and evil. (*SBE*, 10 : 1. 94.)

5. OTHER PRINCIPAL FEATURES OF BUDDHISM

Buddhism did not start with the belief in an adorable supreme being. Nor is it the philosophical elaboration of a consistent system, except as a happy ending of a pessimistic world view. Accordingly, Buddhism contains a number of features, not all of which are coherently connected.

(1) *The Law of Karma*

The supreme power which is actually operating in the world is the "law of the deed"—an inescapable, inexorable, impersonal principle of justice and moral retribution.

Not in the sky, not in the midst of the sea, not if we enter into the clefts of the mountains, is there known a spot where a man might be freed from an evil deed. (*Dhamma-pada*, 127; *SBE*, 10 : 1. 35.)

The blame for the consequences of a person's evil deeds must be placed upon himself, not upon heredity, society, fate,

God, or devil. Buddha had great faith in the reform which would be accomplished, if only people could be made to realize that in accordance with the law of Karma most of their troubles have been brought upon themselves by themselves.

Surely if living creatures saw the consequences of all their evil deeds, self-visited, with hatred would they turn and leave them. (*SBE,* 19 : 158.)

The final judgment scene is depicted as follows:

The warders of hell drag the wicked before the king of hell, Yama, who says to them: "Did you not, when on earth, see the five messengers sent to warn you,—the child, the old man, the sick, the criminal suffering punishment, and the dead corpse?" And the wicked man answers: "I did see them." "And didst thou not think within thyself: 'I also am subject to birth, old age, death! Let me be careful to do good works!'" And the wicked man answers: "I did not, sire. I neglected in my folly to think of these things." Then King Yama pronounces his doom: "These thy evil deeds are not the work of thy mother, father, relations, friends, advisers. Thou alone hast done them all. Thou alone must gather the fruit." (Monier-Williams, *Buddhism,* 114–115; quoted from Oldenberg, *Buddha,* 244–245; Warren, *Buddhism,* 255–257; *Anguttara Nikaya* 3. 35.)

(2) *The Delusion of Self*

The fundamental subtle danger which every wise person must himself eradicate from himself is selfishness.

First banish every ground of "self." This thought of "self" shades every lofty good aim, even as the ashes that conceal the fire, treading on which the foot is burned. (*SBE,* 19 : 261.)
Cut out the love of self, like an autumn lotus, with thy hand.
(*SBE,* 10 : 1. 69.)

The so-called "ego" is not a genuine personality, but only a temporary worthless conglomeration of desires and psychic tendencies, just as:

The word "chariot" is but a convenient designation and name for pole, axle, wheels, chariot-body, and banner-staff.
(Warren, *BT,* 132.)

(3) *The Three Characteristics of Being*

There is no such thing as mere existence. According to Buddha's pessimistic analysis of the universe, to be means to be evanescent, miserable, and impersonal.

Whether Buddhas [*i. e.*, Enlightened Ones] arise, or whether Buddhas do not arise, it is a fact and a fixed and necessary constitution of being that all its constituents are transitory, miserable, lacking in an ego. (Warren, *BT*, p. xiv.)

(4) *Transmigration*

The particular manner in which the law of Karma operates is to produce reincarnation in this same miserable world according unto a person's deeds.[1] The problem arises, how there can be a transmigration of the soul when there really is no soul. However, since Buddha himself at his enlightenment experienced the sense of relief from the dreaded necessity of transmigration, the same hope is offered to every Buddhist (*SBE*, 10 : 2. 58, 198; 11 : 25, 213; 13 : 101; 17 : 9).

(5) *Nirvana*

The technical term in Buddhism which has become most familiar in English is probably the word "Nirvana." This is represented as "the highest happiness" (*SBE*, 10 : 1. 9, 55). But scholars disagree on the question whether Nirvana involves complete annihilation.[2] An utter extinction of personality and consciousness would seem to be implied by the fundamental principles of Buddhism and also by explicit statements of Buddha, such as:

[1] It is not at all unusual to find among well-educated Buddhists, especially in Northern Buddhism, those who declare that the Buddha never really taught the doctrine of rebirth in a literal sense.

[2] For a discussion of the meaning of Nirvana, see Charles S. Braden, *Man's Quest for Salvation*, Chicago, Willett, Clark and Co. (1941), pp. 57–63. A much fuller treatment is that of L. de la Vallee de Poussin, *The Way to Nirvana* (Cambridge University Press, 1917). He comes at last to the conclusion that "the most exact and authoritative definition of Nirvana is not annihilation but 'unqualified deliverance,' a deliverance of which we have no right to predicate anything." P. 22.

Those whose minds are disgusted with a future existence, the wise who have destroyed the seeds of existence, and whose desires do not increase, go out like this lamp. (*SBE*, 10 : 2. 39.)

However, Nirvana certainly does mean the highest conceivable freedom from all disturbances. It is chiefly a negative condition—passionless peace.

(6) *The Buddhist Congregation*

Theoretically Buddhism, with its distinctively individualistic anti-social doctrines, would seem to have no place for society. Yet Buddha was practical enough to organize his converts into a new monastic order. The most important formula in Buddhism is the "Three Refuges," which is a convenient summary of Buddhism, and which is used in the ceremony of admitting initiates.

I take refuge in the Buddha, the Law, the Order. (*SBE*, 10 : 2. 37–40; 13 : 109, 115.)

Candidates for admission must pass the following tests:

Are you afflicted with the following diseases: leprosy, boils, dry leprosy, consumption, and fits? Are you a man? Are you a male? Are you a freeman? Have you no debts? Are you not in royal service? Have your father and mother given their consent? Are you full twenty years old? Are your alms-bowl and your robes in due state? (*SBE*, 13 : 230.)

However, women were admitted later, but to a distinctly lower position (*SBE*, 20 : 322–326). The Buddhist "church," if such it may be called without any worship, is directed to meet for recitation of the words of Buddha and for confession.

Every half month it behooves all to train themselves according thereto in concord, in pleasantness, without dispute. (*SBE*, 13 : 69.)

The 227 rules which must be repeated in the assembly every fortnight occupy the first of the "Three Baskets."

Buddhist monasticism varies from country to country. For example, in both Burma and Thailand, theoretically every boy is supposed to enter the order for at least six months, and a surprising percentage of them do so. This accounts for the very large number of monks to be seen in those countries. In Burma, also, it is quite a common practice for laymen to return to the monastic discipline for brief periods. But in addition to the monasteries there are numerous temples and stupas, or dagobas, or pagodas (the name varies) where the layman performs his worship. As in Jainism, for the instructed, it is a subjective matter, for the Buddha can help no one. But for one watching the ordinary layman praying before a Buddha image, it is impossible to see any difference between their worship and that of the frankly objective worshippers in Hinduism and other religions who believe that the god to whom they pray can help them.

6. THE SACRED SCRIPTURES OF BUDDHISM

The *Tripitaka*, meaning "Three Baskets" of Wisdom, consists of the *Vinaya Pitaka* (Discipline Basket), containing rules for the initiates in the order, or higher class of Buddhists; the *Sutta Pitaka* (Teaching Basket), containing the discourses of Buddha; and the *Abhidhamma Pitaka* (Higher Doctrine or Metaphysical Basket), containing expositions of the intricate points of Buddhist psychology and doctrine.

The *Tripitaka* is preserved in the Pali language, a literary dialect closely related to the Maghadi which was the spoken dialect used by Gautama and his followers. It is the canon recognized by the Southern school of Buddhism, or the Hinayana. Is is also known as the Theravada canon. The scriptures of Mahayana or Northern Buddhism are preserved in Sanskrit, as are also many writings which are not considered as canonical.

The *Tripitaka* contains twenty-nine subdivisions, ranging in length from 10 pages to 1,839 pages. All of it has not been translated into English, nor even published in its original Pali. Under the leadership of the late Professor Rhys Davids of Manchester University and with the co-operation of various European scholars, the Pali Text Society of London has been active on a program of publishing the original documents and

English translations. The full text of the canonical scriptures, when completed, will probably occupy 10,000 pages.

A translation of the Buddhist scriptures into English would be about four times as long as the English Bible. (Rhys Davids, *Buddhism, a Sketch*, 20.)

The first English translation of any part of the *Tripitaka* was of the short *Dhamma-pada* ("Way of Virtue"), made in 1870 by the late Professor Max Müller of Oxford University. Buddhism has been a fascinating subject to the English-speaking world even before any of its sacred scriptures were available in translation. A generation ago the New York Public Library alone contained over two hundred books and important articles published on this religion in English before the date of 1870. That first-translated document of the *Tripitaka*, and the other one which is included in the tenth volume of the *Sacred Books of the East*, have received high commendation.

The *Dhamma-pada* and the *Sutta-Nipata* deserve to be read by all who care for the unseen riches of the soul. By their simple earnestness, their quaint use of parable and metaphor, and their mingling of the homeliest things with the highest truths, these books take rank among the most impressive of the religious books of the world. (Menzies, *History of Religion*, 373.)

Another section of the Buddhist *Tripitaka* has evoked from a professor of comparative religion at Manchester University the following, perhaps extravagant, comparison with one of the finest Greek philosophers:

Scholars will revere this book as one of the most priceless of the treasures of antiquity still preserved to us. And it is quite inevitable that, as soon as it is properly translated and understood, this collection of the Dialogues of Gotama will come to be placed, in our schools of philosophy and history, on a level with the Dialogues of Plato. (Rhys Davids, *Buddhism, Its History and Literature*, 59.)

The *Tripitaka* contains some reminiscences of Buddha, some elaborate doctrinal expositions, and much advice for a quiet life. Yet the canonical scriptures, certainly of Hinayana Buddhism, contain no complete biography of the founder, no report of any later leader continuing the work of the founder, no historic application of the highest Buddhist principles to the regeneration of society, no intimation of a creative purpose or power in the world, and no prophetic vision of a glorious abundant life here or hereafter.

In the Mahayana *Sutras* there is a very detailed description of the Western Paradise which is very appealing to the Buddhists of the popular Mahayana sects. It is to be found in the *Sukhavati-Vyuha,* translated in Vol. 40 of the *Sacred Books of the East.* Here is to be found not only peace and quietude, but beauty and richness of color, jeweled trees, wonderful lotus blossoms, no day or night, no distinction of gods or men, perfect beauty and happiness.

7. THE HISTORY OF BUDDHISM

In India Buddhism began its life some twenty-four hundred years ago. This long stretch of history has included some brilliant periods under devout and generous kings, such as Asoka, Kanishka, Chandragupta II, and Harsha. But about a thousand years after the founder the Buddhists of India allowed themselves to become corrupt in doctrine and distraught over petty matters. The Chinese Buddhist pilgrim, Hiuen Tsiang, who made the long journey to India in 629–645 A. D., and who has left an important record of his visit to the holy land of his faith, reports that the Greater Vehicle and the Lesser Vehicle were mutually exclusive, and that the eighteen main sects were wrangling about the size and cut of their robes.

The different schools are constantly at variance, and their contending utterances rise like the angry waves of the sea. (Beal, *Buddhist Records of the Western World,* 1 : 80.)

Accordingly, decadent Buddhism soon faded away before the pressure of another religion, Islam, which arrived in India with a God of power, a God-enthused founder, and a vigorous anti-idolatrous monotheism. According to the recent census records Buddhism is virtually extinct in the land of its birth.

The first foreign missionary enterprise of Buddhism was conducted in Ceylon by the son of King Asoka about 250 B. C. The impression which was left by those early Buddhist missionaries is recorded in the *Great Chronicle of Ceylon.*

As the All-merciful Conqueror [*i. e.,* Buddha] renounced his own blessedness, so these renounced the happiness they had won, and in this place and that toiled for the world's welfare. For, when the world's welfare is concerned, who would be slothful or indifferent? (*Mahavamsa,* 12 : 55.)

In the neighboring countries, Ceylon, Tibet, Burma and Siam, now called Thailand, Buddhism encountered none of the great ethnic faiths in any strength, but more primitive forms of native religion, chiefly animistic in belief and practice. These still exist alongside Buddhism, though considerably affected by it. And it must be said also that Buddhism at the popular level, at least, has been much affected by these simpler faiths. This is quite evident to those who visit their temples and watch the humble worshippers perform their worship, sometimes before old native divinities who have been admitted to the temples. The Buddhism of Tibet represents a very definite blending together of the native Bon religion and Mahayana Buddhism. The resultant Buddhism, called Lamaism, is quite different in many respects from that found anywhere else in the world. But the Bon religion itself was probably the result of a combination of the primitive Tibetan religion and Taoism before the arrival of Buddhism.

In China and Japan, geographically farthest away from its original home, Buddhism has won its largest and most active groups of followers. And here its doctrines have been most changed from their original form. In these countries it exists alongside of other religions, viz., the national religions of Confucianism, Taoism, and Shinto. In China the most popular Buddhist deity is a female, Kwan-yin, the goddess of mercy. In Japan the modern Buddhists have been adopting certain successful Christian methods; for example, congregational worship and singing, Sunday-schools for children, Young Men's Buddhist Association, woman's societies, social service and schools for the education of the laity. In both China and Japan, along with the original characteristic of general quietism, the Buddhists have developed certain tendencies which are radically inconsistent with the primitive system, such as a more active social and æsthetic appreciation, the hope of salvation through faith in Buddha, a picturesque heaven and hell, and a pantheon of deities.

Over all the Far East Buddha has succeeded in making the people feel more like one another than like the people of the Occident, because they have actually been brought under the influence of such common religious ideals as, that the perfect human life is a life of patient, long-suffering quietude; that no human individual, much less a woman or a child, possesses enduring religious worth; that the supreme power in the world is not a person, but is impersonal; and that the final beatitude is for the most part an escape from life rather than a continually enlarging life.

8. A COMPARISON OF HINDUISM, JAINISM, AND BUDDHISM

The three religions originating in India, and each with a history more than 500 years longer than the history of Christianity, are noticeably similar in certain respects, yet also noticeably dissimilar in other respects.

(1) *Points of Agreement between All Three Religions*

General pessimism concerning the worth of human life in the midst of the material and social world.

The specific worthlessness of the human body.

The specific worthlessness of human activity.

The specific worthlessness of the individual as such.

A common tendency to ascetic monastic orders.

A common tendency to sectarian subdivisions.

No program of organized social amelioration.

A common ideal of the greatest good as consisting in subservience, quiescence or passivity, certainly not universally beneficial.

A common ideal of salvation to be obtained by methods largely negative or repressive, certainly not self-expressive.

A common appreciation of a certain religious value in sufferings borne, even voluntarily self-imposed, for self-benefit.

A common belief in many prophets in the same religion, teaching the same eternal doctrines of that particular system.

A common belief in Karma and transmigration.

(2) *Points of Agreement between Jainism and Buddhism against Hinduism*

Rejection of the Hindu *Vedas*, as being in the ancient Sanskrit language, no longer intelligible nor even available for the common people. Then the two protesting movements produced their scriptures in vernaculars, Jainism its *Angas* in the Prakrit dialect, and Buddhism its *Tripitaka* in the Pali dialect; but both of these languages are now no longer in use, and the two sets of sacred scriptures are not easily available for their respective followers.

Rejection of the Hindu philosophic system. Then Jainism produced a dualistic philosophy, and Buddhism produced a nihilistic philosophy.

Rejection of the whole Hindu theistic, pantheistic, and polytheistic system. Then both Jainism and Buddhism deified their atheistic founders, and worshipped them even idolatrously, as well as twenty-four saviors incarnate.

Rejection of the whole Hindu sacrificial system. Then both the protesting systems taught kindness to animals; Jainism taught the sacrifice of one's body, and Buddhism taught the sacrifice of one's desires and individuality.

Rejection of the domination of the Hindu caste system. Then both the protesting movements advocated a voluntary religious order. Jainism established the oldest living church in the world today, and Buddhism established the second oldest church.

(3) Points of Disagreement among the Three Religions

	NATURE OF EVIL	METHOD OF OVERCOMING EVIL	RESULTING SALVATION
Philosophic Hinduism:	Intellectual—ignorance of Brahma	By knowledge of pantheism	Mystical reabsorption into the Infinite
Jainism:	Physical—encumbrance of body	By asceticism of body	Freedom of soul from worldly attachments
Fundamental Buddhism:	Emotional—unsatisfied desires	By suppression of desires	Passionless peace, Nirvana

	MATERIAL WORLD	INDIVIDUAL SOUL	SUPREME SOUL
Philosophic Hinduism:	Unreal, an illusion	Unreal, a temporary emanation	The only Real, the All
Jainism:	Real	Real	Unreal
Fundamental Buddhism:	Unreal	Unreal	Unreal

	VALUE OF ASCETICISM	VALUE OF MORALITY
Philosophic Hinduism:	Optional, though theoretically unnecessary	Unimportant; ultimately illusory
Jainism:	Obligatory; the chief means of salvation	Relatively unimportant; list of prohibitions
Fundamental Buddhism:	Of desires, rather than of only the body	Quite important, yet distinctly subordinate

9. PARTIAL SIMILARITIES BETWEEN BUDDHISM AND CHRISTIANITY

Both religions originated in Asia, received a missionary impulse from the founder, and have become international. But Buddhism has not extended itself generally beyond Asia, and has expanded little geographically during the last seven centuries. Christianity has spread through East and West, has made its greatest increase of missionary activity in recent centuries, and of all the living religions gives the greatest promise of actually becoming universal.

Both religions emphasize a moral life. But Buddhism enjoins a morality which is apart from deity. Christianity enjoins a morality which is like unto the character of God, and which is to be realized with the help of God.

Both religions exalt a cosmic moral law encompassing human destinies, unbribable and inescapable. But Buddhism's Karma is an impersonal principle, which finally destroys individuality. Christianity teaches that the Supreme Being is a supremely perfect Person, who uses universal moral law to produce perfect human personalities.

Both religions diagnose selfishness as the immediate cause of human misery. But Buddhism prescribes as the cure a negative self-suppression which is chiefly self-benefiting and subtly self-centered. Christianity prescribes as the cure a positive love of others, which is altruistic and socially centered.

Both religions teach a gospel of salvation. But Buddhism teaches the salvation of the individual apart from society. Christianity teaches the salvation of the individual and of society.

Both religions have produced monastic institutions. But Buddhism regards the monkish life as intrinsically superior. Christianity teaches the sacredness of all social life.

Both religions revere their founder for a certain superb manner of living. But Buddha attained the Buddhistic ideal of ethical culture only in the latter part of his life, after he had tried and successively abandoned three other ideals, viz., the life of self-indulgence, of philosophical speculation, and of bodily asceticism. Jesus continuously, from boyhood, lived a wholesome joyful life with God and with men, which he offered as normal for all mankind.

Both religions were started by a notably self-sacrificing founder. But Buddha died, an old man of eighty years, from dysentery after eating a heavy meal. Jesus died, a young man of about thirty, on the cross because men did not appreciate his service of love.

10. RADICAL DISSIMILARITIES BETWEEN BUDDHISM AND CHRISTIANITY

A personal God in Buddhism is denied, except as Buddha himself was deified; and then many gods have been worshipped. In Christianity there is one Supreme Being—God, to be obeyed, loved and trusted.

Man in Buddhism is a worthless, temporary conglomerate. In Christianity every human individual is a child of God.

The human body in Buddhism is only a miserable hindrance. In Christianity it is a fit instrument for the spiritual life.

Desire, for any kind of individual life, in Buddhism is evil.[1] In Christianity the desire for a righteous life is indispensable, and will be fulfilled.

Activity in Buddhism is, perhaps, temporarily unavoidable, but is evil and ultimately to be overcome. In Christianity activity is essential to holy living.

Vicarious suffering in Buddhism is inconsistent with the fundamental doctrine of individualism. In Christianity suffering unjustly caused is a terrible fact, yet it may be used as a means of blessing.

Sin, against a Divine Being, is denied in Buddhism. In Christianity a sinner sins against God and against other human beings and against his own higher self.

Life in Buddhism, because of its sufferings, is hardly worth

[1] This would not be true of certain sects of Mahayana Buddhism.

living. In Christianity life, despite its sufferings, is progressively worthful.

11. ELEMENTS OF STRENGTH IN BUDDHISM

The urgency and assurance of its gospel.
Its emphasis on a person's inner attitude.
A certain noble earnestness in its ethics.
Self-renunciation as a condition of salvation.
Its admirable first five commandments.
Its teaching of a moral law.
Certain admirable qualities in its founder.
Its successful repudiation of caste.

12. ELEMENTS OF WEAKNESS IN BUDDHISM

Its original atheism.
Its fundamental impersonalism.
Its low estimate of human life and the human body.
Its low estimate of woman and the family.
Its low estimate of the environing world.
Its checking of individual initiative.
Its refusal of social responsibilities.
Its repudiation of the idea of progress.
Its excessive emphasis on self-saving.
Its generally negative method of salvation.
Its empty idea of a blissful Nirvana.
Its general pessimism.
Its loss of an original missionary aim.

V

SIKHISM

The Religion of Disciples of the One True God

1. INTRODUCTION: AMONG THE WORLD'S LIVING RELIGIONS

Chronologically, Sikhism stands the very latest among the eleven living religions.

Numerically, Sikhism's 6,219,314 (1951 Census) adherents place it ninth in size. Only Jainism and Zoroastrianism have a smaller following.

Geographically, Sikhism is to be found almost exclusively in the one land of India, and there, too, in the one province of the Punjab. Yet in less than 200 years after its foundation it had extended itself clear across the north of India and southward to Ceylon. Most of the provincial governors of India have bodyguards composed of stalwart Sikhs. They are also used for police patrols on the streets of Penang and Singapore, Hongkong, and Shanghai, and other Far Eastern cities where Great Britain has exercised rule. However, 95 per cent of all the Sikhs in the world are concentrated in northwest India in the same region where their religion originated.

Politically, Sikhism is the only religion in the history of the world which has given birth to a nation, with the exception of Judaism. Its chief place in history has been political more than religious. In its case, as also in the case of Judaism,[1] political independence has been destroyed, while religiously and every other wise the people have continued strikingly able and distinctive.

[1] It is true that an independent Jewish state, Israel, has recently been set up in Palestine, but it includes only a relatively small percentage of the Jewish people of the world. Judaism as a faith knows no one nationality.

Architecturally, Sikhism's central shrine, the Golden Temple in the Pool of Immortality at Amritsar,

may be said to rank next to the Taj at Agra as one of the most striking sights of India. In the centre of the water rises the beautiful temple with its gilded dome and cupolas, approached by a marble causeway,—one of those rare sights seen at intervals during life which fix themselves indelibly on the memory. (Sir Monier-Williams, *Brahmanism and Hinduism, or Religious Thought and Life in India,* 175–176.)

Theologically, there is nothing clearly distinctive in Sikhism. It arose as a conscious attempt to harmonize the two most powerful rival religions in India. This latest development among the world's living religions represents a certain fusing together of the stern anti-idolatrous monotheism of Islam and Hinduism's vague mystic pantheism with its notorious tendency toward idolatry. This combination was accomplished through the personal religious experience and the continued personal influence of a great irenic reformer who was a contemporary of Luther, another remarkable religious reformer in Europe.

2. THE LIFE OF THE FOUNDER, NANAK (1469–1538 A. D.)

The primary sources of information are extra-canonical *Janam-sakhis,* "Life-Stories."

(1) *Religious Aspirations and Discontent until Thirty-six*

The birthplace of Nanak is situated about thirty miles southwest of Lahore, the capital of the Punjab, on the river Ravi, which the Greek historians call the Hydaspes. The little village had been known as Talwandi, but in honor of this distinguished son the name has subsequently been changed to Nanakara, "Nanak's Place." His parents were common villagers—the father a Hindu of the second caste, in the employ of an Islamic feudal lord, the mother very pious and devoted. At the age of seven, when first taken to school, the precocious boy exhorted the Hindu teacher to know the True Name of God by His mercy, rather than study all the Hindu *Vedas* (8–

9).[1] At nine years of age, according to the report in a late Janam-sakhi, the young boy began the study of Persian, the language of some parts of Sikhism's sacred scriptures (15). An important passage in the canonical *Granth* is assigned by one of the biographies as the utterance of Nanak at the age of nine. At any rate, the Sikhs do generally believe that, on the occasion when he was being invested with the sacred thread of Hinduism, this religiously minded boy gave instruction to the officiating Brahman priests concerning the spiritual significance of the material sacrament (16–18).

Many incidents are narrated showing how ordinary avocations were distasteful to him, how he preferred a life of quiet meditation and religious devotion, and how supernatural power was with him in difficult situations. Because of his aversion to manual labor or any physical or commercial activity, his relatives and friends were in despair over him; they thought him hopelessly useless and a disgrace to his family (21–23). An honorable government position with a brother-in-law in another town was secured for him, but he remained pensively unhappy (23–26).

His wife and two children he left behind at Talwandi, his domestic life being unhappy. Nothing is reported prejudicial to his wife. (Trumpp, translation of the *Granth,* iv.)

Unable to eat or drink, he was sick from need of God (26–29). So he retired to the desert and passed his time under trees in religious contemplation (29). He gave away to holy men money which had been entrusted to him by his father for purchases. He was punished by his father, but remained unrepentant (31).

He used to pause, and several times repeat, "I am Thine, O Lord." (33.)

(2) *The Divine Call and Commission*

One day after bathing, Nanak disappeared in the forest, and was taken in a vision to God's presence. He was offered a cup of nectar,

---

[1] In this chapter all the reference numbers are to pages in the first of the six volumes of Macauliffe, *Sikh Religion: Its Gurus, Sacred Writings and Authors.*

which he gratefully accepted. God said to him: "I am with thee. I have made thee happy, and also those who shall take thy name. Go, and repeat Mine, and cause others to do likewise. Abide uncontaminated by the world. Practise the repetition of My Name, charity, ablutions, worship, and meditation. . . . My Name is God, the primal Brahma. And thou art the divine Guru." (33–35.) After three days the Guru came forth from the forest, went home, gave all that he had to the poor. It was the general belief at this time that Nanak was possessed with an evil spirit, and a Mulla or Muhammadan priest was summoned to exorcise it. (36.)

The lamentable social and religious situation which was prevailing at that period is described by Nanak in the *Granth*. The Kal (Dark) Age is a knife. Kings are butchers. Justice hath taken wings, and fled. In this completely dark night of falsehood the moon of truth is never seen to rise. (170.)

Nanak now assumed the garb of a religious ascetic, a simple loin-cloth.

He remained silent for one day, and the next he uttered the pregnant announcement: "There is no Hindu and no Musalman!" (37.)

This amazing repudiation of all popular religious ideas was received with consternation, but was interpreted as presenting a more spiritual and inclusive religion (37–41).

Then the Kazi (Islamic ruler) came, and fell down at his feet, and said: "Wonderful, wonderful! On this one is the favour of God!" Then the Kazi believed. Nanak uttered a *slok* (stanza):

"He is a Musalman who clears away his own self,
Who is sincere, patient, of pure words,
That Musalman will go to paradise."

Then the people, Hindus and Musalmans, began to say that God was speaking in Nanak. (Trumpp, xiii.)

(3) *Nanak's Missionary Journeys*

Then Nanak took Mardana, a Mohammedan, who had formerly been a servant. With him as a musical accompanist, Nanak started forth to deliver more widely the gospel of discipleship of the One True God of all people, both of the rich and of the poor (58–59).

The Guru (teacher) arrayed himself in a strange motley of Hindu and Muhammadan religious habiliments. He put on a mango-coloured jacket, over which he threw a white *safa* or sheet. On his head he carried a hat of a Musalman, *Qalandar,* while he wore a necklace of bones, and imprinted a saffron mark on his forehead in the style of Hindus. This was an evidence of his earnest desire to found a religion which should be acceptable both to Hindus and Muhammadans without conforming to either faith. (58.)

The pair presented in their own persons a strange combination of the two chief religions prevailing in India. They achieved remarkable success, preaching and singing together. They travelled widely over north India, visiting many famous pilgrimage places of Hinduism, viz., Kurukshetra, Hardwar, Panipat, Delhi, Brindraban, Gorakhmata, Benares, the Brahma-putra River, Puri and the Temple of Jagannath, and the Himalaya Mountains.

Mardana had by this time had enough of travel, hardship, and hunger. (95.)

So after twelve years' absence the pair returned to their home in the Punjab, but again set out for further evangelistic effort. The second missionary journey was more extensive. They went to Madras, a Jain temple in south India, and the island of Ceylon, where Nanak preached to the king and queen.

The Guru then went to an island in the ocean governed by an in-human tyrant. (152c)

He also visited the extreme northwest of India, Srinagar in Kashmir, Mount Sumeru among the Himalayas, and Peshawar on the frontier (163–172). The persistent prophet carried his gospel far westward in Asia, even to the heart and citadels of the Islamic world. Disguised in the dress of an Islamic pilgrim, Nanak was perhaps the first Hindu to make the pilgrimage (Haj) to Mecca. There his simple preaching of the universality of God produced a miraculous effect in front of the sacred Kaaba stone [1] (174–175; Trumpp, xli–xlii).

[1] The story of Nanak's visit to Mecca as well as to some other distant places may be only legend rather than fact, according to the belief of some scholars, but that he did travel widely there can be no doubt.

In due time the Guru proceeded to Medina, where he vanquished the Muhammadan priests in argument. Thence he journeyed to Baghdad. He shouted the call to prayer. The high priest of Baghdad inquired who he was, and to what sect he belonged. The Guru replied: "I have appeared in this age to indicate the way unto men. I reject all sects, and only know one God, whom I recognize in the earth, the heavens, and in all directions." (179.)

The records of his ambitious plans, extensive journeys, and successful preaching resemble in some respects the records of the first great Christian missionary, Paul.

(4) *Nanak's Missionary Methods*

When imprisoned unjustly, he preached to the Islamic official, who then released him (111–114). When attacked by a band of robbers,

the Guru gave them spiritual instruction, and said that their sins would be wiped out when they had abandoned their evil career, turned to agriculture, and bestowed charity out of the spoils in their possession. They acted on his suggestions, began to repeat the Name, and to reform their lives. (71; Trumpp, xviii–xix.)

By humble preaching he converted a notorious villain, and advised him:

At the throne of God grace is obtained by two things: open confession and reparation for wrong. . . . He did so, whereupon the Guru told him to give all his possessions to the poor. (47; Trumpp, xiv.)

In "a country whose women were famous for their skill in incantation and magic" (73) he preached to a group of sorceresses and their queen. Whereupon they

fell at the Guru's feet, and asked how they could obtain salvation. The Guru told them to repeat God's name, conscientiously perform their domestic duties, renounce magic. . . . They became followers of Guru Nanak, and thus secured salvation. (78.)

He denounced Hindu ascetic practices, and offended Hindu susceptibilities by his own liberal practices (47–49, 51, 60–61, 135–136). Yet he made many, even notable, conversions of individual Hindus by means of a spiritual reinterpretation of

Hinduism (49, 130, 145–146). Similarly, he reinterpreted "being a Musalman" (38, 40), and made many, even notable, conversions of individual Muslims (37–41, 58–59). A Jain priest was shocked by Nanak's practices:

After this the Guru launched out into a satire on the Jains. "They have their hair plucked out. They drink dirty water. They beg, and eat others' leavings." . . . The Jain priest fell at his feet, and became a convert to his faith. (150, 152.)

Once in the wilderness Nanak is reported as having been tempted by Satan.

Kaljug offered the Guru the wealth of the world, if he would abandon his mission. "I will bring thee very beautiful women, and give thee the power of working miracles, and confer upon thee the sovereignty of the East and the West." The Guru informed him that he himself had renounced all sovereignty. . . . Then Kaljug in adoration fell at his feet, and took his departure. (79–80.)

Nanak repeatedly affirmed his faith in the one true sustaining omnipotent God (97, 98, 101, 110, 114, 141, 171).

(5) *Nanak's Marvellous Death*

The Guru, knowing that his end was approaching, appointed Angad his successor. The Guru's sons had not obeyed him. Their minds were insincere, and they had rebelled and deserted him. . . . Then it became known to his people that Guru Nanak was about to die. (187–188.)
Guru Nanak went and sat under a withered acacia tree, when lo! it became green, and produced leaves and blossoms. (188.)
The Musalmans, who had received God's name from the Guru, said they would bury him after his death. His Hindu followers, on the contrary, said they would cremate him. When the Guru was invited to decide the discussion, he said: "Let the Hindus place flowers on my right, and the Musalmans on my left. They whose flowers are found fresh in the morning, may have the disposal of my body." Guru Nanak then ordered the crowd to sing: "O my friends, pray for me that I may meet my Lord." The Guru drew a sheet over him, made obeisance to God, and blended his light with Guru Angad's [his successor]. . . . When the sheet was removed the next morning, there was nothing found beneath it. The flowers on both sides

were in bloom. All the Sikhs reverently saluted the spot on which the Guru had lain . . . at Kartepur in the Punjab. The Sikhs erected a shrine, and the Muhammadans a tomb in his honour on the margin of the Ravi. Both have since been washed away by the river. (190–191.)

3. THE VENERATION OF GURU NANAK

(1) *His Shortcomings in the Scriptures of Sikhism*

Guru Nanak's own words are reported in the canonical documents, in which he makes confession, and pleads for mercy and pardon.

The True, the Inapprehensible, the Infinite Himself does all. I am a sinner; Thou art the Pardoner. (Trumpp, 503; also translated in Hastings, *ERE,* 9 : 183.)

Thou art omnipresent, though I thought Thee distant. Thou beholdest mine acts, yet I deny them. I have not done Thy work, or uttered Thy name. (35; Trumpp, 39.)

My demerits cannot be numbered! My sins are numerous, as the waters of the sea and the ocean! Bestow compassion! Extend a little mercy! Save me, who am like a sinking stone! (30; Trumpp, 220.)

I utter calumny day and night. I am base and worthless. I covet my neighbour's house. Lust and anger, which are Pariahs, dwell in my heart. O Creator! I remain in the guise of a huntsman. In saint's dress I meditate to entrap others. I am a cheat in a country of cheats. Ungrateful that I was, I did not appreciate what Thou didst for me. How can I, who am wicked and dishonest, show my face! Humble Nanak expresseth his thoughts. (184; Trumpp, 38.)

I am not chaste nor truthful nor learned. Foolish am I from birth. (Hastings, *ERE,* 9 : 183. The original words in the Punjabi language are cited in Macauliffe, *Life,* 280.)

Even in the latter part of his life, when he lamented the grievous religious situation in his native land, he lamented his own perplexity and darkness in his earnest quest for deliverance.

I have become perplexed in my search. In the darkness I find no way. Devoted to pride, I weep in sorrow, saith Nanak. How shall deliverance be obtained? (170; Trumpp, 202.)

(2) *His Shortcomings in the Extra-Canonical Biographies*

Nanak is reported during the first thirty-six years of his life to have been useless, sick, unhappy, even in his search for religious truth.

I first feel the pain of separation from God, then a pang of hunger for contemplation on Him. I fear also the pain which death's myrmidons may inflict. I feel pain that my body shall perish by disease. I forgot God, and devoted myself to pleasure. Then this bodily illness befell me. The wicked heart is punished. (27.)
I have consulted the four Vedas. But these writings find not God's limits. I have consulted the four books of the Muhammadans. But God's worth is not described in them. I have consulted the nine regions of the earth. Having turned my heart into a boat, I have searched in every sea. I have dwelt by rivers and streams, and bathed at the sixty-eight places of pilgrimage. (179.)

(3) *His Miracles in the Extra-Canonical Biographies*

He is reported to have revivified a withered fig-tree (59–61), and also a withered acacia-tree (188; Trumpp, xlv). He revivified a dead elephant (56; Trumpp, xv), and a dying man (94–95). He cured and converted a leper (107). He produced water from dry ground (172). He wrought many marvels and conversions (113–114).

(4) *Revered Immediately, even as a Divine Savior*

The most frequent title for Nanak has been "Guru," meaning "Religious Teacher." He has also been designated honorifically as "Chief," or "King," Nanak "Shah," and endearingly as "Father," "Baba" Nanak. During the latter part of his life he was revered as a saint and even as a divine savior.

The people began to think him a god, and prayed him to pardon them and grant them salvation. (51.)

(5) *Subsequent Superlative Veneration of Nanak*

In the East the progress from the homage paid to a religious teacher to his deification is tempting and easy. In the short space of sixty years, between his demise and the completion of Gurdas' "Wars," he was made by his loving followers, not only a worker of stupendous miracles, but the Supreme God Himself. "Guru Nanak is God, the Supreme Brahma." (*Gurdas*, 13 : 25.) . . . All this testimony leaves no doubt in the minds of the majority of the Sikhs regarding the divinity of their inspired and holy Guru. (Macauliffe, *Life of Guru Nanak*, 280–281.)

Modern educated Sikhs ascribe superlative adoration to their founder without any theological complexities or perplexities, and even along with respectful reverence for Jesus.

In his character we do not find any improvement being made, for he was thorough in his childhood. He had no extravagancies to prune off, no eccentricities to return from. Guru Nanak presents a character thorough and consistent all around, and without a parallel in the history of the world. Christianity had not yet reached India; and we therefore do not find him anywhere referring to it. But so far as the general tenor of his doctrine is concerned, it may be safely said that he was not a Christian, yet the noblest of all Christians. His great work was to have made himself beloved in the highest degree by his disciples; and his doctrine was so little dogmatic that he never dreamed of writing, or of causing it to be written. For about 400 years past the Sikhs have believed, and do now believe, his sayings to be inspired. This sublime being we may call divine. In Guru Nanak, whom we may well describe as a man among men and a god among gods, was concentrated all that was good and lofty in human nature. Infallible he was not, but he conquered all those passions which we fight against.

> "Grave it on brass with adamantine pen!
> 'Tis God Himself becomes apparent, when
> God's wisdom and God's goodness are displayed,
> For, God of these His attributes is made."
> (Matthew Arnold.)

(Sewaram Singh Thapar, B.A., LL.B., *A Critical Study of the Life and Teachings of Sri Guru Nanak Dev* [*i. e.*, God]. *The Founder of Sikhism*, 173–179, Rawalpindi, Commercial Union Press, 1904.)

4. THE SACRED SCRIPTURES OF SIKHISM

The title *Granth* is a common noun derived ultimately from Sanskrit, meaning "book." But as a technical term it is used to designate "the Book" pre-eminently. It is an anthology of many poems, some of them quite short, totalling some 29,480 rhymed verses, arranged partly according to authors, but mainly according to the thirty-one different metres used. It is a miscellaneous collection of meditations on God and exhortations on life, somewhat like the Hebrew Psalms and Wisdom literature. The "Original Granth," *Adi Granth*, was compiled in 1604, by the fifth Guru from material which had come down from Nanak and the intervening teachers. Subsequently there have been added a few short pieces by the ninth and tenth Gurus. The text as printed at the Government Press, Lahore, contains 1,570 pages, and slightly less than a million words. Most orthodox sikhs recognize as authoritative another composite collection a hundred years later, entitled *Dasam Granth*, or "The Granth of the Tenth Guru." The authors comprised in the *Adi Granth* number thirty-seven. In addition to seven of the ten official heads of the Sikh Church, they include various Sikh bards and also Islamic and Hindu "saints," Bhagats. Two of the latter are Kabir and Ramananda, who started reform movements recognized as Hindu sects. The languages contained within the *Granth* are six in number, viz.: Punjabi, Multani, Persian, Prakrit, Hindi, and Marathi, besides several varieties of dialect. Thus the sacred scriptures of Sikhism are composed in a larger variety of languages than is the case in any other religion in the world. The latest translator into English estimates that there are not ten persons living who are able to read the entire Granth in its original text intelligently.

Of these, few or none is capable of giving an English interpretation. . . . The Granth Saheb thus becomes the most difficult work, sacred or profane, that exists. (v–vi.)

Absolute authority is ascribed to the *Granth* by the Sikhs. Yet "The Book" has been practically neglected. At least 90 per cent of the Sikhs do not know the contents of their sacred scriptures. At the same time the *Granth* is treated with a reverence which is virtual idolatry. The most common designation for it is *Granth Sahib*, which means "Lord Book." Actually, at the central shrine of Sikhism at Amristar,

although the temple is free from images, and is dedicated to the one God, . . . a visible representation of the invisible God is believed to be present in the sacred book. The Granth is, in fact, the real divinity of the shrine, and is treated as if it had a veritable personal existence. Every morning it is dressed out in costly brocade, and reverently placed on a low throne under a jewelled canopy. Every evening it is made to repose for the night in a golden bed within a consecrated chamber, railed off and protected from all profane intrusion by bolts and bars. (Monier-Williams, *Brahmanism and Hinduism, or Religious Thought and Life in India,* 177.)

At one side of the temple another copy of the book is being read aloud continuously day and night, month after month, year after year by relays of temple officials intoning, among others of its teachings, the passage:

> Why worship any one who is born and dieth!
> Remember the one God, who pervadeth sea and land.
> (Macauliffe, *Life of Guru Nanak*, p. 280.)

The Hindu reformer, Swami Dayanand Saraswati, founder of the Arya Samaj, the most popular religious reform started in all India during the nineteenth century, criticized especially this feature of the Sikh worship:

Though they perform no idol-worship, they worship their Granth more idolatrously. Is it not idolatry? Idolatry is bowing down to, or worshipping, any material object. They have done exactly the same things as the idolaters, who have made their idolatry a very lucrative business. Just as the idolaters exhibit their idols to the people at large and receive presents for their gods, so do the followers of the religion of Nanak worship the Granth, allow it to be worshipped, and receive presents for it. (*Satyartha Prakash,* English translation, 63.)

5. THE CONCEPTION OF THE SUPREME BEING IN SIKHISM

Mystic monotheism was the chief theoretical teaching of the founder, and has been of his followers ever since. Nanak's first utterance, when he felt the divine call, constitutes now the first two sentences in the sacred scriptures, and is prescribed as the first utterance for every Sikh every day:

There is but one God, whose name is True, Creator, devoid of fear and enmity, immortal, unborn, self-existent, great and bountiful. The True One was in the beginning. The True One is, was, and also shall be. (35, 195.)

Mystic rhapsodies on God bulk large in the *Granth,* much more so than in the sacred scriptures of any other religion in the world. The unity of the Supreme Being is a doctrine which is frequently proclaimed in the *Granth,* even as also in the *Koran* and the *Upanishads.*

The Lord is one. There is none other, my brethren! (149; Trumpp, 589.)
Thou hast no partner who is brought near. (Trumpp, 431.)
Whom shall I call the second? There is none! In all is that one Spotless Supreme. (Trumpp, xcviii, 320.)
Like Thee there is no other. Thou art in all ages the only One. Always, always Thou art One. Without Thee there is no other. (Trumpp, 17.)

The sovereignty of God is absolute and inscrutable. Nanak might have taken this doctrine almost verbatim from the *Koran,* or from certain scriptures in Hinduism:

Imprisonment and release is made by Thy decree. Nobody can interfere with it. (209; Trumpp, 8.)
He doeth what pleaseth Himself. No order may be issued to Him. He is King, the King of kings. All remain subject to His will. (212; Trumpp, 10.)
As it pleaseth God, He directeth them by His orders. He beholdeth, but is not seen by them. (213; Trumpp, 11.)
What is pleasure to Thee, that exists. What Thou thyself doest, that is done. What is pleasing to Thee, that will be done. (Trumpp, 17.)

Many names may be used for God on account of his manifold manifestations, although ultimately He is unitary. In this respect also may be seen Nanak's effort to syncretize Islam and Hinduism. The *Granth* uses for the Supreme Being

Islamic names Allah and Khudda "the Glorious," interchangeably with the names and descriptions of some of the Hindu
deities, *e. g.*, Brahma, Param Brahma or "the Supreme Brahma,"
Parameshvar "the Supreme Lord," Hari "the Kindly," Rama,
Govind, and Narayan.

Thou, O Lord, art One. But many are Thy manifestations. (310;
Trumpp, 504, similarly 400.)

Another simple, vital designation for deity which is used by
Nanak is "Guru" (Teacher). Thus Sikhism is unique among
the religions of the world in the fact that its sacred scriptures
refer to the Supreme Being as "Teacher." And the very name
which is used for the religion, "Sikh," denotes that its followers should be "pupils" or "disciples."

The chief designation for the deity in Sikhism is "Sat Nam,"
meaning "True Name." These two words are the first two words
in the text of the sacred scriptures. They recur at the beginning
of each hymn in the *Granth* and frequently throughout the
book. They are used mystically as an efficacious saving formula. The phrase is itself venerated mystically, as if it were a
pantheistic kind of deity.

The Guru was asked why the words "Sat Nam"—the True Name
—were always written as an introduction to his hymns. He replied:
"The Name is the God of all gods. . . . The Guru's Sikhs worship
the True Name, and thus remove all obstacles to salvation. Accordingly the prefatory words, 'the True Name,' are written in all com-
positions." (138.)

They who forget the Name, go astray. . . . How can a man be
saved without the Name? (149; Trumpp, 589.)

I abide in the Name, and the Name abideth in my heart. (135;
Trumpp, 77.)

6. THE CONCEPTION OF THE WORLD AND OF MAN

In comparison with the omnipotent and eternal God the
world is vain and transitory.

With whom contract friendship? The whole world passeth away.
. . . Except Thee, O God, everything is thoroughly false. (131,
231; Trumpp, 642.)

The affairs of this world are transitory, only for four days. We must assuredly proceed onwards. . . . This world is an illusion. (188–189.)

In comparison with the omnipotent and eternal God man is a helpless, submissive creature.

Nanak is His slave; He is the Supreme God. (Trumpp, 644.)
As long as man thinks that anything is done by him, he gets no happiness whatever. (Trumpp, 400.)
By God's order all were produced. By God's order they perform their functions. By God's order they are in the power of death. By God's order they are absorbed in the True One. Nanak! What pleaseth God, shall happen. There is nothing whatever in the power of His creatures. (135; Trumpp, 78.)
If it pleases Him, then He gives honour. If it pleases him, then He inflicts punishment. What is pleasing to Him, that is done. Nanak says: What is man? (Trumpp, 585.)

7. THE METHOD OF SALVATION

The Sikh religion teaches that salvation consists in knowing God, or in obtaining God, or in being absorbed into God. The general method of salvation is fairly consistent with the fundamental doctrine of the supremacy of an inscrutable God, and with the accompanying doctrines of the worthlessness of the world and the helplessness of man.

Divine knowledge is not sought by mere words. . . . By God's grace man obtaineth it. . . . If the Kind One looks with kindness, then is the true Guru obtained. (223; Trumpp, 638.)
The worshippers on whom God bestoweth kindness, worship Him. . . . The Kind One saveth those on whom He looketh with favour. (57, 224; Trumpp, 638.)

This doctrine of salvation by the grace of God had been stated at least four times in the Hindu *Upanishads*, viz., Katha, 2 : 20; Svetasvatara, 1 : 6; 3 : 20; Mundaka, 3 : 2, 3.

He himself createth, and He himself again destroyeth. Some have chains on their necks, and some ride on many horses. It is God who causeth to act, and who acteth himself. To whom shall I cry out? (248; Trumpp, 652.)

This idea of absolute submission before the world potentate was the distinctive method of salvation in Islam.

By whom his own self is known as *"so 'ham"* [*i. e.*, I am that World-Soul], he believes in the secret of the word. (Trumpp, 84.)

This method of obtaining salvation by a pantheistic merging of the individual self with the mystical world soul is identical with the method of salvation which had been taught in the Hindu *Upanishads:*

Whoever thus knows "I am Brahma," becomes this All. (*Brihad-Aranyaka Upanishad,* 1 : 4. 10.)
That Soul! That art thou. (*Chandogya Upanishad,* 6 : 8–16; nine times.)

But in general Guru Nanak seems to advocate not the lonely meditation of the Hindu mystic, but *Bhakti,* that is, the way of faith, love or devotion as the way of salvation. And while it is true that mergence in God is the ultimate goal to be sought after, man is thought of as caught on the wheel as in Hinduism and may have to pass through many lives before reaching salvation. The *Granth* also speaks frequently of heaven and hell, and a particular paradise called *Sach Khand* is promised to the blest. This is indentified by some learned Sikhs with Nirvana.

8. WORSHIP AND ORGANIZATION IN SIKHISM

The main method of worship in Sikhism is meditation on God, particularly in the form of a repetition of the "True Name."

Meditation on the Supreme Being is the only religious ceremony, my brother. (335.)
The highest duty of all is to repeat the Name of the One God. (234.)
The pure Name is my support. (Trumpp, 577.)
Remember the very pure name of Ram. Give up other things. (Trumpp, 582.)
Repeat the Name. Hear the Name. Deal in the Name. (118; Trumpp, 587.)
Fix thine attention on God. Repeat His name at every inspiration

and expiration. And thy soul shall be absorbed in the light of God. (181.)

The absence of sacrifices and of idols has been a marked feature of Sikhism. This method of worship is in exact conformity with Islam and also with certain phases of Hinduism, although in direct opposition to certain other phases of Hinduism.

Another important feature of Sikhism has been the need of a *Guru* or teacher as a means of salvation. This emphasis is strictly in conformity with the emphasis which has been made both in Hinduism with its veneration of many human Gurus and also in Islam with its veneration of the pre-eminent prophet Mohammed.

By the Guru's instructions to his disciples this knowledge is obtained. (57.)
The true Guru is a boat. Few there are who consider this. And those who do, he mercifully saveth. (236; Trumpp, 645.)
Without the true Guru you shall not find the way. (237; Trumpp, 646.)
Without the Guru no one hath obtained God, however much the matter may be debated. (149; Trumpp, 589.)

The Pure (*khalsa*) Congregation (*Sangat*) of Sikh "Disciples" has been another important feature of Sikhism. The formation of this new voluntary church in India was one of the definite achievements in the religious movement initiated by Guru Nanak. It was strengthened by successive Gurus, especially by the tenth Guru, who ceremonialized it. This religious-social organization has undoubtedly been one of the elements of strength in Sikhism.

9. THE HISTORY OF SIKHISM

The beginnings of this religion are closely connected with the history of its ten Gurus.

(1) Guru Nanak, before his death in 1538, found that neither of his two sons was qualified to become his successor. Therefore he appointed an extremely devoted disciple, a rope-

maker, Lahina, whose name he changed to Angad, "Body-giving."

(2) Guru Angad (1538–1552) rendered an important linguistic service to all the Punjab through his systematic rearrangement of the letters in the old Guru-mukhi alphabet. He introduced another important innovation in that he "began to regard Nanak as the equal to God" (Court, translation of the *Sikkhan de Raj di Vikhia, or History of the Sikhs*, from Panjabi, p. 11, Lahore, 1888).

(3) Guru Amardas (1552–1574), a gentle but enthusiastic convert, did much to organize, differentiate, and strengthen the Sikh community.

(4) Guru Ramdas (1574–1581), another enthusiastic convert, centralized Sikh worship in the Har-mandir, "Temple of God," which he built in a small lake thirty miles southeast of Lahore. This place, which he named Amritsar, or "Immortality," has subsequently become the central shrine of Sikhism. Himself the son-in-law of his predecessor, he introduced the principle of hereditary succession by appointing his own son as the next Guru of Sikhism.

(5) Guru Arjan (1581–1606) is especially memorable for having compiled the *Granth*. He did this from the literary remains of the four preceding Gurus and from the writings of other saints along with some of his own writings. He relinquished the distinctive religious attire, dressed in more costly clothing, and instituted the system of collecting religious tithes or taxes from all the Sikhs. He extended the Sikh faith vigorously, and met his death in a struggle against the king of Delhi.

(6) Guru Har Govind (1606–1638) first assumed the sword as a badge of his leadership, built the first Sikh stronghold, added recruits for military purposes, and definitely transformed the Sikhs from a company of quiet religious devotees into a band of soldiers fighting against the Moghul Islamic rulers of India.

(7) Guru Har Rai (1638–1660) continued military opera-

tions against the reigning Moghul, Aurangzib, and was defeated.

(8) Guru Har Kishan (1660–1664) continued in contest with the Islamic ruler of Delhi, Aurangzib.

(9) Guru Tegh Bahadur (1664–1675) was a doughty warrior, who in person carried the influence to Sikhism far afield, even to the farthest northeast corner of India and southward to Ceylon. He was not personally opposed to the Islamic religion; but he spent much of his life in successfully fighting against Muslims, so that after a certain battle "from that day the Muhammadans never ventured to fight with the Guru" (*Travels of the Guru Tegh Bahadur*, translated by Sirdar Attah Singh, Lahore, 1876, p. 58). Some of the writings of this ninth Guru were incorporated into the *Adi Granth*.

(10) Guru Govind Singh (1675–1708) continued with the tendency to transform Sikhism into a militant theocracy. Under him, Dacca, which is now the capital of the province of Eastern Bengal and Assam, became famed as a stronghold of Sikhism. He assumed, and he required all Sikhs likewise to assume, the surname Singh, meaning "Lion," so that they all might be welded together into one valiant family of the Pure (Khalsa).

For formal initiation into the Sikh assembly or fraternity he instituted a new baptismal rite. The initiates were required to drink, and also to be sprinkled with, sweetened water which had been stirred in an iron basin with a sharp sword. This nectar, *amrit*, is supposed to confer ceremonial purity, and also immunity in battle.

Guru Govind Singh introduced another innovation into Sikhism, when he wrote the *Granth of the Tenth Guru*, and declared it to be a supplementary authority along with the *Adi Granth*.

The Guru discovered that, from reading the original Granth, the Sikhs became very feeble-hearted. He therefore determined himself to compose such a Granth that, from reading it, his disciples should become fit for fighting. . . . "After my death do all you people regard the book of the Granth Saheb as your Guru." (Court, *Sikkhan de Raj di Vikhia, or History of the Sikhs*, 43, 56.)

After the death of the tenth Guru, in 1708, after a series of marked changes in Sikhism during the two centuries under ten successive Gurus, the supreme loyalty of the Sikhs was transferred from the personal Guru to the book, the *Granth Sahib*.

Upon the downfall of the Sikh monarchy the community broke up into several feudal states. However, in 1765 the national Sikh Assembly, Khalsa, at Amritsar, minted coins, with the inscription "the world, the sword, and unfailing victory"; this connected absolute faith in their religion with world conquest. But the political organization in Sikhism as a militant church state became extinct in March, 1849, when after the second Sikh War the last independent Sikh king, Maharaja Dhulip Singh, made complete surrender to the British arms, and gave his world-famous Koh-i-nur diamond to Queen Victoria. Shortly afterward, in 1858, she became Empress of India, and he embraced Christianity.

At the present time the Sikhs are still proudly conscious of their historic name, "the Lions of the Punjab." Most of them are located within the confines of their original ancestral home, living the lives of peaceful agriculturists.

Since the partition of India, granting autonomy to the Muslims who formed the new state of Pakistan, there has been agitation among some of the Sikhs for the right to form an independent Sikh state, since they once did constitute a separate political unit.

10. SECTS IN SIKHISM

There are two chief divisions among the Sikhs. The quietistic Nanak-panthis cling closely to the teachings of the founder. The more energetic Khalsa Siks adhere to the tenth Guru, Govind Singh.

There are also five main sects: Udasis, *i. e.*, "indifferent" to the world; Suthre, *i. e.*, "pure" mendicants; Diwane Sadhu, *i. e.*, "mad saint" devotees; Nirimale Sadhu, *i. e.*, "spotless saint" celibates; and Akalis, *i. e.*, worshippers of the "Timeless" Eternal.

In all, there are more than a score of sects. Some differ

concerning the color of their garments, whether white, or blue, or reddish yellow. Others differ concerning the proper length of their garments. Others differ concerning the propriety of shaving the face and cutting the hair.

11. A COMPARISON OF SIKHISM WITH HINDUISM

(1) *Points of Agreement*

Theoretically, belief in a mystical Supreme Unity.
Practically, great variety of designations for deity.
A certain theistic application of pantheism, even as in some of the Hindu *Upanishads* and the *Bhagavad Gita*.
Salvation by faith in the grace of God.
The doctrine of Karma.

As man soweth, so shall he reap. (124; Court, *History*, 48.)

Transmigration of souls.

It is he himself soweth, and he himself eateth. Man suffereth transmigration by God's order. (206; Trumpp, 7.)
Man, my brother, is born in the world as a result of bad and good acts. (335.)

Great importance in repeating prescribed prayers or formulas (*mantras*).

(2) *Points of Disagreement*

Hindu caste repudiated in favor of unity among all Sikhs.

Castes and no caste do not please Him, if He makes one great. (Trumpp, 75.)
Castes are but raillery. (Trumpp, 114.)
If a beggar at the gate raises a cry, the Lord hears it in His palace, and does not ask after his caste; for, in the other world there is no caste. (Trumpp, 494.)

Hindu idolatry repudiated in favor of worship of the Formless One.

The Hindus have forgotten God, and are going the wrong way. . . . The ignorant fools take stones, and worship them. O Hindus, how shall the stone, which itself sinketh, carry you across? (326.)

My brethren, you worship goddesses and gods. What can you ask them? And what can they give you? Even if a stone be washed with water, it will again sink in it. (336.)

Hindu polytheism repudiated, in favor of a monistic pantheism.

Hindu pilgrimages, ritualism, and hermit asceticism repudiated, in favor of pure worship of the Pure One.

Man is led astray by the reading of words. Ritualists are very proud. What availeth it to bathe at a place of pilgrimage, if the filth of pride be in the heart? (272.)

He who worshippeth stones, visiteth places of pilgrimage, dwelleth in forests, renounceth the world, wandereth and wavereth,—how can his filthy mind become pure? (339.)

Hindu scriptures repudiated, in favor of the Sikh scriptures.

A fetter is the Veda, dispute and pride. (Trumpp, 584.)

Hindu degradation of women repudiated, in favor of a higher regard for women.

Hindu infanticide repudiated, in favor of a more vigorous populating.

Hindu vegetarianism repudiated, in favor of a more vigorous meat-eating.

12. A COMPARISON OF SIKHISM WITH ISLAM

(1) *Points of Agreement*

Unity of the Supreme Personal Being.

Sovereignty of the Supreme Absolute Ruler.

A certain mercifulness attributed to the inscrutable deity, along with an uncomplainable arbitrariness.

Salvation through submission to God.

Worship through repetition of the name of the deity.

Great importance in repeating prescribed prayers.

Devotion to the founder as God's prophet.

Extreme reverence for sacred scripture.

The first section in the sacred scripture, a kind of Lord's

Prayer, composed by the founder at a crisis in his early life when seeking for God, and subsequently prescribed for daily repetition by all his followers.

A series of subsequent leaders after the original founder.

A long, powerful, militaristic church state.

Unity among believers, despite subsequent sects.

A very important central shrine—Mecca and Amritsar.

Vehement denunciation of idolatry.

(2) *Points of Disagreement*

Sikhism's founder not so ruthless or violent as Islam's.

Sikhism's deity not so ruthless or violent as Islam's.

Sikhism's sacred scriptures ascribed to many teachers, at least thirty-seven; not to one, as in Islam.

No fasting prescribed to Sikhs, as to Muslims in month of Ramadan.

No decisive judgment-day in Sikhism, as in Islam.

13. ELEMENTS OF STRENGTH IN SIKHISM

The strong reforming and peacemaking effort of the founder.

The enthusiastic and successful missionary activity of the founder.

The strongly monotheistic teaching.

The teaching that to be a religionist means to be a learner.

The strong organized solidarity of the adherents in their congregation, despite their subordinate sects.

14. ELEMENTS OF WEAKNESS IN SIKHISM

The largely mystical character of its Supreme Being.

The repetitiousness and mystical contentlessness of its worship.

The conception of the world as not worthful.

The attitude of almost helplessly submissive fatalism.

The heterogeneous and almost inaccessible contents of its sacred scripture, the Granth.

The virtually idolatrous worship of the book, the *Granth.*

The present generally self-centered condition of the Sikhs.

VI

CONFUCIANISM

The Religion of Social Propriety

1. INTRODUCTION: AMONG THE WORLD'S LIVING RELIGIONS

Confucianism has been the chief religion of the oldest self-governing nation now living in the world. Some authorities claim that Confucianism can hardly be classified as a religion, but rather as an ethic, because the founder discouraged belief in a personal God and the practice of prayer, and common worship of the Supreme Being. However, it has always taught, not only the existence of a Supreme Being, but also divine supervision over the world. There has always been official worship of the Supreme Being, until that ancient practice was discontinued in 1915 by the newly established Republic of China. Confucianism has indeed prevented the common people from approaching the Supreme Ruler of the world, any more than they would be allowed to approach the emperor of China; but it has taught them to worship various other beings. It has functioned as a religion, whatever may have been its degree of efficiency.

The secret of China's long vitality has been religious strength. An enormous man-power might, under a different ideal of life, have been made to produce surpassing military strength. But religion in China has never recognized the military class as the highest social rank. The secret of China's long life has not been isolation from the rest of the world. At several periods that nation has undergone humiliating subjection from foreign nations, and its actual isolation has tended toward stagnation rather than toward progress. The secret of China's long vitality has not been some peculiar form of political government, for that has never been strong. China possesses great natural resources in fields, forests, and mines; but these have never been properly utilized. Until 1905 a remarkable system of examinations in the Confucian scriptures was the basis of appointment to civil service; yet that system was chiefly memorizing, and popular education has never existed in China until recent years.

Confucianism has enabled China to demonstrate, on a larger scale than has been done before in human history, the abundant success of the principle of filial obedience under a religious sanction, as formulated by Moses.

Honor thy father and thy mother, that thy days may be long in the land which the Lord thy God giveth thee. (Exodus 20 : 12.)

The comparative statement might almost be made that in no other religious group has there been such actual insistence upon the principle of every individual performing properly his several and reciprocal social duties. According to the Confucian *Book of History*, the record of China's history goes back to a date which, in the Christian calendar, is to be identified as 2356 B. C.[1] At that early period social justice, communal welfare, and governmental responsibility for the common people are represented as going hand in hand with religious belief and worship.

The state religion of China had flourished thus for 1,800 years on the basis of the older chronology, yet it had not been organized into a system of teachings until about 500 years before Christ. Then in a period of special depression, there arose a great teacher whose name has subsequently been given to this previously unnamed religion.[2]

[1] According to earlier scholars. More recent critical scholarship tends to revise this chronology downward on the basis of archæological evidence and other considerations. See, for example, H. G. Creel, *The Birth of China*, New York, Reynal and Hitchcock, 1937.

[2] Actually, the term "Confucianism" is one used by Westerners, not by the Chinese. They are accustomed to speak of *Ju Chiao*, which might be translated as the "teaching of the sage" or "scholar." The term "Sinism" has sometimes been used to designate ancient Chinese religion, before the coming of Confucius. See, H. G. Creel, *Sinism, A Study of the Evolution of the Chinese World View*, Chicago, Open Court, 1929.

Again the world fell into decay, and principles faded away. Perverse speakings and oppressive deeds waxed rife again. There were instances of Ministers [of State] who murdered their rulers, and of sons who murdered their fathers. Confucius was afraid, and [undertook a work of reform.]. (*Mencius,* 3 : 2. 9. 7–8.)

2. LIFE OF THE FOUNDER, CONFUCIUS (551–479 B. C.)

More details about the life of Confucius are contained in the *Analects* than are known about most other founders of the great world religions.

(1) *Humble Youth* (*Aged* 1–21)

Confucius was born and buried in the province of Shantung, which district has since been regarded by the Chinese as their holy land. He was the youngest child and the only able-bodied son among eleven children. The father died when Confucius was three years old, and he was obliged to work hard in order to help support the family (9 : 6. 3).[1]

At fifteen I had my mind bent on learning. (2 : 4. 1.)

He was married at nineteen. No reference to his wife is to be found in any of the Confucian scriptures, except that Confucius reprimanded his son for mourning the death of his mother (*SBE,* 27 : 122, n. 2; 27 : 131, n. 2). Confucius was austere toward his only son (16 : 13. 1–5). He was exemplarily faithful in his first employed position (*Mencius,* 5 : 2. 5. 4).

(2) *A Successful Teacher* (*Aged* 21–51)

The private school which he started grew till he had 3,000 pupils. He was so generous that he never turned away a poor pupil who was in earnest (7 : 7). But he required studiousness (7 : 8). He had varied interests and subjects of teaching: history, poetry, literature, proprieties, government, natural science, music (7 : 17, 24, 31; 8 : 8. 1–3; 16 : 13. 1–3; 17 : 9. 1–7). The subjects which he avoided were prodigies, feats of strength, disorder, and the supernatural (7 : 20). He had

---

[1] The reference numbers in this chapter are to the *Analects*.

special pride in those pupils who displayed abilities: virtuous, oratorical, administrative, and literary (11 : 2. 2).

(3) A Successful High Official (Aged 51–55)

The famous local sage was appointed chief magistrate of the town. He was advanced successively to become Assistant Superintendent of Works and Chief Justice of the state. Both in internal administration and in interprovincial affairs Confucius was successful in obtaining obedience, peace, order, and even the beginnings of disarmament. He declared that the prime requisite in government should be, not revenue, but proper performance of function by all persons (12 : 11. 1–3). However, some internal intrigues and also jealousy from a neighboring state led to his resignation (*Mencius,* 6 : 2. 6. 6).

(4) An Itinerant Preacher (Aged 55–68)

Undauntedly confident of his own ability as a social and administrative reformer, he sought a government position in another state, but unsuccessfully (13 : 10). Nevertheless, his confidence continued in the efficacy of good government to secure all needed reforms, even the reform of human nature (13 : 11). He enthused his own disappointed disciples with confident zeal for the reform of society among the states of China (11 : 25. 3–5). In a casual interview he enthused a subordinate official with his heaven-sent mission as a righteous reformer (3 : 24). Even when in danger of his life, he continued confident of his Heaven-produced virtue (7 : 22). Mobbed and almost assassinated in the town of Kwang, he yet remained triumphantly confident of Heaven's protection in his mission of truth (9 : 5. 1–3). Again he was put in danger of his life (*Mencius,* 5 : 1. 8. 3). Even when destitute, he was uncomplainingly joyful in righteousness (7 : 15). Though suffering along with his discouraged followers, he yet remained undemoralized (15 : 1. 2–3). Instead of withdrawing into retirement, he was determined to help save a troubled world (18 : 6. 3–4). Though sometimes discouraged and tempted, he was never deserted by a faithful disciple (5 : 6).

(5) *Final Literary Labors* (*Aged* 68–72)

During this period he completed the compilation of what now are known as the *Confucian Classics*. Among them was only one original production, "Spring and Autumn," Annals of the State of Lu, which is reported as having produced a very remarkable reforming effect.

Rebellious ministers and villainous sons were struck with terror. (*Mencius,* 3 : 2. 9. 11.)

He died a disappointed, apparently unsuccessful, old man, crooning to himself:

"The great mountain must crumble! The strong beam must break! And the wise man wither away like a plant! There is not one in the empire that will make me his master! My time has come to die!" (Legge, *Life and Teachings of Confucius,"* 87–88; Douglas, *Confucianism and Taouism,* 62; Soothill, *Analects,* 56.)

His disciples mourned him for three years, one of them remaining six years at his grave (*Mencius,* 3 : 1. 4. 13).

Such is the picture of the Sage as he is found in the so-called *Sacred Books of China.* And there is great deal of obviously legendary material concerning him in later writings. Was Confucius what he seems in these sources to be?

Modern critical scholarship, both Chinese and Western, has occupied itself in the attempt to discover just what is authentic and what must be considered as legendary. So far, it must be reported that there is by no means entire agreement among scholars, beyond the fact that there has been an undoubted growth of tradition concerning the sage. There is still much work of a critical nature to be done on the sources before anything approaching a final answer can be given. Typical of the work of more recent scholars is the book of H. G. Creel, *Confucius, Man or Myth* (Chicago, The University of Chicago Press, 1949), who finds a substantial part of the older picture of Confucius to be based on other than early and dependable sources, and therefore of doubtful authenticity. (For other studies of Confucius, see the Bibliography.)

Meanwhile, it may be observed that Confucian teaching as it has come to be accepted by later generations, not what it really was, is what has influenced China; and that Confucius as he came to be regarded by the Chinese people, not the real Confucius, if there is a difference, is the figure who has exercised the enormous influence which it is admitted the Sage had over the Chinese people.

3. THE VENERATION OF CONFUCIUS

Esteem for Confucius has risen in a very remarkable manner.

(1) *His Own Humble Estimate of Himself*

He claimed to be only "a transmitter, not an originator" (7 : 1). He was no more than an indefatigable learner and teacher (7 : 2). He frankly confessed certain specific moral inabilities (7 : 3). But he hoped for improvement, if only he could have fifty years more for study (7 : 16).

The Master said: "In letters I am perhaps equal to other men. But the character of the superior man, carrying out in his conduct what he professes, is what I have not yet attained to." (7 : 32.)

He confessed four shortcomings of being "a superior man" (*Doctrine of the Mean*, 13 : 4; also *Li Ki*, 28 : 1. 33; *SBE*, 28 : 305–306). He acknowledged himself defective in four duties, including "not to be overcome with wine" (9 : 15). However, his disciples report:

It was only in wine that he laid down no limit to himself, but he did not allow himself to be confused by it. (10 : 8. 4.)

(2) *His Immediate Disciples' Estimate of Confucius*

There were four things from which the Master was entirely free. He had no foregone conclusions, no arbitrary predeterminations, no obstinacy, no egoism. (9 : 4.)

He was undauntedly persevering, even though not immediately successful (14 : 41). He was far above ordinary men, far above even the appreciation of ordinary men. He was unappreciably above comparison (19 : 23–25).

Our Master cannot be attained to, just in the same way as the heavens cannot be gone up to by the steps of a stair. (19 : 25. 3.)

(3) *Later Appreciation of Confucius in the* Books

He was incomparably and universally supreme.

Therefore his fame overspreads the Middle Kingdom, and extends to all barbarous tribes. Wherever ships and carriages reach, wherever the heavens overshadow and the earth sustains, wherever the sun and moon shine, wherever frosts and dews fall, all who have blood and breath unfeignedly love and honor him. Hence it is said: "He is the equal of Heaven." (*Doctrine of the Mean,* 30 : 2; 31 : 3; also *Li Ki,* 28 : 2. 53–56; *SBE,* 28 : 326–327.)

He was unequalled in the entire history of mankind.

No! Since there were living men until now, there never was another Confucius! (*Mencius,* 2 : 1. 2. 23; again in a similar strain, 2 : 1. 2. 27–28.)

He was a model of propriety, "a complete concert" in himself, a harmonious combination of strength and wisdom (*Mencius,* 5 : 2. 1. 4–7).

(4) *Subsequent Progressive Governmental Elevation of Confucius*

From before the beginning of the Christian era, and even into the twentieth century, he has won increasing official veneration.

B. C.

195   The Emperor of China offered animal sacrifice at the tomb of Confucius.

A. D.

1   He was given the imperial title "Duke Ni, All-complete and Illustrious."

57   Regular sacrifice to Confucius was ordered at the imperial and provincial colleges.

89   He was raised to the higher imperial rank of "Earl."

267   More elaborate animal sacrifices to Confucius were decreed four times yearly.

492   He was canonized as "The Venerable, the Accom-
              plished Sage."
555   Separate temples for the worship of Confucius were
              ordered at the capital of every prefecture in China.
740   The statue of Confucius was moved from the side to
              the center of the Imperial College, to stand with
              the historic kings of China.
1068–1086   Confucius was raised to the full rank of Emperor.
1906   December 31. An Imperial Rescript raised him to the
              rank of Co-assessor with the deities Heaven and
              Earth. (Soothill, *Analects,* 60; Moore, *History of
              Religions,* 1 : 22.)
1914   The worship of Confucius was continued by the first
              President of the Republic of China, Yuan Shi Kai.

(5) *The Actual Temple-Worship of Confucius*

For at least 1,200 years, twice every year, in the temple of
Confucius at the national capital of Peking, the emperor of
China conducted religious worship of Confucius, with a ritual
of praise and sacrificial offerings (Douglas, *Confucianism and
Taouism,* 163–164).

And in some 1,560 local temples in every city of China down
to those of the third rank, the local officials twice every year
with elaborate ceremonies, and twice every month with less
elaborate ceremonies, worshipped Confucius, offering some
62,606 animals annually on the altars (Douglas, *Confucianism
and Taouism,* 165; Wells Williams, *Middle Kingdom,* 2 : 203).

But in recent years the temples of Confucius have been
notoriously neglected.

(6) *The Active Principle in the Veneration of Confucius, and Its Historic Effect*

The main concern of the humble social reformer was to encourage proper social duties. He actually discouraged prayer
(3 : 13; 7 : 34) and all concern for the supernatural or for
spiritual beings (6 : 20). He would have been horrified at
the religious veneration which has been offered to him,
especially at the slaughter of animals in the sacrifice. However,
he did explicitly enunciate the principle that wide-reaching

service for the benefit of men is to be regarded as a mark of extraordinary or perfect virtue (6 : 28), or possibly "of divine virtue" (Giles, *Sayings of Confucius*, 60).

In its more than forty centuries of continuous self-government, a stretch of history which is unparalleled by any other present national administration, China has produced no figure who has been so intensely admired as this Sage of Shantung. The result of such devotion to him has been that the character of the people of China has been more nearly the creation of this one great teacher than is the case with the people of any other single country in the history of the world.

What will the future of Confucius be in a China dominated by Communism? The general anti-religious attitude of Communism, though recently modified in practice for reasons of expediency to permit a degree of religious freedom, makes it altogether unlikely that religious veneration of Confucius will receive encouragement from the Communist state. Indeed it is reported that the few remaining temples of Confucius, except the one associated with his burial in the province of Shantung, have been taken over to be used as schools or offices or even barracks for soldiers. His strong emphasis on family loyalty stands directly in the way of utter loyalty to the state which is demanded by Communism, so there is a fundamental and irreconcilable conflict between the two systems. Which will win out? No one can say. But China which has had a definitely Confucian background for many centuries has seen invaders come and go, or, staying, be absorbed in the environing Confucian Chinese culture. Will it be otherwise this time?

4. THE SACRED SCRIPTURES: *CLASSICS* AND *BOOKS*

Among the nine personally founded religions, Confucius is unusual in being a founder who was also an author. The exceptions are that Zoroaster wrote part of the *Avesta*, and that Lao-tze is credited with writing the short *Tao-Teh-King*.

Although Confucius did not contribute a single new idea, practice, or experience to the inherited religion of his country, yet he did render a very important service in supplying a body of writings which have been virtually "sacred scriptures" for Confucianism. Without these the old religious system probably would not have been perpetuated with so little change through the subsequent almost twenty-five centuries.

Yet, even in respect of this literary contribution to the religious history of China, Confucius shows notable lack of originality as an author as well as a thinker. In the first group of Confucian scriptures, the five, or possibly six, *classics*, which are indeed attributed to Confucius, are all compilations reputed to have been collated or edited by him; only one of them is strictly an original work. And that one, the Chun Chiu, or "Spring and Autumn [Annals]," is a rather dry-as-dust chronicle of his local state of Lu.

The second group, the four *Books, Ssu Shu,* were written either about him personally, or about his doctrines by various followers, immediate or subsequent.

(1) *The Five (or Six) Canonical* Classics

Canon of History, *Shu King:* China's history reviewed.
Canon of Poetry, *Shi King:* a secular and religious anthology.
Canon of Changes, *I King:* a system of divination.
Book of Rites, *Li Ki:* a compendium of proprieties.
Spring and Autumn [Annals], *Chun Chiu:* a local history.
In another classification there is also added: "Book of Filial Piety," *Hsiao King:* a special exposition of that virtue.

(2) *The Four* Books

"Great Learning," *Ta Hsio:* teaching concerning virtue.
"Doctrine of the Mean," *Chung Yung:* perfect moderation.
"Analects," *Lun Yu:* collected sayings of Confucius.
"Mencius," *Meng-tze:* works of the great expositor of Confucius.

No theological doctrine of inspiration or supernatural authority has ever been evolved concerning these nine or ten books. Yet they have been actually the most formative single agency in the production and maintenance of the Chinese ideal of character.

There have been some important writings of later philo-

sophical ethicists, Moh Ti (fifth century B. C.), Wang Chung
(first century A. D.), and Chu Hsi (1130–1200 A. D.). But
none of these have been so much studied, memorized, com-
mented upon, and made the basis of examination in appointment to public office as have the works of and about Confucius.

5. THE ETHICS OF CONFUCIANISM

The fundamental practical principle in Confucianism is
social propriety. This was concisely summarized by Confucius himself:

Tsze-kung asked, saying: "Is there one word which may serve as
a rule of practice for all one's life?" The Master said: "Is not reciprocity such a word? What you do not want done to yourself, do
not do to others." (15 : 23. This "Silver Rule," as it has sometimes
been designated, occurs in five other places in the Confucian scriptures: 5 : 11; 12 : 2; *Great Learning*, 10 : 2; *Doctrine of the Mean*,
13 : 3; *Li Ki*, 28 : 1. 32.)

This principle of reciprocal propriety is to be applied especially in the Five Relationships.

There are the relations of ruler and subject, father and son, husband and wife, elder brother and younger, friend and friend. . . .
No one, intelligent or stupid, can dispense with these for a single
day. If beside these, beyond your proper lot, you go about to seek
for some refined and mysterious dogmas and to engage in strange
and marvellous performances, you will show yourself to be a very
bad man. (Wang Yu-Po's paraphrase of the Sacred Edict of the
Emperor Kang-hsi; Legge, *Religions of China*, 105.)

Of these five relationships Confucius probably had more to
say about the relationship between ruler and subject than
any other. This was a major preoccupation of the Sage, who
was more a political scientist than a religionist. But across the
centuries the filial relationship has been more stressed popularly. It was the basis of the strong family system which has
been probably the major element in China's enduring culture.
The inculcation of filial piety has been a principal concern
of those charged with the education of children and youth.

The appeal to filial devotion has been one of the most potent of all in securing conformity to the accepted ethical ideals of the Chinese people. He must not do this or that because of the bad effect it would have upon his parents, or positively, he must do this or that because of the good effect upon his parents. This came to have a very broad application.

In general, the Confucian ethical ideal is simply for every person to do his proper part in the immediate relationships of life.

The "Superior Man" is the specific formulation of the Confucian ethical ideal for the individual. This is described one hundred and five times in the *Analects,* often by contrast with the behavior of the "mean man." It is distinctly a masculine concept. The *Analects* contain no picture of a "superior woman." Indeed, except for the list of proper designations for the wife of a prince (16 : 14), the only reference to the female sex in the *Analects* is decidedly derogatory (17 : 25).

Various virtues are exhorted, *e. g.*, propriety, sincerity, faithfulness, studiousness, justice, benevolence, reverence, moderation, calmness, truth-seeking.

Wisdom, benevolence, and fortitude,—these are the universal virtues. (*Doctrine of the Mean,* 20 : 8; *Li Ki,* 28 : 2. 9; *SBE,* 28 : 313.)

But limitations are distinctly set upon certain virtues.

Have no friends not equal to yourself. (1 : 8. 3; also 9 : 24.)
Recompense injury with justice, and recompense kindness with kindness. (14 : 36. 3.)
Filial piety does not require testifying to misconduct of father or of son. (13 : 18. 2.)

The ethics of Confucianism are the ethics of a dignified aristocracy which prided itself on a long-established social order, and which despised outlandish barbarians. No other ethical system in the world has so emphatically prescribed to rulers duties for the welfare of the people in the state. The ethics of Confucianism were clearly formulated in an age self-contained and self-satisfied. They do not contain provisions for problems of industrialism, democracy, and internationalism.

But while it is true that there is little appeal to religious sanctions in Confucius' ethical teaching, it would be a mistake to think that there is no religious basis for ethics in the Confucian system. If Confucius is responsible for editing the *Book of History* in its present form, he certainly held that there was a moral order in the universe and that Heaven or God judged rulers as good or evil and rewarded or punished them accordingly. Certainly also in the later books, popularly regarded as Confucian, even though he may not himself have written or even edited them, there is definitely a conception of God or Heaven as guarantor of the moral order of the world.

6. THE CONCEPTION OF DEITY

Although the chief interest of Confucianism is ethical rather than religious, yet even for its ethical system there is made a genuine religious postulate, viz., the inherent goodness of human nature as being divinely implanted.

The great God has conferred even on the inferior people a moral sense, compliance with which would show their nature invariably right. (*SBE*, 3. 89–90.)
Man is born for uprightness. (6 : 17.)
What Heaven has conferred is called the nature. (*Doctrine of the Mean*, 1 : 1.)
The tendency of man's nature is good. There are none but have this tendency to good. (*Mencius*, 6 : 1. 2. 2.)

Every one of the Confucian scriptures makes direct allusion to the supreme power of the world. Three different designations are used. "Shang Ti," meaning literally "Supreme Ruler," is a personal designation which, in the *Sacred Books of the East*, is always translated by the English word "God." "Tien," meaning literally "Heaven," refers to the supreme moral rule or order of the world in impersonal terms. This designation occurs about three times as frequently as the personal term. However, they are often used together and interchangeably. The third designation is also impersonal, "Ming," meaning "Decree" or "Fate." The last section in the Analects connects ethics closely with faith in the Supreme Being.

The Master said: "Without recognizing the ordinances of Heaven it is impossible to be a superior man. Without acquaintance with the rules of propriety it is impossible for the character to be established." (20 : 3. 1–2.)

However, Confucius used the personal name for the Supreme Being only once (20 : 1. 3), and that only in the course of a poetical quotation. The evidence is ample and explicit that the ethico-religious system which Confucius organized included belief in and worship of a Supreme Deity, but that his own influence tended to depersonalize that faith and to secularize its ethic.

Numerous deities are worshipped in Confucianism, both in the ancient literary records and also in the modern actual practices.

He sacrificed specially, but with the ordinary forms, to God; sacrificed with reverent purity to the Six Honoured Ones; offered their appropriate sacrifices to the hills and rivers; and extended his worship to a host of spirits. (SBE, 3 : 39.)

Some of them, like Heaven, are prominent objects or forces in nature, for example, Earth, Sun, Moon, the important mountains and rivers in China. Some of them are minor nature spirits. Some are mythical or historical figures, like Confucius, and an ancient Chinese emperor, Kwang Ti, who has been deified as the God of War, to whom there were 1,600 state temples. The worship of these different deities was definitely apportioned among the emperor, the various officials, and the people.

The Son of Heaven sacrificed to Heaven and Earth, to all the famous hills and great streams under the sky, the five mountains and the four rivers. The Princes of the States sacrificed to the spirits of the land and grain, to the famous hills and great streams which were in their own territories. (SBE, 27 : 225.)

7. THE STATE RELIGION IN CONFUCIANISM

There has never been a separate priesthood in Confucianism. However, some distinctly priestly functions were performed by the regular government officials. The local mandarins perpetuated the national veneration of Confucius, while the higher officials perpetuated the nature-worship.

The formal worship of the Supreme Ruler of the world, Heaven, was conducted by the supreme ruler of China, the emperor, on behalf of his nation. This was, perhaps, the longest-lived religious ceremony anywhere in the world. The worship of Heaven was conducted regularly every year after the night of the winter solstice, December 22, with whole burnt-offerings of bullocks, foods, silks, and wine, with music, lights, processions, and graded groups of participants. The ceremony took place on and around the huge, round, three-terraced white marble altar of Heaven, which stands south of the city of Peking, and which is the largest altar in the history of the world. The prayer which was offered on this occasion by the emperor of China, in the year 1539, contains the following:

The Great and Lofty One sends down his favour and regard. As a potter, hast Thou made all living things. What limit, what measure can there be while we celebrate His great name! For ever He setteth fast the high heavens, and shapeth the solid earth. His government is everlasting. All the ends of the earth look up to Him. All human beings, all things on the earth, rejoice together in the great Name. (Legge, *The Religion of China*, 47–51.)

After the overthrow of the Manchu dynasty there was no emperor on the ancient throne of China to continue the annual ceremony. But the first president of the new republic of China, Yuan Shi Kai, continued it in spite of the radically different form of political government. However, the centuries-old religious ceremony of the worship of Heaven has quietly lapsed amid the new activities and perplexities in China. The beautiful historic altar of Heaven is being neglected, and is gradually falling into ruin along with the numerous temples of Confucius.

The worship of Earth is another correlated, but inferior, nature-worship. It was conducted by government officials annually on the occasion of the summer solstice, at the altar of Earth, which stands north of Peking, and which, symbolically, is square and surrounded by water.

Worship of the sun was conducted annually at the spring equinox at the east gate of the capital, and worship of the moon annually at the autumn equinox at the west gate.

Thus, at the four quarters of the year in the four cardinal directions from the capital, there were systematic formal religious observances, conducted by high government officials as part of their regular duties of state. But all this official religion in Confucianism has lapsed in recent years.

8. POPULAR RELIGION IN CONFUCIANISM

A very definite religious worship has been prescribed by Confucianism for the common people of China, as well as for the officials. Ancestor-worship has been the special and long-continued popular cultus. All the books covering the period prior to Confucius contain references to the ancestral temples and other details of this ritual. In the Analects a great moral value is attached to ancestor-worship.

Let there be a careful attention to perform the funeral rites to parents when dead; and let them be followed, when long gone, with the ceremonies of sacrifice. Then the virtue of the people will resume its proper excellence. (1 : 9.)

This practice of ancestor-worship is a continuation, after the parents' death, of the absolutely devoted filial piety which Confucianism requires all its adherents to show to parents, even while they are still alive.

Filial piety is the root of all virtue, and the stem out of which grows all moral teaching. Our bodies, to every hair and bit of skin, are received by us from our parents; and we must not presume to injure or wound them. (SBE, 3 : 466.)
The services of love and reverence to parents when alive, and those of grief and sorrow to them when they are dead: these completely discharge the fundamental duty of living men. (SBE, 3 : 488.)

The condition of the dead ancestors is neither feared nor craved. They are believed to be simply continuing in existence, hovering close around their old abode in the family home and around the grave. The food which is laid out before them on stated occasions is not an expiatory sacrifice, but is a sacred joint communion meal.

Its feature of ancestor-worship effects a notable foreshortening of Confucianism's ethical demands. It more exclusively than any other religion in the world centers its requirements upon a moral life, yet it teaches no great future judgment or any method of finally vindicating its own ideals of human morality. So far as an individual himself is concerned, he experiences no subsequent advantage or disadvantage, whether he has lived well or ill during the years of this present life. There is no better form of life after death for which to hope and strive. In fact, a loyal Confucianist because of his filial piety would be horrified at the thought that any ancestor of his might be in hell, or that any living person should fail to offer worship even to those ancestors who had lived wickedly. The cost of funerals and also of the sacrificial ceremonies in connection with the anniversaries of the death of parents and other forebears has formed a weighty part of the economic problems of the poor people in China.

There have been those, both in the East and the West, who have denied that the ancestral cult is really religious. They say that it is only a practice similar to that of the West of venerating the dead, laying wreaths of flowers on their tombs, eulogizing them, paying them honor. The Roman Catholic church has officially given its approval to the celebration of ancestral rites by its converts, though Protestant churches have generally forbidden it. Certainly at the popular level it has all the earmarks of a religious practice, and it seems effectively to have filled the place of a religion in the lives of the Chinese masses.

Under the impact of the Western world and the modern scientific age, Chinese religion has undergone many changes. Many old religious practices and beliefs have been given up. Even the ancestral cult in time began to fade out, though its resistance to the encroachment of the modern world was long and formidable. It was the extension of the filial devotion principle to those beyond the grave. And filial devotion had been deeply embedded in the Chinese character. To what extent it is still practiced, it is impossible to know. There is little doubt that in the interior, in the more remote sections of the country, the cult survives. It gets no encouragement from Communism which tends to regard all religion as an enemy to the ends it seeks, and since the perpetuation of the principle of family solidarity seems to them irreconcilable with the complete loyalty to the state which Communism demands, they may be expected to discourage it, if they do not actually forbid it.

A high theoretical and practical regard is held by the common people of China, not only for the spirits of their deceased ancestors, but also for the innumerable spirits which are believed to inhabit the earth and air. *Feng-shui,* or fear of offending the spirits of "wind and water," has been a potent factor in the practical religious life of Confucianists.

This regard for the spirits diminishes steadily under the impact of the modern world upon China. As more and more of the people are educated in the schools which in ever-increasing numbers are being established, the newer understanding of the functioning of the natural world will tend to destroy these popular beliefs. What religion, if any, will replace the old cult of spirits? Will Communism fill the void thus created? Or will the old semi-humanism of the great Sage come back to dominate the mind of China? Will some of the Western religions provide the answer? Or will some new religion which may result from a blending of various of these faiths and others arise to meet China's need?

9. ELEMENTS OF STRENGTH IN CONFUCIANISM

Its emphasis on morality, obligatory on all persons.

They will even sacrifice their lives to preserve their virtues complete. (15 : 8.)

Its confidence in the moral supervision of the world.

The Master said: "Virtue is more to man than either water or fire. I have seen men die from treading on water and fire, but I have never seen a man die from treading the course of virtue." (15 : 34.)

Its confidence in the fundamental divine goodness of human nature.

Its teaching of the invincible human will.

The Master said: "The commander of the forces of a large state may be carried off; but the will of even a common man cannot be taken from him." (9 : 25.)

Its teaching of inescapable social duties.

Its teaching of reciprocal social responsibilities.

Its teaching of the principle of the "Golden Rule."

Its emphasis on the value of the family.

Its latent universalism, even though not applied.

All within the four seas, brothers. (12 : 5. 4.)

Its teaching of a religious value in the state.

Its emphasis on the need and value of education (13 : 9. 1–4; 17 : 4. 3).

Good government does not lay hold of the people so much as good instructions. Good government is feared by the people, while good instructions are loved by them. Good government gets the people's wealth, but good instructions get their hearts. (*Mencius,* 7 : 1. 14. 2–3; also 1 : 1. 3. 4; 3 : 1. 4. 8; also *SBE,* 28 : 82–83.)

Its emphasis on the efficacy of the good example of superiors.

The Master said: "He who exercises government by means of his virtue, may be compared to the north polar star, which keeps its place and all the stars turn toward it." (2 : 1.)

The Master said: "When a Prince's personal conduct is correct, his government is effective without the issuing of orders. If his personal conduct is not correct, he may issue orders, but they will not be followed." (13 : 6; also 2 : 3. 1–2; 8 : 2. 1–2; 12 : 18; 13 : 1; 13 : 4. 3; 13 : 13; 14 : 44.)

Its founder so self-sacrificingly devoted to the welfare of the people.

Its teaching of respect for the wisdom of the past.

10. ELEMENTS OF WEAKNESS IN CONFUCIANISM

Its lack of a supreme personal deity accessible for all people, instead of to the emperor alone.

Its actual polytheism, despite its one "Supreme Ruler."

Its excessively self-saving scheme of salvation.

What the superior man seeks is in himself. (15 : 20.)

Its lack of a sufficiently enthusiastic, inner dynamic.

Its excessive emphasis on commands, forms, ceremonies.

It embraces the three hundred rules of ceremony and the three thousand rules of demeanor. (*Doctrine of the Mean,* 27 : 3; also *Li Ki,* 28 : 2. 38; *SBE,* 28 : 323.)

Its lack of the principle of self-sacrificing, redemptive love.

The inadequate religious basis even for its own ethics.

Its negative form of the "Golden Rule" principle.

Its inadequate treatment of the moral evils in human nature.

Its lack of a program for real social amelioration, especially for the uplift of the lower units in society.

Its generally inferior position assigned to women.

The woman follows and obeys the man. In her youth she follows her father and elder brother. When married, she follows her husband. When her husband is dead, she follows her son. (*SBE,* 27 : 441.)

If no distinction were observed between males and females, disorder would arise and grow. (*SBE,* 28 : 104; also 27 : 77–78, 380, 439, 441, 454–455, 458, 479.)

Its retrospective, unprogressive ideal; perfect society in the past; no forward-looking creative goal ahead.

Its inadequate interpretation and use of physical facts.

VII

TAOISM

The Religion of the Divine Way

1. INTRODUCTION: AMONG THE WORLD'S LIVING RELIGIONS

According to the older chronologies of China, Taoism, at least in its philosophic aspects, is older than Confucianism. More recent scholarship is not sure that this is true. The question has been seriously raised as to whether original Taoism was a religion at all, or only a philosophy. The first professor of the Chinese language and literature at Oxford University declared, with regard to its primary scripture:

There is not a word in the Tao-Teh-King of the sixth century B. C., that savors either of superstition or religion. (Legge, *The Religions of China*, 164.)

Perhaps, as another eminent European sinologist has declared, Taoism did not become organized as a religion until the Han dynasty in China, shortly before the Christian era (DeGroot, *The Religion of the Chinese*, 132). Taoism has had what has been erroneously called a "pope" from the first century until very recently. He was more properly "Heavenly Teacher," a lineal descendent of Chang Ling, the reputed founder of so-called religious Taoism. He never had the power of a pope but was rather the custodian of a body of knowledge than a spiritual leader or an arbiter of morals. He seems to have had, at least in more recent times, little or no influence or control over Taoist priests who were ordained locally.

Taoism has been steadily in decline for a long time. Many regard it as already a dead religion. If it has not yet disappeared, there is very little likelihood that it will come back.

A distinguished Chinese scholar has said: "There is no doubt that Taoism is approaching extinction," and he gives five reasons for its disintegration. (See Wing-tsit Chan, *Religious Trends in Modern China*, New York, Columbia University Press, 1953.)

Nobody knows how many Taoists there are left in China. Estimates run as high as fifty million, but it is only possible to guess at the number, since, as observed above, the Chinese do not hold their religion in the exclusive fashion of the West, but may at the same time be also Confucian and Buddhist and feel no inner contradiction between them.

Among the religions of China it is one of the officially recognized "San Chiao," or "Three Religions," Confucianism, Taoism, and Buddhism. The last was introduced into China about 71 A. D. So the three have been in that country about as long as Christianity has been in the world. They have not only coexisted, but intermingled. Innumerable Chinese worshippers participate in the ceremonies and contribute to the maintenance of the three religions. However, the distinctive emphases are clear. According to Confucianism, religion consists in obeying the rules of proper conduct between the superior and inferior members of human society. According to Buddhism in China, religion consists in meditative world-renouncing self-discipline with faith in a personalized deity. According to Taoism, religion consists in a mystical following of the divine Way of the universe. The contrast with the sociological scheme of Confucianism, the chief religion of China, is clearly stated in the inscription in the Taoist temple at the birthplace of Lao-Tze:

The Three Hundred Rules of Ceremony could not control men's natures. The Three Thousand Rules of Punishments were not sufficient to put a stop to their treacherous villainies. But he who knows how to cleanse the current of a stream, begins by clearing out its source. And he who would straighten the end of a process, must commence with making its beginning correct. Is not the Great Tao the Grand Source and the Grand Origin of all things? (*SBE*, 40 : 313.)

Among the religions of the world Taoism like Buddhism, comes near to Christianity in teaching that a person should return good for evil.

2. LIFE OF THE FOUNDER, LAO-TZE (604–517? B. C.)

Only little is known concerning the biography of the humble individual who first among the religious teachers of the world taught the principle of universal unrequiting goodness. The main source of information is a short sketch of 248 Chinese words by the Herodotus of Chinese history, Ssu-ma Chien, about 500 years later.

According to this source, Lao-Tze was born in the province of Honan, Central China, about fifty years before Confucius. So meager is the information concerning his life that some scholars have doubted if he was really an historic figure at all. H. G. Creel in one of his books refuses to speak of Lao-tze as an historical figure, but he does speak of the thought of Taoism as found in the Tao Teh King and the Chwang-tzu. (*Chinese Thought from Confucius to Mao Tse-tung*, Chicago: University of Chicago Press, 1953, p. 98.) Older scholars fix the date of his birth as in the late seventh or early sixth century. More recent scholarship fixes it as late as in the fourth century. (Feng Yu-lan *A History of Chinese Philosophy to about 100 B. C.*, translated by Derk Bodde, Peiping, 1937, pp. 170 ff.)

On the basis of the older chronology he was an older contemporary of Confucius. This would mean that he lived not far from the time of Zoroaster in Persia, Mahavira and Buddha in India, and the great Hebrew prophets, Jeremiah, Ezekiel, and the Isaiah of the Exile. He was keeper of archives at the court of the Chinese dynasty of Chou. It is related that on account of his official position and great learning the "Venerable Philosopher" was visited by Confucius, who then was thirty-four years old. Lao-tze chided that historian-to-be and busy young reformer, who desired to search out the ancient history of China and to restore its passing glory by a scheme of social proprieties.

The men about whom you talk are dead, and their bones are mouldered to dust. Put away your proud airs and many desires. (*SBE*, 39 : 34.)

Instead, Lao-tze urged Confucius to search quietly and personally for the Tao, which is the mystic principle of the universe, and which alone can furnish the key to religion and life. When the young man asserted that he had been studying diligently in books for twenty years past, Lao-tze replied:

If the Tao could be offered to men, who would not wish to offer it to his Prince? If it could be presented to men, who would not wish to present it to his parents? If it could be announced to men, who would not wish to announce it to his brethren? If it could be transmitted to men, who would not wish to transmit it to his children? Why do you not obtain it? This is the reason: Because you do not give it an asylum in your heart. (Douglas, *Confucianism and Taouism*, 184; *Kwang Tze*, 14. 2. 7. 5; *SBE*, 39. 355; Giles, *Chuang Tzu*, 183.)

After this interview Confucius, who later was to be recognized as the most famous scholar and teacher of all China, said to his disciples:

I know how the birds fly, how the fishes swim, how animals run. But there is the Dragon. I cannot tell how it mounts on the wind through the clouds, and flies through Heaven. To-day I have seen Lao-tze, and I can only compare him to the Dragon [*i.e.*, supramundane and unintelligible mystery]. (*SBE*, 39 : 34–35.)

Lao-tze must have appeared to Confucius like an otherworldly dreamer, soaring among the clouds of his own speculations. And Confucius must have seemed to Lao-tze like a busybody, meddling in everybody's affairs. The two most influential men of China were indeed different from one another in their interests, aims, methods, and general systems.

All that is known of the rest of the life of Lao-tze is contained in the conclusion of Ssu-ma Chien's biography.

Lao-tze practised reason and virtue. His doctrine aims at self-concealment and namelessness.

Lao-tze resided in Chou most of his life. When he foresaw the decay of Chou, he departed and came to the frontier. The custom-house officer, Yin-Hi, said: "Sir, since it pleases you to retire, I request you for my sake to write a book." Thereupon Lao-tze wrote a book of two parts consisting of five thousand and odd words, in which he discussed the concepts of reason and virtue. Then he departed. No one knows where he died. (Carus, *Canon of Reason and Virtue,* 71–72.)

3. THE CHARACTER OF LAO-TZE

According to Confucianism the guiding principle of life is appropriate reciprocity; so, if a man has done an injury, he should be punished with exact retributive justice.

Recompense injury with justice, and recompense kindness with kindness. (*Analects* of Confucius, 14 : 36. 3.)

But according to Lao-tze an injury should be met by a superior goodness.

Recompense injury with kindness. (*TTK,* 63 : 2.)
To those who are good to me, I am good. And to those who are not good to me, I am also good. And thus all get to be good. To those who are sincere with me, I am sincere. And to those who are not sincere with me, I am also sincere. And thus all get to be sincere. (*TTK,* 49 : 2.)

This avowal of personal conduct, according to the principle of universal unrequiting goodness, has been equalled among the founders of the non-Christian religions only by the Buddha. However, under circumstances more trying than those which troubled Lao-tze, Jesus taught and showed self-sacrificing forgiveness to wrong-doers (Luke 6 : 27; 23 : 34). And Jesus connected this principle of treating other people better than they deserve, as Lao-tze did not, with a personal God who gives that same kind of treatment to all men (Matthew 5 : 38–48).

According to Christian standards Lao-tze professed a principle of meeting evil which is superior to that of Confucius. Yet his actual conduct must be estimated as decidedly inferior to Confucius. The two contemporary founders of religion in China lived in the same general social situation. Lao-tze also lamented "the poverty of the people," "the greater disorder," "crafty dexterity," "thieves and robbers" (*TTK*, 57 : 2), the destructive bravado, the unthriftiness and self-seeking of the time (*TTK*, 67 : 3). But, instead of resolutely facing the evils and attempting to apply his principle concretely, as Confucius did, Lao-tze only talked some sage advice; and then he resigned from his government post into convenient irresponsibility, as many another Chinese official has done even to modern times.

To withdraw into obscurity is the way of Heaven. (*TTK*, 9 : 2; *SBE*, 39 : 53.)

So he simply withdrew from the troubles of China, and went west.

4. THE VENERATION OF LAO-TZE

The founder of Taoism was confident concerning his principles, although he was humble concerning himself.

The multitudes of men are happy, so happy! I alone remain quiet. Forlorn am I, O so forlorn! . . . I alone appear empty. Ignorant am I, O so ignorant! I am dull! . . . I alone am confused, so confused! I alone am awkward, and a rustic too! I alone differ from others. But I prize seeking sustenance from our Mother [the cosmic Tao]. (*TTK*, 20 : 3–9; Carus's translation, *Canon of Reason and Virtue*, 86–87.)

All in the world call me great. But I resemble the unlikely. . . . [However,] I have three treasures which I cherish and prize, compassion, economy, and humility. (*TTK*, 67 : 1–2; Carus's translation, 121–122.)

My words are very easy to know and very easy to practise. But there is no one in the world who is able to know and able to practise them. There is an originating and all-comprehending principle in my words, and an authoritative law. It is because they do not know these, that men do not know me. (*TTK*, 70 : 1–2; *SBE*, 39 : 112–113.)

Subsequently there has been a remarkable increase in appreciation of Lao-tze, even a governmental and theological elevation. In 156 A. D. the state first ordered sacrifices to be offered to Lao-tze. In the fourth century A. D. there started the dogma of a supernatural conception of the "Venerable Philosopher," or, as his honorific title has also been translated, "the Old Boy." Having been born with white hair, and having been so precociously wise, he was declared to have been born not an ordinary infant, but a mature person, who had been carried in his mother's womb for seventy-two or eighty-one years (*SBE*, 39 : 35, note 1). In 586 A. D., when the temple at his birthplace was being repaired, an inscription was placed, stating the dogma of the repeated reincarnation of Lao-tze (*SBE*, 40 : 311–313). The emperor of China who reigned 650–684 A. D. proclaimed Lao-tze as a former emperor. In 713–742 he was canonized as "the Great Sage Ancestor." At a later date, not exactly determinable, he was made a member of a Taoist Trinity. The second member is a metaphysical principle, named Pan-ku, "the Demiurge." The third member of the Taoist Trinity is another historic personage, commonly known as "the Pearly Emperor," who was apotheosized in 1116 A. D. (Soothill, *Three Religions of China*, 82–83).

Lao-tze's admiring followers do not lay up against him his own words of dejection, which he wrote at the time when he was withdrawing from the world into final obscurity and death, and which now are contained in the sacred scriptures of this religion. Rather do his followers believe that he who had taught them to believe in and follow universal goodness must himself have been divine. Lao-tze did not teach a personal Supreme Being, and his teaching about persistent goodness to be shown unto evil people was not fully exemplified in his own conduct. Yet millions of his followers in China have recognized in their great sage and religious teacher an actual manifestation of the Divine Being. The history of China might be pointed to as furnishing a concrete fulfilment with regard to his own person of the principle which in the twenty-eighth chapter of his book he taught concerning humility being ultimately recognized and exalted.

He who knows the light and at the same time keeps the shade, will be the whole world's model. Being the whole world's model, eternal virtue will not miss him; and he will return home to the Absolute. (Douglas, *Confucianism and Taouism*, 195.)

Lao-tze was, in certain respects, a wise "old philosopher," but he was not a "suffering servant" of China. He gave to his religion a certain noble idealism, but not himself. Six others among the world's personally founded religions have been designated from names of their respective founders: Jainism, Buddhism, Confucianism, Zoroastrianism, Christianity, and Islam. But Taoism has been designated, not from the personality or example of its greatest teacher, but from its chief teaching concerning the impersonal principle "Tao."

5. THE SACRED SCRIPTURES OF TAOISM

The chief literary treasure of Taoism is a document which is usually attributed to the founder himself. The title *Tao-Teh-King* has been treated variously by more than a dozen English translators. Usually it is left untranslated, being cited in its original form as a compound of three Chinese nouns. It has been translated as *The Classic of Tau and of Virtue* (Chalmers), *The Book of the Path of Virtue* (Old), *The Providential Grace Classic* (Parker), *The Principle of Nature and Its Attributes* (Balfour), *Thoughts on the Nature and Manifestations of God* (Alexander). Arthur Waley calls it *The Way and Its Power*, Lin Yutang, *The Book of Tao*. Perhaps as simple and exact a rendering as any is *Canon of Reason and Virtue* (Carus).

The work of translating this sacred scripture of Taoism, even into half a dozen European languages, has proved fascinating, but difficult. It was translated into Latin in 1788 A. D., by the Roman Catholic missionary, Father Gramont, with the erroneous belief that "the Mysteries of the Most Holy Trinity and of the Incarnate God were anciently known to the Chinese nation" (*SBE*, 39 : xiii). The earliest translation of the *Tao-Teh-King* into a modern European language was into French, in the year 1823, by Father Remusat, under the title *Memoirs on the Life and Opinions of Lao-Tze, a Chinese Philosopher of the Sixth Century before Our Era, Who Professed the Opinions Commonly Attributed to Pythagoras, to Plato, and to their Disciples.*

That French translation of the *Tao-Teh-King* startled the scholars of Europe by its report that the word "Jehovah," which was the special name for deity among the Hebrews, had been found in the fourteenth chapter of the book of this Chinese philosopher of the sixth century B. C.

The contents of the *Tao-Teh-King* are a series of unsystematically arranged generalizations and counsellings. Besides the three chapters which contain autobiographical allusions (*TTK*, 20 : 3–9; 67 : 1–2; 70 : 1–2) and a few general references to the contemporary social situation, there are no historical references whatsoever, cither to specific persons or to any events in China. In all the eighty-one brief chapters of the book there occurs not a single proper name.

The history of the *Tao-Teh-King* has included some notable appreciations of its importance. The Emperor Ching Ti (156–140 B. C.), first officially recognized it as a "Classic." The Emperor Ming Ti (227–239 A. D.) used to deliver lectures on this rather dry book to his assembled ministers of state, with a severe reprimand to "any official who either stretched, yawned, or expectorated during the discourse" (H. A. Giles, *Confucianism and Its Rivals*, 181; L. Giles, *Sayings of Lao-Tze*, 13).

By successive edicts the Tao-Teh-King was made obligatory at the examination for graduates of the second degree; every one was required to possess a copy of the work; and it was cut on stone at both capitals. Later on printed copies were distributed to all directors of education; and it was translated into the language of the Nu-chen Tartars. (Giles, *Sayings*, 13.)

The monument of the Nestorian Christians in Hsian-Fu, province of Shen-si, China, shows that before 781 A. D. they were acquainted with the *Tao-Teh-King*. Modern western translators and comparers of religion have expressed high estimates of the intrinsic value of the *Tao-Teh-King*.

A work so recondite, and yet so clear and simple, . . . so surprising an accordance with the latest teachings of philosophy and science . . . Its precision, its analysis, its teachings, and its methods are above praise. And in purity it is spotless. (Heysinger, *The Light of China, the Tao-Teh-King,* 5, 8.)
Nothing like this book. . . . So lofty, so vital, so restful, at the roots of strength; in structure as wonderful as in its spirit. Terse aphorism of a mystical and universal wisdom. (Rev. Samuel Johnson, in a three-volume study, *Oriental Religions and Their Relations to Universal Religion : China,* 862.)

A German treatise by I. Hesse on "Lao-tze, A Pre-Christian Witness to Truth," contains a list of two hundred and sixty-eight parallels between verses in the *Tao-Teh-King* and verses in the *Bible* (Basel, Missions-buchhandlung, 1914).

No higher tribute has been paid to the book than that by a distinguished Chinese writer who has given, if not the most exact translation of the book into English, certainly the most readable, Mr. Lin Yutang. (*The Wisdom of China and India,* New York: Random House, 1942, pp. 583–624. London: Michael Joseph, Ltd.) In the introduction to his translation he writes:

"If there is one book in the whole of Oriental literature which one should read above all others, it is, in my opinion, Laotse's *Book of Tao.* If there is one book that can claim to interpret for us the spirit of the Orient, or that is necessary to the understanding of characteristic Chinese behavior, including literally 'the ways that are dark,' it is *The Book of Tao.* For Laotse's book contains the first enunciated philosophy of camouflage in the world; it teaches the wisdom of appearing foolish, the success of appearing to fail, the strength of weakness and the advantage of lying low, the benefit of yielding to your adversary, and the futility of contending for power. It accounts for any mellowness that may be seen in Chinese social and individual behavior. . . . I would go further and say that if I were asked what antidote could be found in Oriental literature and philosophy to cure the contentious modern world of its inveterate belief in force and struggle for power, I would name this book of "5000 words" written some 2,400 years ago. For Laotse (born about B. C. 570) has the knack of making Hitler and other dreamers of world mastery appear foolish and ridiculous. The chaos of the modern world, I believe, is due to the total lack of a philosophy of the rhythm of life such as we find in Laotse and his brilliant disciple, Chwangtse, or anything remotely resembling it. And furthermore, if there is one book advising against the multifarious activities and futile busy-ness of the modern man, I would again say it is Laotse's *Book of Tao*. It is one of the profoundest books in the world's philosophy." (P. 579)

Standing in relation to Lao-tze very much as Mencius stood to Confucius was Chwangtse (written variously Chuang-tzu, Kwang-tze, Chwang-tze, Chuangtse, etc.), a mystic follower who lived some two hundred years after his master, in terms of the older chronology. The teaching of Lao-tze was being eclipsed by a revival of Confucianism. The bold activism of Confucius was in sharp contrast to the passivism of Lao-tze, expressed in his fundamental principle, *wu-wei* or non-action. So Chwangtse came to the defense of the man he so deeply admired, and wrote extensively, setting forth in fresh terms much of what his teacher had taught, though he went beyond him in some respects. He was a brilliant writer. Rated as one of China's greatest literary figures, he succeeded in giving a currency to Lao-tze's writing which it could never have gotten otherwise. He was, writes Lionel Giles, "the first to show to what heights of eloquence and beauty his native language could attain. . . . His master-hand sounded chords that have vibrated to no other touch." (*Musings of a Chinese Mystic,* London: John Murray, 1927, p. 36.) Lin Yutang speaks of the "brilliance of his style and the depth of his thought." (*Op. cit.,* p. 625.)

His writings are a delight to read. Whimsical, humorous, yet profound, they have carried the major principles of Lao-tze into Chinese life to become if not the dominant force, yet a powerful influence which has had a most notable effect upon Chinese literature, art, and social relationships. Lin Yutang has said of it that it has had the effect of "humanizing the humanists themselves," providing the "only safe, romantic release from the severe Confucian classics restraint." (*Op. cit.,* p. 626.) His work constitutes an important part of what may be called the Scriptures of Taoism, though, as in Confucianism, there is of course no claim to anything like divine inspiration for what he has written. (For books concerning Chwangtse and his work, see Bibliography, in the Appendix.)

Another much later Taoist scripture is the *Tai-Shang Kang-Ying Pien,* "Tractate of Actions and Their Retributions." This is highly esteemed by the Taoists themselves and also by students of the world's living religions for the reach of its ethical ideals. Along with some crudely primitive teachings it contains some passages which, for ethical worth, are unsurpassed among the non-Christian religions. Several parallels from the *Bible* might be adduced for the following description of "the Good Man."

He will not tread in devious by-ways. He will amass virtue, and accumulate deeds of merit. He will feel kindly towards all creatures. He will be loyal, filial, loving to his younger brothers, and submissive to his elder. He will make himself correct, and so transform others. He will pity orphans, and compassionate widows. He will respect the old, and cherish the young. Even the insect tribes, grass and trees he should not hurt. He ought to pity the malignant tendencies of others; to rejoice over their excellencies; to help them in their straits; to rescue them from their perils; to regard their gains as if they were his own, and their losses in the same way; not to publish their shortcomings; not to vaunt his own superiorities; to put a stop to what is evil, and exalt and display what is good; to yield much, and take little for himself; to receive insult without resenting it, and honor with an appearance of apprehension; to bestow favors without seeking for a return, and to give to others without any subsequent regret. This is what is called a good man. All other men respect him. Heaven in its course protects him. Happiness and emolument follow him. All evil things keep far from him. What he does, is sure to succeed. He may hope to become immaterial and immortal. (*SBE,* 40 : 237–238.)

However, this scripture also includes a long series of important and trivial commands:

Never divulge the faults of your parents. Never confuse right and wrong. Don't reward the unrighteous. Don't punish the innocent. Don't scold the wind, nor abuse the rain. Don't listen to what your wife and concubines say. Don't disobey the instructions of your father and mother. Don't let new things make you forget the old. Repay what you have borrowed. Don't seek to obtain anything beyond the lot appointed you by Heaven. Don't use a short foot or an unfair measure, a light balance, or a small pint. Don't sing and dance on the last day of the month, or on the last day of the year. Don't shout or get angry on the first day of the month, or in the morning. Don't weep or spit toward the north. Don't spit toward shooting stars. Don't point at a rainbow. If a man who has done wrong repents and corrects himself, if he abstains from evil deeds, and accomplishes all sorts of good works, he will at length obtain joy and felicity. Why then do we not force ourselves to do good? (Douglas, *Confucianism and Taouism*, 260–271.)

6. THE CENTRAL CONCEPT, "THE TAO"

The primary etymological meaning is clearly that "Tao" as a common noun designates "Way," "Path," "Road." The same Chinese word, "Tao," in its simplest, untechnical meaning occurs in the name of another of the world's living religions, Shinto, or "Shintao," meaning "The Way of the Gods." Christianity also was first referred to simply as "The Way" (Acts 9 : 2, 19 : 9; 19 : 23; 22 : 4; 24 : 14; 24 : 22).

The Confucian scriptures also use this same religious idea to indicate the "way" of the perfect human religionist and, too, the "method" of the Supreme Being.

the Path (Tao): What you do not like when done to yourself, do not do unto others. (*Doctrine of the Mean*, 13 : 3.)
The way of Heaven (Tien-tao) is to bless the good and make the bad miserable. (*SBE*, 3 : 90.)

At least three different meanings of "Tao" have been developed from the primary idea of "way," viz., the moral and physical order of the world; the path of reason, truth, principle; and the way of perfect virtue, or the right way of life which Heaven approves, and which Heaven itself follows. In its highest technical meaning "Tao" designates the philosophic Absolute, the religious Supreme Being. Carus always renders the word by the English equivalent "Reason"; Parker, "Providence"; Alexander, "God." The French translation by Remusat uses "Supreme Being," "Reason," "Word," and "Logos" to represent the Chinese "Tao." The translation of the Christian "Gospel according to St. John" into Chinese starts with the first verse thus: "In the beginning was the Tao, and the Tao was with God, and the Tao was God."

7. THE CONCEPTION OF THE SUPREME BEING

The chief religious teaching in the *Tao-Teh-King* is concerning one eternal, impersonal, mystical Supreme Being. In the whole book there is only one occurrence of the personal designation (Ti, literally "Ruler") which in the *Sacred Books of the East* is rendered God."

I do not know whose son it is. It might appear to have been before God. Tao-Teh-King 4. 3.[1] (*SBE*, 39 : 50.)

The Tao fundamentally is inactive and indescribable, yet the *Tao-Teh-King* attempts to describe its activities and attributes.

Original, primeval, before heaven and earth, the Ultimate, still, formless, unchanging, nameless. (25 : 1–4.)
The one abounding sustaining source of all things. (39 : 1–2.)
Unostentatiously producing, and sustaining all things. (51 : 3–4.)
All-pervading, unpretentious, creative. (34 : 1–2.)
Heaven's Way (Tien-tao) is quietly, unselfishly effective for good. (7 : 1–2; 9 : 1–2; 47 : 1; 68 : 1–2; 73 : 2; 79 : 3; 81 : 3.)
To be known solely by intuition. (47 : 1–2; 81 : 1.)
"To know the eternal is enlightenment." (Carus, 16 : 4; 55 : 3.)
"Possessed of the Tao, he endures long." (16 : 4; *SBE*, 39 : 60.)
The Tao is inexpressible, unnamable, indescribably great. (1 : 1; 14 : 1–3; 25 : 1–4; 32 : 1; 37 : 3.)
Yet, as it were, an All-father. (4 : 1.)
Also like a mother. (1 : 2; 6 : 1; 20 : 2; 25 : 1; 52 : 1–2.)
Makes its knower "the noblest man under heaven." (56 : 1–3.)
Makes its knower long-enduring, his body undecaying. (16 : 2.)
Makes its knower fearless, invulnerable, immortal. "He does not belong to the realm of death." (Carus, 50 : 1–4.)
Strictly, the Tao is unstriving and non-active. (37 : 1; 63 : 1.)

---

[1] The reference numbers in this section and the next are to chapter and verse in the *Tao-Teh-King*.

8. THE ETHICS OF TAOISM

The ethical ideal inculcated in the *Tao-Teh-King* is a quiet, restful, simplicity, like that of Heaven itself. The ideal Taoist is calm and peaceful like the Tao. At least eight Chinese synonyms are used to describe the abiding admirable quietude of the eternal Tao and of the perfect individual. Humility is stressed repeatedly.

Heaven is long-enduring, and earth continues long, because they do not live of, or for, themselves. Therefore the sage puts his own person last, and yet it is found in the foremost place. The highest excellence, like that of water, appears in its benefiting all things, and in its occupying, without striving, the low place which all men dislike. (7 : 1–2; 8 : 1; *SBE*, 39 : 52.)

Perhaps the two finest passages in the whole document are the two following:

To those who are good to me, I am good; and to those who are not good to me, I am also good; and thus all get to be good. To those who are sincere with me, I am sincere; and to those who are not sincere to me, I am also sincere; and thus all get to be sincere. (49 : 2; *SBE*, 39 : 91.)
Recompense injury with kindness. (63 : 1; *SBE*, 39 : 106.)

Yet the perfect individual is chiefly placid, self-contented, indifferent toward all people and all things, even like the Supreme Being.

"Aim at extreme disinterestedness, and maintain the utmost possible calm." (16 : 1, Parker's translation.)
"The sage keeps his mind in a state of indifference to all." (49 : 3.)
"There is no guilt greater than to sanction ambition; no calamity greater than to be discontented with one's lot; no fault greater than the wish to be getting. Therefore, the sufficiency of content- ment is an enduring and unchanging sufficiency." (46 : 2.)
"Heaven and earth exhibit no benevolence; to them the ten-thou- sand things are like straw dogs. The holy man exhibits no benev- olence; to him the hundred families are like straw dogs." (5 : 1; Carus, *Lao-Tze's Tao-Teh-King*, 99.)

The most characteristic single phrase in Taoism is "wu-wei," *i. e.*, "do-nothing," or "non-striving," or "inactivity."

It is the condition of universal good order. (2 : 3.)
Only quiet non-striving is successful. (29 : 1.)
Therefore, the holy man says: "I practise wu-wei." (57 : 3, Carus's translation.)
Return to a state of natural simplicity which is contentment, without war, government, writing, travel, or fear of death. (80 : 1–5.)

The ethical ideal in the late "Tractate," Tai-Shang, is similarly a combination of noble and ignoble elements.

9. LATER LEADERS OF TAOISM

No outstanding leader appeared for a century and a quarter after the death of the founder.

Lieh-tze, in the fifth century B. C., taught some remarkably high religious ideals, as translated by Lionel Giles in *Taoist Teachings:*

"My secret is one whereby every man, woman and child in the empire shall be inspired with the friendly desire to love and do good to one another. If you are sincere in your purpose, all the people within the four borders of your realm will be made happy." (56–57.)
"The man who achieves harmony with Tao enters into close unison with external objects, and none of them has the power to harm or hinder him. Passing through solid metal or stone, walking in the midst of fire or on the surface of water—all these things become possible to him." (51.)

The latter quotation illustrates also the combination of lower ideals, as taught by Lieh-tze. All distinctions are repudiated, even ethical distinctions (Giles, *Taoist Teachings*, 41–42). Miracle and magic are mingled in the knowledge of Tao (44–45). "Following Nature" ends in animalism (54–55). Absent-mindedness is a blessing (71). Complete indifference to life and society is the mark of the true sage who has received divine enlightenment (78–79).

Kwang-tze, in the fourth century B. C., was the Taoist author whose writings are the most widely enjoyed. Somewhat like John Bunyan through *Pilgrim's Progress*, he conveyed religious ideals by means of graphic narratives, imaginative conversations, meaningful proper names, incisive proverbs, and quaint paradoxes. By 600 A. D. "the editions of his work amounted to nearly a score" (*SBE*, 39 : 9). In 742 A.D., he was canonized as a sage, by imperial order. Kwang-tze reiterated the fundamental Taoist principles.

The cosmic Tao is invisible, inaudible, unnamable, undiscussable, inexpressible. (*SBE*, 40 : 68–69.)
The perfect man is peaceful like the Tao. (*SBE*, 39 : 192–193.)
The ideal condition is a by-gone utopian simplicity in a state of nature. (*SBE*, 39 : 278.)
"Vacancy, stillness, placidity, tastelessness, quietude, silence, nonaction—this is the level of Heaven and Earth, and the perfection of the Tao." (*SBE*, 39 : 331.)
Perhaps the most remarkable case of doubting one's personality in all serious literature is Kwang-tze's famous "butterfly dream." "I did not know whether it had been formerly Kwang-tze dreaming that he was a butterfly, or it was now a butterfly dreaming that it was Kwang-tze." (*SBE*, 39 : 197.)

10. THE HISTORY OF TAOISM

Throughout its possibly 2,500 years of existence Taoism has stood opposed to Confucianism, which has been the chief religious system of China. During the Christian era there has been a third rival religion, Buddhism, from India. A few emperors of China have actually favored Taoism. But for the most part Taoism has been in disrepute on account of its degradation. Taoism has had no foreign-missionary activity, and few reformers. The outstanding dates in its history have been the periods of favor and disfavor with the emperors of China.

B. C.
212   Emperor Shi Huang Ti burned Confucian books, and established Taoism; sent naval expeditions to Fairy Islands to discover the herb of immortality.

A. D.
1   The leading Taoist in China endeavored to compound a pill of immortality.
156   Emperor Hwan of China first sacrificed to Lao-tze.

574–581   Emperor Wu arranged order of precedence, viz., Confucianism, first; Taoism, second; and Buddhism third; but soon became disgusted with Taoism and Buddhism, and ordered their abolition. The next emperor, Tsing, re-established both non-Confucian religions.

650–684   Lao-tze canonized as an emperor; his writings included among subjects for government examinations.

713–742   Emperor Kai Yuen distributed copies of the *Tao-Teh-King* throughout the empire; took a dose of Taoist "gold-stone" medicine; magicry increased.

825–827   Emperor Pao-Li banished all Taoist doctors on account of their intrigues and pretensions away to the two southernmost provinces of China.

841–847   Emperor Wu Tsung ordered all Taoist and Buddhist monasteries and nunneries closed. Later he restored Taoism to imperial favor, and stigmatized Buddhism as "a foreign religion." Took Taoist medicine to etherealize his bones, so as to fly through the air like the fairies.

1661–1721   Emperor Kang Hsi ordered punishment not only of the Taoist quacks, but also of the patients; forbade Taoist assemblies and processions; endeavored to suppress the various Taoist sects.

1900   The Boxer Uprising originated in a sect of specially ardent Taoists who believed their bodies would be immune against foreigners' bullets, trusting the exact words of the founder: "When coming among soldiers, he need not fear arms and weapons." (*TTK*, 50 : 4; Carus's translation.)

11. MODERN TAOISM

The actual outworkings of the system have been quite different from the high theories of its founder. Yet the *Tao-Teh-King* itself presents some basis for most of the later developments of Taoism. Taoists have lost almost totally their founder's original protest against social disorders and his measure of ethical idealism. Taoism has always been mystical, but through most of its history it has interpreted the mysterious mostly in magical and anti-scientific terms. Taoism presents a pathetic history. It started with some admirable features, but it has degraded fearfully into polytheism, demonolatry, witchcraft, and occultism.

The functions of the modern Pope [so-called] are chiefly to bless and sell charms and amulets to be used against disease and similar machinations of evil spirits. (Giles, *Confucianism and Its Rivals*, 178.)

The social morality of the Taoist priests is in general ill repute. The easiest approximation to the unperturbed condition of the immortal Tao is now conceived to be accomplished through the method of retiring into a monastery or a nunnery, and there living inactively so as to produce prodigious longevity. Every one of the authorities who deals with Taoism from personal knowledge of it utters condemnation.

This doctrine has degenerated into vagaries, such as pulmonary gymnastics and searches after elixirs of life. (DeGroot, *The Religion of the Chinese*, 153.)
Sunk lower in the estimation of their fellow men than any but the most degraded of idolaters. (Douglas, *Confucianism and Taouism*, 287.)
For centuries, Taoism, a by-word of reproach. . . . This cult is little more than an inextricable mass of jugglery and fraud, . . . conducted by a body of priests recruited from the very dregs of the empire. (L. Giles, *The Sayings of Lao-tze*, 17–18.)
As a religion in actual practice it is of a rather low form, full of idolatry and superstition. In China it is the religion of the unlearned and ignorant. (Y. C. Yang, *China's Religious Heritage*, 167.)

12. ITS TEACHING CONCERNING THE AFTER LIFE

Confucianism has nothing to say concerning the afterlife, though Confucian books include rules for the observance of the ancestral cult which implies belief in an ongoing life. But Taoism, that is Taoism as a religion, has a great deal to say about it. Whether this grew originally out of the teaching of Lao-tze may be questioned. Scholars think that it was due chiefly to the influence of Buddhism which brought well-developed ideas concerning multiple heavens and hells into

China. It has been suggested that it was because of this lack
of concern for a future life in the religions native to China
which made Buddhism so welcome to the Chinese people.

Whatever its origin may have been, Taoism came to place
a very strong emphasis on the life hereafter. Over against the
humanistic ethics of Confucianism which appealed chiefly,
though not wholly, to social and this-worldly sanctions in its
ethical teachings, Taoism invoked other-worldly sanctions in
the form of numerous heavens and hells which rewarded the
good and punished evil conduct. A prominent feature of Taoist
temples was the physical representation of the fate, especially
of the evil, after death. All the methods of torture conceivable
are graphically represented, presumably as a deterrent to those
who would do evil.

It seems very certain that Taoism as a cult is deteriorating
rapidly. For more than a thousand years, says one authority,
there has been no outstanding priest, philosopher, or teacher
in Taoism. The same writer says that Taoism has been the
unquestioned basis of the religion of the Chinese masses. What
will become of the religion of the masses? Complicated as it
is by the incoming of a strong new ideology, Communism,
it is impossible to say. New religious societies of importance
have arisen in recent years, some of them as a result of the
flowing together of various streams of religion. There has
been an active, conscious syncretism, embracing elements
from Confucianism, from Taoism, from Christianity, Buddhism,
Islam and Judaism, and all these are to some extent combined
with old folk beliefs and practices. No consistent pattern has
as yet appeared.

There can be little doubt that Taoist philosophy will
always remain. As education becomes more general among
the masses, this will become a part of their heritage, thinks
Dr. Wing-tsit Chan, the authority mentioned above, furnishing a useful counterpart to Confucian humanism. He thinks
also that its doctrine of *wu-wei,* or non-action, is needed even
in a dynamic, restless period like our own, and that its principles of spontaneity, simplicity and rhythmic vitality will

persist as an influence in Chinese art and poetry. (See further, Wing-tsit Chan, *Religious Trends in Modern China*, New York: Columbia Univ. Press, 1953, pp. 146 ff.)

He quotes Professor Dubs as saying: "Philosophical Taoism with its exaltation of mysticism, naturalism and simplicity, securing solace in misfortune by cultivating inward calm, laissez faire, skepticism of doctrinaire programs, and optimism, cultivating bodily as well as spiritual health, is likely to remain an important part of China's heritage." (P. 154.)

13. ELEMENTS OF STRENGTH IN TAOISM

Its intimate connection of each human individual with the Supreme Being.

Its teaching that the perfect man must follow the divine "Way."

Its founder's teaching to return good for evil.

Its ideal of "a good man" continuing even into the later degraded periods.

14. ELEMENTS OF WEAKNESS IN TAOISM

Its not sufficiently personal and responsible Supreme Being.

Its founder's positively ignoble example of withdrawing from difficulty; not organizing for reform.

Its inadequate recognition of the evils in the world.

Its inadequate appreciation of physical facts and resources, discouraging to scientific inquiry.

Its over-emphasis on inactivity (*wu-wei*), belittling to human effort.

Its lack of a commanding enthusiastic principle for living; mostly negative advice.

Its ethical ideal of indifference and irresponsibility.

Its inadequate conception of immortal life; merely a protracted existence.

Its lack of a program for the uplift of society; only a return to an uncivilized simplicity.

Its relapse into polytheism, demonolatry, and practice of magic.

VIII

SHINTO

The Religion of Nature-Worship,
Emperor-Worship, and Purity

1. AMONG THE RELIGIONS OF THE WORLD

Shinto, the immemorial national religion of Japan, would rank as the third oldest among the religions of the world, if its own traditional chronology is followed back to 660 B. C. Such antiquity is considerably modified by modern critical study. However, Shinto unquestionably represents the distinctive religious genius of Japan from the very beginnings of its history.

Shinto is unique among the religions of the world for the contribution which it has made to the political theory and the national stability of its own adherents. According to its sacred scriptures, the islands of Japan were the first divine creation, and the first Mikado was a literal descendant to earth from the Sun-goddess in heaven.

Do thou, my august grandchild, proceed thither, and govern it. Go! And may prosperity attend thy dynasty. And may it, like Heaven and Earth, endure for ever. (*Nihon-gi*, 1 : 77.) [1]

The belief in the divine origin of the land and government of Japan and in the perpetual duration of the monarchy has been steadfastly fostered in the mind of Japan by its national

[1] The references in this chapter to the *Nihon-gi* are to the volume and page of the two-volume translation by W. A. Aston in *Transactions and Proceedings of the Japan Society,* London. (Trübner, 1896.)

The references to the *Ko-ji-ki* are to the pages of the translation by Professor Basil Hall Chamberlain, in *Transactions of the Asiatic Society of Japan,* Supplement to volume X. (Tokyo, 1882.) The pages of the original edition may be found in the margin of both reprints, viz., the editions of 1906 and of 1920.

religion. The Constitution, which was formulated in 1889 in order to bring Japan into line with the methods of other nations of the world, starts with a reaffirmation of religious faith; the preamble declares that the Mikado sits upon "the throne of a lineal succession unbroken for ages eternal." Historically, Shinto has furnished the vital religious basis for the oldest reigning dynasty in the world.

Shinto is unusual for its active tolerance toward other religions. According to its own records, there have been almost 1,400 years during which Shinto has co-existed and intermingled with two other religions, Confucianism and Buddhism. Taoism also has been in Japan since 600 A. D. The regular Japanese name for this religion is Kami-no Michi, meaning "The Way of the Gods," but the most common designation is a translation of that phrase into Chinese—"Shinto" (or Shin-tao). The last element in this name is the distinctive element in the name of the Chinese religion, "Tao-ism." According to its own record (*Nihon-gi*, 2 : 195), an emperor of Japan "despised the Way of the Gods," and formally adopted the Buddhist religion. Shinto has never proselytized or persecuted, except to require political loyalty. Indeed, Shinto, not being personally founded, does not possess the sharply defined characteristics which are usual in personal religious belief and in personal religious experience.

Late in the nineteenth century, after Japan had become an important modern state, it introduced into Shinto a distinction between what it called State or Shrine Shinto and Sectarian Shinto. The former it declared to be not a religion at all, but a patriotic ceremonial. In it all citizens, regardless of their personal religious views might engage without violation of the principle of religious liberty which, if Japan was to be a modern nation, she felt she must grant to her people. On this basis she felt free to require attendance at the shrines on stated occasions without regard to religious affiliation. To most members of other faiths the government disclaimer was not convincing since most of the associations with the shrines were unquestionably religious. Since the disestablishment of

State Shinto, it has become a commonplace among Shinto leaders themselves to assert that it really was religious.

2. THE SACRED SCRIPTURES OF SHINTO

The most valuable and influential documents in the indigenous literature of Japan have been two, which set forth a story of the deeds and conversations in "The Age of the Gods" before there were any men, then the creation of Japan, and then the reigns of the sovereigns of Japan for somewhat more than a thousand years. These two are the *Ko-ji-ki*, meaning "Records of Ancient Matters," and the *Nihon-gi*, meaning "Chronicles of Japan." From the preface of the former and from a commentary on the latter, written within a hundred years, the dates of their composition may be fixed precisely at 712 A. D. and 720 A. D., respectively. These dates bring the sacred scriptures of Shinto very late in the history of religions,—more than a century after the birth of Mohammed, who founded the latest of the world's great religions, and more than 1,300 years after the earliest event in human history which is recorded in the documents themselves, the accession of the first Mikado, Jimmu Tenno, 660 B. C. Yet even so, the *Ko-ji-ki* and the *Nihon-gi* are the earliest extant specimens in 1,200 years of book-making in Japan.

The author of the *Ko-ji-ki* presents himself in the preface as a court noble of the fifth rank, who was commanded by the emperor to gather up and arrange "the genealogies of the emperors and likewise the words of former ages," particularly as these were repeated to the compiler of the document by a very remarkable "reciter," who could repeat the contents of anything he had ever read and who could remember all that he had ever heard.

Ere many years have elapsed the purport of this the great basis of the country, the foundation of the monarchy, will be destroyed. So now I desire to have the chronicles of the emperors selected and recorded, and the old words examined and ascertained. (*Ko ji-ki*, 1, 9, 11, 13.)

The same author is reported by the commentary on the *Nihon-gi*, to have collaborated with a prince under the same royal authority only eight years later to produce the second document, which is a more extensive collection of varied source material, but arranged with the same royalist purpose.

The absolute reliability of these historical records was first rejected, on critical grounds, in 1893 by a Japanese scholar, Professor Kume, of the Imperial University at Tokyo, who was deprived of his professorship for thus impugning the orthodox Shinto belief.

The utter frankness, amounting to what seems to Western ears to be obscenity in the *Ko-ji-ki* exceeds anything to be found in the sacred scriptures of any other religion in the world. The English translator alludes to this fact five times in his introduction. On at least sixteen pages there are "indecent portions of the text which, from obvious reasons, refuse to lend themselves to translation into English" (*Ko-ji-ki*, p. iv), and which, therefore, he translates into Latin.

A third important document of the Shinto religion is the *Yengi-shiki* ("Institutes of the Period of Yengi") (901–923 A. D.). The first ten of its fifty books are the very earliest source for a knowledge of the cultus. The actual text records twenty-five Nori-to, prayers for various ceremonial occasions. For example, the prescribed prayer at the annual harvest festival contains the following:

If the sovereign gods of the harvest will bestow the late-ripening harvest in many bundled ears, then I will fulfil their praises by setting up the first fruits in a thousand ears and raising high the beer-jars; and, having furnished a white horse, a white boar, and a white cock, will pile up the first fruits like a range of hills, and will tranquilly take the remainder. (Satow, *Transactions of the Asiatic Society of Japan*, 7 : 105, 109, 111.)

A fourth important scripture in Shinto is the *Manyo-shiu*, meaning "Collection of Ten Thousand Leaves." This is an anthology of 4,496 poems, made perhaps in 5th–8th centuries A. D. The following is a specimen:

"When began the earth and heaven,
Met the gods in high assembly.
Myriads upon myriads gathered.
On the Goddess of the Sunlight
They bestowed the realm of Heaven.
To her grandchild they delivered
This the land of fairest rice-ears,
His with god-like sway to govern,
Long as heaven and earth endured."

(Aston, *History of Japanese Literature*, 36.)

The sacred scriptures contain a varied collection of legends, chronicles, ballads, and poems centering on the divine origin and the early history of the island empire of Japan. They report a generally joyous delight in the powers of nature, along with a recognition of some of its gruesome aspects. But the fact is noticeable that the sacred scriptures of Shinto do not contain any of the more tragic and glorious themes of religious literature, such as a conflict of duties, the intricate problems of the moral ideal, the critical struggles of human beings with good and evil, a pre-eminent historic personage, saving assistance coming to an individual in an effort for virtue, the progressive accomplishment of a plan for the whole world, or the momentuous mysteries of a future life.

3. THE CONCEPTION OF DEITY

The regular word for god or deity in the Japanese language is *kami*. Its primary meaning is "upper." The latest elaborate treatise on Shinto published in Japan reviews sixteen different theories concerning the origin and signification of the word, and classifies them under three main ideas: (1) pure or bright, (2) superior, and (3) strange, mysterious, fearful, hidden, supernatural.

There is no other word in the original Japanese language with such a rich and multiform content, with respect to which translators, both Japanese and foreign, have encountered greater difficulties. (Holtom, *TASJ*, 49 : 2. 129.)

Motoori (1730–1801 A. D.), who was the most important theologian in the whole history of Shinto, has expounded the

meaning of this crucial Shinto concept in a passage which has
become of historic influence.

Not only human beings, but birds, beasts, plants and trees, seas
and mountains, and all other things whatsoever which deserve to
be dreaded and revered for the extraordinary and pre-eminent
powers which they possess, are called *Kami*. They need not be
eminent for surpassing nobleness, goodness, or serviceableness.
Malignant and uncanny beings are also called *Kami*, if only they
are the objects of general dread. The successive Mikados, numerous examples of divine human beings in ancient and modern times,
the fox, the tiger, the wolf, the peach, the jewels are called *Kami*.
(Aston, *Revival of Pure Shintau*, 42–43; reprinted in 1883 and
1905 from *TASJ*, vol. III, 1875.)

The number of Shinto deities is usually referred to as 80
myriads in the *Nihon-gi*, and as 800 myriads in the *Ko-ji-ki*.
They are also referred to summarily, without any indication of
their numbers, thus:

"the gods," "the gods of high heaven," "the gods of heaven," "the
gods of heaven and earth," "the gods of the earth and of grain,"
"all the gods of heaven and earth," "all the gods," "all the deities
of the august declivities of the hills, and all the deities of the
reaches of the rivers, without neglecting any." (*Ko-ji-ki*, 175.)

The origin of the deities is declared by both of the chief
scriptures of Shinto as having occurred after the formation
of heaven and earth, which in turn took place after "chaos
had begun to condense" (*Ko-ji-ki*, 4; *Nihon-gi*, 1 : 1–2).

The two chief primeval deities are the famous Izanagi
(Male-who-invites) and Izanami (Female-who-invites). These
together became the progenitors of all subsequent.

The doings of the deities, both male and female, are reported in the Shinto scriptures with much directness. They
are born, wed, beget children, vomit, bathe, become sick,
vexed, jealous, weep, curse, kill, destroy, die, are buried in
a certain place, and subsequently may be raised in rank by
the emperor of Japan.

The moral character of the Shinto deities is as varied as
that of human beings. For example, a whole group of them

are "lying deities" (*Ko-ji-ki,* 229). One of the most important is characterized thus:

This god, Susa-no-wo, was of a wicked nature. (*Nihon-gi,* 1 : 20.) His "behaviour was exceeding rude." (*Nihon-gi,* 1 : 40.) Specifically, this deity, when "impetuous with victory, broke down the divisions of the rice-fields, filled up ditches, and flayed an animal alive." (*Ko-ji-ki,* 52–53; *Nihon-gi,* 1 : 41, 45, 47.) Then "all the gods imposed on Susa-no-wo a fine." (*Nihon-gi,* 1 : 45, 49.) The assembled gods said: "Thy behaviour has been filthy and wicked." In the end they repulsed him. (*Nihon-gi,* 1 : 50.) And he was driven into banishment. (*Nihon-gi,* 1 : 57.) Indeed, "the 800 myriad deities took counsel together, and cut his beard, and even caused the nails of his fingers and toes to be pulled out." (*Ko-ji-ki,* 59; *Nihon-gi,* 1 : 45.)

This is, perhaps, the extreme instance of how the standards of morality in Japan have been advancing beyond the standards which the sacred scriptures of the Shinto religion allow to the deities. No human being in Japan now would be allowed to do with impunity what the God Susa-no-wo is reported to have done, or what the other deities did to him in punishment of his offense. The phallic worship which was quite prevalent prior to 1868 has been notably suppressed since the beginning of the era of Meiji (Enlightenment).

4. THE NATURE DEITIES

The Shinto religion originally was chiefly a nature-worship. Almost all of the deities referred to in the primary documents are objects or forces in nature.

The Sun-goddess, Ama-terasu (the Heaven-Shining-One), is the most important object of worship among the nature deities. Unto her was given the prime appointment among the numerous progeny of the primeval progenitor, Izanagi.

Do Thine Augustness rule the plain of high heaven. (*Ko-ji-ki,* 43; *Nihon-gi,* 1 : 32.)

From her, and not from any male deity, is traced the ancestry of the divine Mikado of Japan. Shinto is unique among the religions of the world in representing the paramount regent of the world as feminine in gender.

The Moon-god, Tsuki-yomi, was appointed second by the primeval male to be a ruler auxiliary to the female solar deity.

Do Thine Augustness rule the dominion of the night. (*Ko-ji-ki,* 43–44; *Nihon-gi,* 1 : 32.)

His radiance was next to that of the Sun in splendour. This god was to be the consort of the Sun-goddess and to share in her government. (*Nihon-gi,* 1 : 19.)

Many other nature deities are mentioned in the two main scriptures of Shinto, such as Kagase-wo (the star god), Susano-wo (the storm god), and Ta-kiri-bima (the mist goddess).

Mount Fuji-yama is the one most venerated among several sacred mountains in Japan. Thus from the Manyo-shiu:

"Of Yamato, the Land of Sunrise,
It is the peace-giver, it is the God."
(Aston, *Shinto, the Way of the Gods,* 17.)

"No words may tell of it.
No name that I know is fit for it.
But a wondrous deity it surely is."
(Aston, *Japanese Literature,* 41.)

5. MIKADO-WORSHIP

The divine origin of the first Mikado in direct lineal descent from the Sun-goddess is alleged in both of the primary documents. Ama-terasu sends one of her offspring down to earth for the express purpose of reigning over the land.

Descend to, dwell in, and rule over, this Luxuriant Reed-Plain-Land-of-Fresh-Rice-Ears. (*Ko-ji-ki,* 106–107.)

Indeed, the exact spot is designated by the sacred writ.

His Augustness, Ho-no-ni-ni-gi, first descended to the peak of Takachi in Tsukushi. (*Ko-ji-ki,* 5, 111–112; *Nihon-gi,* 1 : 78–79.)

The claims of divine origin and divine authority are reiterated by the Mikado himself in several pronouncements and edicts.

Hear, all of you! The dear progenitor and progenitrix, who divinely remain in the plain of high heaven, respectfully gave the mandate with the words: "Our sovereign's grandchild's augustness shall tranquilly rule the Luxuriant Reed-plain Region of Fresh-young Spikes as a peaceful country." (Text of the semi-annual great purification ceremony; *TASJ*, vol. XXVII, part I, p. 59.)

The empire was entrusted by the Sun-goddess to her descendants with the words: "My children, in their capacity of deities, shall rule it." For this reason, this country since heaven and earth began has been a monarchy. . . . The duty has therefore devolved on Us, in Our capacity as Celestial Divinity, to regulate and settle it. (*Nihongi*, 2 : 226–227.)

This is the mandate of the emperor of Japan, who rules the world as a God incarnate. (*Nihon-gi*, 2 : 198, 210.)

The claim of the Mikado's authority and incarnation is also reported as acknowledged by glad subjection.

I therefore, filled with joy and veneration, prostrating myself, address Your Majesty, the Emperor, who now rules the Land of the Eight Islands as an incarnate deity. (*Nihon-gi*, 2 : 217.)

This religious teaching in the ancient scriptures of Shinto concerning the absolute paramountcy and the perpetual sovereignty of the hereditary Mikado was embodied formally into the political constitution and pronouncements of modern Japan up until 1946. The official English translation of the constitution of 1889 contains the following:

Article I: The Empire of Japan shall be reigned over and governed by a line of Emperors unbroken for ages eternal.
Article III: The Emperor is sacred and inviolable.

The famous Imperial Rescript on Education, October 30, 1890, which effectively promoted the era of Meiji, started with a demand for unquestioning devotion to the hereditary monarchy of Japan:

Know ye, our subjects: Guard and maintain the prosperity of our Imperial throne, coeval with heaven and earth, infallible for all ages.

However, the sacred records contain ample evidence that the actual sovereignty of the Mikado over a unified realm was built up only gradually and by a process of fighting over unsubmissive people. Indeed, condemnation of more than one Mikado stands in the text of the sacred *Chronicles of Japan*.

The Sun-goddess in her original instructions pointed out the need of physical force over the inhabitants of Japan.
If the Heavenly Grandchild will use this spear, he will undoubtedly subdue it to tranquillity. (*Nihon-gi*, 1 : 69.)
And the first Emperor, Jimmu, is reported as having been successful in his struggles with various tribes because of divine assistance, "my sword, with which I subdued the land." (*Nihon-gi*, 1 : 115.)
The Emperor Mimaki was wanting in thoroughness. Therefore that Emperor was short-lived. For this reason do thou, our august descendent, now show regret for the shortcomings of the late Emperor, and be watchful in regard to the ceremonies of worship. If thou dost so, thine augustness will be long, and moreover the empire will have peace. (*Nihon-gi*, 1 : 177.)
The Empress Jingo was grieved that the Emperor [her predecessor] would not follow the divine instructions, and had consequently died a premature death. (*Nihon-gi*, 1 : 224.)

For centuries in Japan there was a strict enforcement of the command that no person might be allowed even physically to look down upon Imperial Majesty. By 1922 the general democratizing process had developed to such an extent that the Crown Prince for the first time in the entire history of Japan travelled abroad, and on returning from Europe passed among the common people in various cities of Japan.

Even so, the Emperor himself, down to the time of the end of World War II, was regarded as one apart from all other men, accessible only to a relatively small group of high officials. Even his pictures were guarded jealously from any possibility of destruction. In the immediate pre-war years the doctrine of the uniquely sacred character of the Emperor had been assiduously taught as a support for a developing imperialistic drive for the control of the East.

6. WORSHIP, CENTRALIZED AND PATRIOTIC

If the test be applied of worship of superhuman deity, Shinto is amply evidenced as a religion. Numerous shrines and priests cover the country, yet the number of deities is almost too large and indefinite to permit systematic worship of them all. In fact, the scriptures report the actual worship of only a few.

The Sun-goddess, being the most obvious and eminent, is the chief object of worship in this polytheistic nature religion. She is easily worshipped, individually and locally. Yet there is also an official and formal worship of this great Shinto deity, centralized in Isé for the whole Japanese nation, somewhat as in Judaism the worship of Jehovah used to be centralized in Jerusalem. This most sacred spot in all Japan, the one which is perhaps most frequently visited on religious pilgrimages, is on the seacoast southeast of the ancient capital, Kyoto. Here the Naiku, or "inner temple," is believed by the Japanese to date from the year 4 B. C., and is sacred to the Sun-goddess Ama-terasu, ancestress of the Mikados. In this sanctuary is a round mirror, the precious symbol of the great orb of light in heaven.

Worship in this particular place, even the method of worship, is mentioned in both of the primary documents of Shinto, and is carried back to a time dating from before the beginning of the Christian religion. The mirror is declared to have been given by the Sun-goddess to the first Mikado as a sacred token.

Ama-terasu took in her hand the precious mirror, saying: "My child, when thou lookest upon this mirror, let it be as if thou wert looking on me. Let it be to thee a holy mirror." (*Nihon-gi*, 1 : 83.) Reverence this mirror exactly as it were our august spirit, and reverence it as if reverencing us. (*Ko-ji-ki*, 109.)

According to the sacred *Chronicles of Japan*, the custom has been maintained throughout a period longer than the entire history of Christianity, that a princess of the royal house has been high priestess of the Sun-goddess at the temple at Isé (*Ko-ji-ki*, 174, 186).

Probably all devout Shintoists consider it a privilege and a duty, at least once in a lifetime, to make a religious pilgrimage to Isé, where there stands also the famous Geku, or "outer temple," which is sacred to the food-goddess, Uke-mochi.

Worship of the emperor has already been mentioned as an essential feature of the Shinto religion. Every year prior to 1946 on the Mikado's birthday in every educational institution, by official command, there was conducted a certain solemn ceremony which was largely patriotic, including obeisance to the picture of the emperor.

The significance of this practice, required of all Japanese citizens, taught in all public schools and to all young men inducted into the armed services—Japan practised universal military conscription—can hardly be overestimated. It gave to the commands of the Emperor an authority not only political, but also religious. The result was the creation of armed forces of almost fanatical loyalty who would stop at no sacrifice to carry out what they thought to be his bidding. The twin forces of religion and patriotism were made to converge at a single point. This largely explains what Japan, a relatively small country, poor in natural resources, was able to do in the years preceding and during the Second World War. (See further, D. C. Holtom, *Modern Japan and Shinto Nationalism*, rev. ed., Chicago: University of Chicago Press, 1947.)

The national flag of Japan, with its radiant red sun, was a concrete instance of how the religious faith of Shinto has been directed powerfully to promote patriotic zeal. The full significance of this emblem doubtless carried to intelligent citizens of "The Land of the Rising Sun" the glowing suggestion that for their national and religious rule they should reverently look up on high to the source of all light, and that the subjects of the divinely descended heavenly Mikado might all regard themselves as, through him, a divine progeny dwelling in a holy land.

7. SHRINES AND OFFERINGS

Some of the worship in the Shinto religion can be seen in the numerous shrines in every hamlet, along the wayside, and in almost every picturesque spot throughout Japan. In the tenth century there were 3,132 officially recognized shrines enumerated in the Yengi-shiki. In 1880 the village and un-graded shrines numbered 183,047, but in 1920 they had de-creased to 111,181. However, the shrines maintained by the government had increased during the same period from 55 to 105.[1]

At the outbreak of the Second World War, there were about 110,000 shrines under the control of the national government through the Home Ministry, many of them supported, at least in part, by the state. This number did not include the sectarian shrines which were supported, wholly without state subsidy, either by endowments or the voluntary gifts of the people. Estimates vary as to the number belonging to the sects in the pre-war years from ten to seventeen million, with the probability that the lesser number was nearer to the facts.

The Shinto shrines are always approached through the char-acteristic *tori-i* gateway, the ends of the upper crosspiece curv-ing heavenward. They are often located picturesquely amid lofty cryptomeria trees, or near hillside waterfalls, or near watercourses spanned by high-arched bridges. Thus, even in their setting, the Shinto shrines are designed to promote a re-ligious appreciation of the beautiful in nature.

The actual worship which is performed at Shinto shrines is almost exclusively individual, not congregational. It consists regularly of obeisance, bowing reverentially as in the presence of a superior. Kneeling is not so common. Clapping the hands together, sometimes done silently, is also an act of reverence performed at Shinto shrines. Material offerings for the gods form another part of Shinto worship.

At the present time the daily offerings made to the Sun-goddess and the Food-goddess at Isé consist of four cups of sa-ke [*i. e.,* liquor], sixteen saucers of rice and four of salt, besides fish, birds, fruits, seaweed and vegetables. The annual offerings at the tomb of the first Mikado, Jimmu, are products of mountain, river and sea, including fish, cakes, birds and liquor. (Aston, *Shinto, the Way of the Gods,* 213.)

[1] These statistics are quoted from Holtom, *TASJ*, 49 : 2. 324, where they are cited from the yearly reports of the Department of Home Affairs.

8. PRAYER IN SHINTO

A Shintoist's worship today is usually completed by his coming to a shrine and offering a prayer.

The earliest document in Shinto, the *Records of Ancient Matters*, contains numerous conversations with the deities, but never once any words of prayer addressed to them. Indeed, the entire document contains only two passing references to prayer:

. . . having said prayers. (*Ko-ji-ki*, 104.)
prayerfully reciting grand liturgies. (*Ko-ji-ki*, 57.)

The same almost entire absence of prayer occurs in the other sacred scripture also. Only two out of the forty-two rulers are reported as having prayed in the *Nihon-gi* (1 : 220, 225). Yet a later Shinto scripture, the *Yengi-shiki*, contains the text of twenty-five long official Nori-to litanies. These consist chiefly of announcements to the various deities, ascriptions of praise, and lists of material offerings which have been made, or which will be made. In the first Nori-to litany the phrase "fulfil the praises" of the gods recurs at least nineteen times, and the idea of bargaining in prayer is expressed more than once.

If the sovereign gods will bestow . . . the harvest, I will fulfil their praises by offering firstfruits. (Aston, *SWG*, 281–285; *TASJ*, vol. VII, 1878, pp. 109–112.)

No moral or spiritual blessings are sought in this entire collection of official Shinto prayers. "They contain petitions for rain in time of drought, good harvests, preservation from earthquakes and conflagrations, children, health and long life to the sovereign, and enduring peace and prosperity to his rule, the safety of his ambassadors to foreign countries, the suppression of rebellion, the repulse of invasion, success to the Imperial armies, and general prosperity to the Empire." "Prayers to the Shinto gods, even at the present day, are mostly for material blessings" (Aston, *SWG*, 234, 236; *Shinto, the Ancient Religion of Japan*, 62).

9. CEREMONIALS AND FESTIVALS

All the ritual prayers which are contained in the Nori-to are connected with specific religious ceremonies, which in turn are connected with popular festivals. These are important parts of the Shinto religion, as of all nature religions and of any other religions which are connected with agricultural operations. For example:

When the seed rice is sown in the second month of the year, there is a harvest-praying service (Toshigohi no Matsuri). The ritual prayer for this occasion is the First Nori-to (Aston, *SWG*, 280; *TASJ*, 7 : 104–126).

When the rice-plants are springing up, there is a prescribed ceremonial service of the food-goddess (Hirose-Oho-imi no Matsuri) on the fourth day of the fourth moon of each year. Numerous offerings are made, and the emperor promises still further that:

If the sovereign deity will deign to perfect and bless the harvest-fields . . . I will draw hither the first-fruits, piling them up like a range of hills. (*TASJ*, 7 : 414–415.)

The first tasting of the new rice, Nihi-name (Feast of First-Fruits), in the eleventh month of the year, is an especially elaborate ancient ceremony, referred to many times in the *Nihon-gi*. "It is accompanied by songs and dances, feasting, holiday dress, presents. Strict Shinto devotees would not eat the new season's rice until it had been performed" (Aston, *SWG*, 277).

Great Tasting (Oho-nihe), when the emperor in person conducts the festival of first-fruits in his coronation year.

Hirata's detailed description of this, the most elaborate and solemn festival of the Shinto religion, occupies 480 pages of his Commentary on the Ko-ji-ki. (Aston, *SWG*, 277.)

Other harvest festivals are the Joint-Tasting (Ahi-name, of Ahimbe; *Nihon-gi*, 2 : 335), and the Divine Tasting.

New-moon religious ceremonies, with prayers and offerings.

Monthly festivals (Tsuki-nami no Matsuri) with their three prescribed Nori-to prayers (Aston, *SWG*, 285–286).

10. PURITY IN SHINTO

One of the marked practical characteristics of the Japanese is their personal cleanliness. Their Shinto religion has impressed upon them the obligation to wash themselves assiduously with water. Both of the sacred scriptures of Shinto record that even the deity, Izanagi, who was the prime progenitor, was careful to wash himself for the purpose of personal cleanliness.

I will perform the purification of my august person. (*Ko-ji-ki*, 39.)
It is meet that I should cleanse my body from its pollutions. (*Nihon-gi*, 1 : 26.)
. . . to wash away the defilement. (*Nihon-gi*, 1 : 31.)

The most important among the recurring Shinto ceremonies was "The Great Purification" (Oho-harahi).

It "includes a preliminary lustration, expiatory offerings, and the recitation of a Nori-to formula, in which the Mikado, by virtue of the authority transmitted to him from the Sun-goddess, declares to his ministers and people the absolution of their sins and impurities." (Aston, *SWG*, 294; *SARJ*, 64.)
"The offerings made were thrown into a river or into the sea, and were supposed, like the scapegoat of Israel, to carry with them the sins of the people. The offenses more specifically referred to are various mischievous interferences with agricultural operations." (Aston, *SARJ*, 72.)

Shinto thus teaches emphatically the obligation of purity, and also the sense of communal guilt, which needs continual purification. But the special kind of purity which the Shinto religion enjoins is mostly physical and ceremonial, rather than a purity of heart and thought and social relations.

11. THE ETHICS OF SHINTO

The Shinto religion is remarkable in having neither a definite set of theological beliefs nor a definite code of morality apart from subservience to the Mikado, until recently regarded as a divinely descended "Heavenly Sovereign." In the second of Shinto's sacred scriptures there are a few passages which contain sage advice for government officials.

He who tells the truth, will be uninjured. He who is false, will assuredly suffer harm. (*Nihon-gi*, 1 : 317.)
Cease from gluttony, and abandon covetous desires. Chastise that which is evil, and encourage that which is good. Cease from wrath, and refrain from angry looks. Be not envious. (*Nihon-gi*, 2 : 130–131.)

Among the specific commands for the common people there is the following:

On entering or leaving the Palace Gate, one must kneel on both knees, with both hands pressed on the ground. But it is permitted to stand up and walk when the threshold is passed. (*Nihon-gi*, 2 : 133.)

In both of the primary sacred scriptures of Shinto there is an almost total absence of direct moral teachings for the people at large. Motoori, the great expounder of Shinto in the eighteenth century, explains the lack of moral regulations in accordance with characteristic Shinto orthodoxy:

To the end of time each Mikado is a goddess' son. His mind is in perfect harmony of thought and feeling with hers. He does not seek out new inventions, but rules in accordance with precedents which date from the age of the gods. And if he is ever in doubt, he has resort to divination, which reveals to him the mind of the great goddess. Not only the Mikado, but his ministers and people also, act up to the traditions of the divine age. Hence in ancient times the idea of *Michi*, or way, ethics, was never broached. In ancient times, although there was no prosy system of doctrine in Japan, there were no popular disturbances, and the empire was peacefully ruled. It is because the Japanese were truly moral in their practise that they required no theory of morals. And the fuss made by the Chinese about theoretical morals is owing to their laxity in practice. (*TASJ*, 3 : 24–26.)

However, the earliest "great purification of the land" mentioned in the "Records of Ancient Matters" was on account of the following offenses:

Flaying alive and flaying backwards, breaking down the divisions of rice-fields, filling up ditches, marriages between superiors and inferiors, marriages with horses, marriages with cattle, marriages with fowls, and marriages with dogs. (*Ko-ji-ki,* 230.)

In the liturgy of the semiannual "Great Purification," as prescribed in Nori-to number 10, the offenses for which the Mikado makes purification regularly are as follows:

Now, of the various faults and transgressions to be committed by the celestial race destined more and more to people this land of His peaceful rule, some are of Heaven, to wit: the breaking down of divisions between rice-fields, filling up of irrigation-channels, removing water-pipes, sowing seed over again, planting skewers [perhaps with an act of incantation], flaying alive, flaying backwards. These are distinguished as heavenly offenses.

Earthly offenses which will be committed are the cutting of living bodies, the cutting of dead bodies, leprosy, incest of a man with his mother or daughter, with his mother-in-law or step-daughter, bestiality, calamities from creeping things [*i. e.*, from snakes and centipedes], from the high Gods [*i. e.*, lightning and goblins], and from high birds, killing animals, bewitchments. (Aston, *SWG,* 297–300; *TASJ,* 27 : 60–61.)

The morality as well as the theology of the Shinto religion is naturalistic. There has been, however, a valuable moral development in Japan subsequent to the composition of the sacred scriptures.

Bushido (fighting-knights'-way, or the teachings of knightly behavior) is a code of ethics which developed in the eleventh and twelfth centuries A. D. as a part of feudalism in Japan. It is a feudalistic amalgam of certain practical features of the three religions which have been prevalent in Japan—Shinto's loyalty to the emperor as divine, Confucianism's filial obedience, and Buddhism's serene disdainfulness of life and of death.

The expositors of Bushido wax eloquent over the moral virtues which that system has fostered, such as loyalty, courage, self-sacrifice, proper decorum, benevolence, honor, justice, self-control. But they point to no specific injunctions for those moral virtues, except the Chinese moralists, Confucius and Mencius.

It is not a written code. At best it consists of a few maxims handed down from mouth to mouth, or coming from the pen of some well-known warrior or savant. (Nitobe, *Bushido*, 51.)
The strength and perhaps also the weakness of Bushido lay in this, —that it possessed no written creed. (Nitobe, *The Japanese Nation*, 155–156.)

The moral code of Bushido seems to have grown up, and also ceased, largely with militaristic feudalism in Japan.

12. THE HISTORY OF SHINTO

Five successive periods have seen very varied tendencies.

(1) *The Early Period of Absolute Supremacy* (660 B. C.– 552 A. D.)

For nominally 1,200 years, from the traditional date of the first Mikado, Jimmu, until the introduction of Buddhism, Shinto held undisputed sway over Japan.

(2) *The Period of Buddhism's Early Gains* (552–800)

For 250 years Shinto was still the strongest religion in Japan, although three foreign religions, Confucianism, Taoism, and Buddhism, were coming in from China. Two-fifths of the *Nihon-gi* is devoted to the period of Buddhism's first 150 years in Japan, and contains more than fifty references to the advancing influence of Buddhism.

In the year 645 the Emperor Kotoku "honored the religion of Buddha, and despised the Way of the Gods." (*Nihon-gi*, 2 : 195.) In the year 671 the Heir Apparent "renounced the world, and put on the priestly garb." (*Nihon-gi*, 2 : 302.)

(3) *The Period of Syncretism, or Mixed Shinto* (800–1700)

For 900 years the indigenous religion of Japan was being consciously intermingled with foreign religions.

The Buddhist priest Kobo-Daishi (774–835 A. D.) successfully preached a doctrine, called Ryobu or Mixed Shinto, that the Shinto deities were only transmigrations or incarnations of Buddhist deities. Kitabatake Chikafusa (1293–1354 A. D.) and Ichijo Kaneyoshi

(1465–1500 A. D.) "contended that Shinto, Buddhism and Confucianism were all capable of being welded into a whole." (Brinkley, *History of the Japanese People*, 452.)

The extent to which the actual paramountcy of Shinto even in the court of Japan was weakened in this period of rivalry with foreign religions may be seen from the fact that the greatest Shinto rite of all, the Oho-nihe, or Coronation Ceremony, was in abeyance for eight reigns, from 1465 to 1687 A.' D. (Aston, *SWG*, 364, also 277).

(4) *Indigenous Revival of Shinto* (1700–1868)

For a century and two-thirds, during a period when its official head was so weak that the military regent had usurped the power of the Mikado, four famous literati effected a notable revival of Shinto. Kada (1669–1736 A. D.) revived the study of the archaic Japanese language and edited the ancient texts. Mabuchi (1697–1769 A. D.), his pupil, recalled that

"In ancient times, when men's dispositions were straightforward, a complicated system of morals was unnecessary. So that in those days it was unnecessary to have a doctrine of right and wrong. But the Chinese, being bad at heart, in spite of the teaching which they got, were only good on the outside. The Japanese, being straightforward, could do without teaching." (*TASJ*, 3 : 16.)

Motoori (1730–1801 A. D.) wrote a commentary on the *Ko-ji-ki*, which extends to forty-four printed volumes. He revived the waning glories of Shinto with the following sentiments:

"As foreign countries, China and India, particularly the former, are not under the special domain of the Sun-goddess, they have no permanent rulers; and evil spirits, having found a field of action, have corrupted mankind." (*TASJ*, 3 : 25.)
"It has been asked whether the Kami-no-Michi is not the same as the Taoism of Lao-tze. Lao-tze hated the vain conceits of the Chinese scholars, and honored naturalness, from which a resemblance may be argued. But, as he was born in a dirty country not under the special protection of the Sun-goddess, he had only heard the theories of the succession of so-called Holy Men." (*TASJ*, 3 : 29.)

"The eternal endurance of the dynasty of the Mikados is a complete proof that the 'Way' called Kami-no-Michi, or Shinto, infinitely surpasses the system of all other countries." (*TASJ*, 3 : 27.)

Hirata (1776–1843 A. D.) produced more than a hundred writings, and was the most learned and productive scholar in the whole history of Shinto. He expounded this faith as follows:

"The two fundamental doctrines are: that Japan is the country of the Gods, and her inhabitants are the descendants of the Gods. Between the Japanese people and the Chinese, Hindus, Russians, Dutch, Siamese, Cambodians and other nations of the world there is a difference of kind, rather than of degree." (*TASJ*, 3 : 46.)
"The Mikado is the true Son of Heaven, who is entitled to reign over the four seas and the ten-thousand countries." (*TASJ*, 3 : 52.)
"From the fact of the divine descent of the Japanese people proceeds their immeasurable superiority to the natives of other countries in courage and intelligence." (*TASJ*, 3 : 54.)
They "are honest and upright of heart, and are not given to useless theorizing and falsehoods like other nations." (*TASJ*, 3 : 58.)

Such a religious revival of faith in the Mikado and in the people of Japan led directly to the Restoration of 1868.

(5) *Recent Varied Readjustments* (*since* 1868)

In 1882 the government authorities divided Shinto itself into two divisions, Sectarian Shinto and State Shinto. Sectarian Shinto was to be regarded as a religion, standing on an equality with Buddhism and other systems of religion. And State Shinto was to be regarded, not as a religion, but as a patriotic cult or ritual in which all Japanese subjects might share equally irrespective of their religious beliefs. However, in the course of time this State Shinto became virtually a real State religion, in which the divinity of the Emperor was a cardinal doctrine. Such doctrine has been taught, for example, by an eminent Professor in the chair of Shinto in the Imperial University at Tokyo.

"Shinto has culminated in Mikadoism, or the Worship of the Mikado, or Japanese Emperor, as a divinity during his life-time as well as after his death." (Genchi Kato, *A Study of Shinto, The Religion of the Japanese Nation*, 203.)

Soon after Japan's military success in the First World War there was publicized a noteworthy expansion of nationalism into a triumphant world-outlook.

The Japanese are the chosen people of God, and the presence of God is especially manifested in the Emperor of Japan. Shinto is logically destined to be the universal religion and the saving culture of mankind. The duty of the Japanese people and of the Emperor of Japan is to spread that religion and culture, until the Emperor of Japan shall become the supreme temporal and spiritual ruler of the world. This conquest of the world is to be made by peaceful means; but it seems reasonable that if peaceful means fail, the power of might may be tried. (Reported in the *Biblical World*, July, 1919, p. 434.)

This development has been described in great detail and with full documentation by D. C. Holtom, *Modern Japan and Shinto Nationalism*, Chicago, 1947, rev. ed.

On the first New Year's Day after the military defeat of Japan in 1945, the Emperor Hirohito issued to his people an epoch-making Imperial Rescript, in which he reconstructed certain conceptions prevailing in Shinto. In particular he disavowed the cherished belief concerning his own divine nature, and also the superiority of the Japanese people.

"In greeting the new year, we have to . . . proceed unflinchingly toward elimination of misguided practises of the past. . . . And, through being thoroughly pacific, we will construct a new Japan. . . .

"The ties between Us and Our People . . . do not depend upon mere legends and myths. They are not predicated on the false conception that the Emperor is divine, and that the Japanese people are superior to other races, and are fated to rule the world. The Tenno [Emperor] is not a living god.

"By their [that is, the Japanese people's] supreme endeavors . . . they will be able to render substantial contribution to the welfare and advancement of mankind."

State Shinto was completely disestablished by the Allied Occupation and ceased to be the State religion, if religion it really was. It was permitted to continue, but on precisely the same basis as other religions in Japan. Neither the Emperor nor any public official might take part, in his official capacity, in any of the shrine ceremonies, though as citizens they might. All support from the government was cut off, and the shrines were obliged to find a basis of voluntary support. This resulted in great hardship for those shrines which had been heavily subsidized by the state. There was a great falling off of attendance at the shrines for a number of years, but recent reports indicate that many of them have been more thronged by worshippers lately than before the disestablishment. No doubt some of them have ceased to exist, but the major shrines are very much an influence in the lives of the Japanese people. In the new constitution, complete religious freedom is guaranteed to every citizen. This new freedom has led to the upsurge of numerous new religions and sects. Over 700 such are registered in the department of government which has to do with the religions. Some 600 of these arose during or immediately after the Second World War. They represent every variety of syncretism of two or more religions to form a new one. (See Charles S. Braden, "Religion in Post War Japan," *Journal of Bible and Religion,* Vol. 21, pp. 147 ff.)

Sectarian Shinto

Alongside traditional shrine Shinto there eventually grew up a variety of sects which emphasized some one or more Shinto beliefs or practices more than was done generally, or which developed different emphases while retaining some of the Shinto traditions. Since only Shinto, Buddhism and Christianity were recognized by the government, those which were neither Buddhist nor Christian tended to be listed as Shinto, though some of them had very little that was typically Shinto in their beliefs. Finally thirteen were recognized as Shinto sects. Most of them worshipped some one or more of the Shinto deities, though one of them has no deity taken from Shinto, Konko-kyo, and the chief deity of another, Tenri-kyo is not found among the list of Shinto deities. A number

had personal founders who eventually came to be worshipped
as divinities.

They have been variously classified. D. C. Holtom classifies them as Pure Shinto Sects of which there are three; Confucian sects, two in number; Mountain Sects, three; Purification sects, two; and Faith-healing sects, of which there are
three. Another authority classifies the latter as sects of peasant
origin. In general the sects carry on very much as other religions, some of them being highly evangelistic in their effort
to win followers. Some of them have their own scriptures,
apart from the Shinto scriptures, revealed through their
founders. Some carry on not a little social service as well as
their religious education activities, influenced in this to some
extent by Christian missionary work. Some have congregational forms of worship and preaching. The last-named groups
especially make a great deal of faith healing. For greater detail concerning the individual sects see D. C. Holtom, *The
National Faith of Japan*, New York; E. P. Dutton and Company, New York, 1938, and *Religions in Japan*, Tokyo, 1948,
published by General Headquarters, SCAP.

A fundamental faith of Japan today is doubtless the same
as that expressed by the ancient Japanese poet, Hitomaro
(737 A. D.):

> "Japan is not a land where men need pray,
>   For 'tis itself divine.
>   Yet do I lift my voice in prayer."
> (Chamberlain, *The Classical Poetry of the Japanese*, 88.)

13. ELEMENTS OF STRENGTH IN SHINTO

Reverence for the supernatural present in nature.

No general idolatry, despite round-mirror symbol of Sun-
goddess.

Self-sacrificing reverence for government as a divine institution.

An enthusiastic, unifying patriotism.

An affinity between man and the divine.

Religious value in cleanliness and purity.

Reverence for the beautiful as integral to religion.
Loyalty to the superior, almost the soul of religion.

14. ELEMENTS OF WEAKNESS IN SHINTO

Its heterogeneous polytheism.
Its primitive animism, unsuited to science.
Its fantastic scriptural myths about deity.
Not one deity worthy of veneration as a moral ideal.
No paramount cosmic moral law.
No intrinsic value in a human individual.
No historic founder to standardize and inspire.
No outstanding, historic noble human example.
No magnificent goal for human society.
No glorious hope of a future life.
Its sacred scriptures give no guidance and inspiration for noble living.
Not much help available from deity.
No historic service actually rendered to outsiders.
No place for non-Japanese, except recently.

IX

JUDAISM

The Religion of Obedience
to the Righteous God

1. INTRODUCTION: AMONG THE WORLD'S LIVING RELIGIONS

The word "Judaism," which occurs in the *New Testament* (Galatians 1 : 13), was first used about 100 B. C. in Græco-Jewish literature (II Maccabees 2 : 21; 8 : 1) to designate the religion of the Hebrews. There is no other one word to cover the entire history of this religion.

Judaism is the oldest of nine personally founded religions. It is the oldest of five living religions which originated from the belief that a personal deity had made a special divine revelation through an individual founder. The other later religions of this type are Zoroastrianism, Christianity, Islam, and Sikhism.

Judaism is the earliest of three religions which teach that there exists one supreme Person, Creator of the whole world, and God over all men. This great religious faith was conveyed through Judaism to two other monotheistic religions, Christianity and Islam.

Judaism is the earlier of two religions whose sacred scriptures proclaim an ideal order which is surely to be realized upon earth under the rule of God. This glowing hope of Judaism is shared in certain respects by only one other religion. But Christianity lays upon all its adherents a responsibility for active co-operation with God to help bring the longed-for kingdom throughout the earth.

Judaism has the unique distinction of being a religion whose followers have been scattered abroad for a longer period than previously they had been in their original national home, Palestine; yet they have not lost their marked religious and racial characteristics, despite more destructive persecutions than have been suffered by any other religious group in the world.

During its long career Judaism has undergone various internal developments. Like all religions, it has borrowed. Yet it has contributed still more. Indeed, Judaism is the parent of the two religions most active in missionary work, Christianity and Islam. Ethical monotheism has been Judaism's noblest feature, and also its noblest contribution to the religious thought of the world.

2. THE SACRED SCRIPTURES OF JUDAISM

The sacred scriptures of Judaism are a collection of twenty-four documents, arranged in three groups known as The Law, The Prophets, and The Writings (or *Hagiographa*). They were all composed in Hebrew, except that about half the book of Daniel, some official documents in Ezra, and a single verse in Jeremiah are in Aramaic. They must be read in the original language in all orthodox synagogues even to the present day. These documents have become more widely known as the *Old Testament* of Christianity, where they have been rearranged into thirty-nine books.

These sacred scriptures represent a literary activity of perhaps ten centuries. They traverse a succession of many stages of religious growth in the knowledge of God. The orthodox Jews regard as peculiarly sacred the first five books, or the Law (*Torah*), which deal with the origin of the world, their nation, and their religion. But as expressing the highest attainment of religious faith, the last book of The Law (Deuteronomy) and the Psalms and the Prophets are more valuable. It was from this latter phase of Judaism as the religion of personal devotion to God that Christianity sprang.

3. BEGINNINGS FROM PRIMITIVE SEMITIC RELIGION (BEFORE 1200 B. C.)

Judaism was the first living religion to spring from the primitive religious life of the Semites. Those uncultured, yet religiously minded, nomads are still represented by the modern Bedouin tribes. Their original belief was that various objects, either natural like a mountain or a spring, or artificially consecrated like a post or an ark, were intimately connected with their special deity. Their social unit was the clan, each recognizing some particular deity at its head. All members, including the deity, were expected to promote the material interests of the clan and to injure its enemies. Thus the conception of deity was essentially that of a hereditary tribal leader. This kind of a religion prescribed no moral obligations outside of the clan. And even within the clan the relations were simple and rudimentary, represented by the communion meal in which the deity partook symbolically through offerings or the shedding of blood.

Out of such a primitive polytheistic background, with only a few moral ideals, there was gradually developed the distinctive ethical monotheism of Judaism through the influence of outstanding personalities such as Abraham, Moses, Elijah, and the prophets of Israel.

The Abraham portrayed in Genesis would not serve at the present time as a model of monogamy or truthfulness or general morality. He lied about his wife (Genesis 12 : 11–19). He was ready to make his son a religious sacrifice (Genesis 22 : 10). He was a man of his age in many respects. Yet he was truly a great man who made a venture of faith and broke away from his inherited polytheism.

The Lord appeared to Abraham, and said unto him: "I am God Almighty: walk before me, and be thou perfect." (Genesis 17 : 1.)

Jews and Christians regard Abraham as "the father of the faithful" because "he believed in the Lord, and he counted it to him for righteousness" (Genesis 15 : 6). Abraham believed that, on account of his religious faith in "the Lord God of heaven and the God of the earth" (Genesis 24 : 3), he would become the head of a countless progeny upon earth and prove a world-wide blessing. Indeed, the sacred scriptures both of Judaism and of Christianity characterize Abraham as a "friend of God" (II Chronicles 20 : 7; Isaiah 41 : 8; James 2 : 23).

That Abraham conceived of God as the highly ethical, monotheistic divinity which He later came to be regarded, is doubted by many modern scholars. On the basis of much study they have come to the conclusion that the religious and ethical ideals which are found in parts of the earlier books of the *Bible* were developed at a later time and projected back into the ancient narratives by their later editors, doubtless with the sincere belief that they had been held at that time. Conservative scholarship does not agree at this point. However, he did nothing further to organize or propagate his faith (Genesis 12 : 2–3; 22 : 17–18). Therefore although Abraham is the first outstanding figure in the history of Judaism, he can hardly be regarded as its founder.

4. MOSES, THE ORGANIZER OF JEHOVAH-WORSHIP (ABOUT 1200 B. C.)

The religion of the people who have been variously known as Israelites, Hebrews, and Jews was first organized out of a momentous religious experience. Moses, a Hebrew in Egypt who had risen to a remarkably high position at the court, killed an Egyptian who had abused a Hebrew, and fled to the wilderness. There he felt that Jehovah was calling him to help deliver his people from their oppression (Exodus, chapters 2 and 3). Thereupon, Moses appeared as a champion of Hebrew liberty in the name of the "I Am That I Am." This special name for deity in Judaism has long been known as "Jehovah," though the original form probably was "Jahveh" or "Yahweh" (Exodus 3 : 14). Through various vicissitudes Moses succeeded in leading the children of Israel out of their servitude in Egypt, and then through forty years to the borders of their Promised Land in Palestine. At Mount Horeb

(Sinai) amid impressive natural phenomena of clouds and thunderings, Moses presented the Ten Commandments as delivered by God Himself (Exodus 20 : 1–17; Deuteronomy 5 : 1–21). Gratitude for blessings experienced in time of distress, and loyalty to God's commandments, rather than an intellectual solution of the speculative problems of the universe, formed Israel's approach to the conception of God.

One of the most significant advances which has ever been made among the religions of mankind was made under Moses. He led a people through an unforgettable experience, which he interpreted as their deliverance by a righteous God from a condition of social injustice. Moses first established the religion of Israel as an individual and communal faith in a personal God of righteousness.

5. THE MINGLING OF RELIGIONS IN PALESTINE (1200–900 B. C.)

When the Hebrews first entered Canaan, they felt themselves religiously justified in a certain amount of extermination of the inhabitants of the land (Joshua 10 : 22–26; 11 : 2–9, 21). But after they had established themselves firmly, and had changed from a nomadic type of life into one of settled agriculture, their religion also underwent certain noticeable changes. They tended toward a policy of accommodation to environment rather than superiority above environment. They gradually absorbed the local Canaanites, and also assimilated many features of the Canaanitish religion. Thus, the Hebrews began to join in the worship of the Baals (deities regarded as lords or owners of the soil) and of the local Ashteroth (female Semitic goddesses). The people who had been taught by Moses to maintain the religion of Jehovah sternly aloof, now adopted the Canaanitish festivals of spring and autumn, harvest and vintage.

They also built them high places and pillars and Asherim on every high hill and under every green tree. They did also according to all the abominations of the nations which Jehovah drove out before the children of Israel. (I Kings 14 : 23.)

And they served idols, wherof Jehovah had said unto them, "Ye shall not do this thing." (II Kings 17 : 10–12.)

This large increment of heathenism slowed down the religious growth of Israel perceptibly. Centuries later the prophet Ezekiel, speaking of Jerusalem, declared: "Your mother was a Hittite, and your father an Amorite" (Ezekiel 16 : 45), that is to say, the city was ever a hotbed of paganism mingled with the Hebrew religion.

Under Samuel, Saul, David, and Solomon the Hebrews achieved an effective nationalism under Jehovah's protection. The division of Solomon's empire into two rival states weakened this unity. Yet when the bold Jezebel introduced the Phœnician deity, Elijah was able to rouse the people's latent loyalty to Jehovah and to bring about the ultimate expulsion of the invading Baal (I Kings 16 : 31–33; 18 : 20–40).

6. THE BEGINNINGS OF JEWISH RELIGIOUS
LITERATURE (900–750 B. C.)

When the prophets Amos and Hosea preached in the eighth century B. C., they evidently assumed that the people of Israel were acquainted with the general facts of the previous history as these have come down to us. We consequently may assume that most of the prophetic narratives from Genesis to II Kings had been taking shape in the period immediately prior to 750 B. C. The first five of these books are attributed by their titles to Moses as author. But he could hardly have written the account of his own death and the comparison of himself with other subsequent prophets (Deuteronomy 34 : 5–10). Scholarly research has shown that the first six books of the *Old Testament* are composite, their major sections dating from the period between Solomon and the earlier of the literary prophets.

During this period there seem to have been two distinct prophetic attempts to put the previous history of the Hebrews into a continuous narrative, both of which have been merged into the history as we read it today. This indicates tendencies leading to the production of religious literature which came to be regarded as sacred. Historical materials were put together in attractive and proportionate form, and were generally accepted, under the conviction that the early history of the world and of the nation was of the utmost significance in manifesting the creative and redemptive purpose of God.

7. THE PRE-EXILIC HEBREW PROPHETS
(750–586 B. C.)

For about two centuries prior to the Babylonian Captivity the Hebrew people were educated in some of the highest ideas of their religion by a series of eight remarkable preachers or prophets of God. The first four in the half-century before 700 B. C. did their special work by shifting the emphasis in religion from form and sacrifices to ethical obedience.

Amos proclaimed the need of personal and national obedience to a righteous God; otherwise the worshippers of Jehovah would be punished, as well as the worshippers of the gods of the other nations whom the Hebrews despised (Amos 2 : 6–7; 3 : 1–2; 4 : 1–5; 5 : 18–22).

Take away from me the noise of thy songs, for I will not bear the melody of thy voice. But let justice roll down as waters, and righteousness as a mighty stream. (Amos 5 : 23–24.)

Hosea added to Amos's message of the uncompromising justice of Jehovah, the very earliest declaration among the religions of the world, that God loves human beings. Through a distressing domestic experience Hosea came to the lofty religious conviction that God loves persistently, and that therefore He is ready to forgive a repentant sinner, though He will not flinch from punishment.

I desire loving kindness and not sacrifice, and the knowledge of God rather than burnt offerings. (Hosea 6 : 6.)
Therefore turn thou to thy God. Keep kindness and justice. (Hosea 12 : 6.)

Isaiah began his work as a religious leader with a vision of the majestic holiness of Jehovah.

Holy, holy, holy is the Lord of hosts. The whole earth is full of His glory. (Isaiah 6 : 3.)

Amid distressing national and international problems Isaiah, like his contemporaries, continued to enlarge the moral content and the practical application of the inherited faith in their tribal deity Jehovah. The first chapter in the collection of his sermons contains some choice examples of Isaiah's teachings concerning Jehovah, for example, that His chief interest is not in heredity nor in ceremonial sacrifices, but in righteousness and in the redemption of the sinful (Isaiah 1 : 1–20; see also 2 : 2–4; 8 : 19–20; 28 : 7–22). Isaiah pictured concretely a glorious future for Israel, in spite of the inevitable punishment which Jehovah must inflict upon the nation's continued sinfulness.

Micah definitely rejected the original belief of the Jews that their deity would be sure to protect their material interests. Instead, he insisted that for the sake of their moral interests Jehovah would be sure to punish the nation, even by the hand of other nations (Micah 3 : 11–12). Like a towering mountain peak among the ranges of the world's living religions stands Micah's summary of religious duty:

To do justly, and to love kindness and to walk humbly with thy God. (Micah 6 : 8.)

The second group of the pre-exilic prophets belongs to the closing years of the monarchy. Zephaniah, like Amos, delivered a rousing message of judgment from God upon persistent sinfulness. Nahum taught that God is both good and strict, and that He is supreme among the nations. Habakkuk preached a comprehensive message of judgment and of hope from the righteous God. Centuries later, three outstanding Christian leaders, Paul, Augustine, and Luther, were powerfully influenced by a sentence from this ancient Hebrew prophet ". . . The just shall live by his faith" (Habakkuk 2 : 4). Jeremiah was the prophet who contributed most clearly to religious advance in this period. In bitter personal sorrows, Jeremiah learned the healing consciousness of fellowship with God. He preached also of religious responsibility and God's renewing influence in the heart.

Behold, saith Jehovah, I will make a new covenant. . . . I will put my law in their inward parts, and in their heart will I write it. (Jeremiah 31 : 31–33.)

Jeremiah saw that the righteous individual, rather than the group to which he belongs, is the immediate agent which God uses in promoting His loving purposes for the world. That principle opened the way for an active monotheism, which is much more than simply a personally satisfying religion. Jeremiah perhaps first furnished the basis for the missionary interpretation of religion which was later elaborated and dropped by Judaism, but which prevails among Christians today.

8. THE TWO GREAT RELIGIOUS LEADERS OF THE EXILE (586–539 B. C.)

During the half-century of the Exile in Babylonia two prophets greatly influenced the religious thinking of the Hebrew captives.

Ezekiel preached the sovereignty of God along with divine mercy and forgiveness. He declared that in deportation from their homeland the people had received the punishment which they deserved for their unrighteousness. Yet Ezekiel taught that this hard experience was not merely a penalty, but also a means of purification and discipline. Again, belief had been that according to the Second Commandment in the Mosaic Decalogue God would continue to mete out punishment for sin even unto the third and fourth generation later (Exodus 20 : 5; Deuteronomy 5 : 9). Ezekiel, proceeding upon the basis of Jeremiah's individualism, brought a message of hope; he taught a person's own responsibility and opportunity before God, irrespective of heredity.

The soul that sinneth, it shall die. (Ezekiel 18 : 5, 20.)

Indeed, God Himself would put a new heart into the sinner (Ezekiel 11 : 19; 36 : 26). Ezekiel also brought comfort, encouragement, and inspiration through his sketch of the new community and temple (chapters 40–48). This was really the bold assurance that religious life would be begun again in Palestine without the old political complications. He wanted to organize religious worship so thoroughly as to promote, and almost to insure, the blessings which Jehovah would give. The main idea was noble, but the focus of the picture was upon ceremonial details centering in Jerusalem.

Thus saith the Lord Jehovah: "No foreigner, uncircumcised in heart and uncircumcised in flesh, shall enter into my sanctuary." (Ezekiel 44 : 9.)

So Ezekiel became the father of "Judaism" in the narrower technical meaning of the term, as designating the religion of the Hebrews who after the Exile were called "Jews."

Isaiah 40–55 is a collection of religious teachings, which seem to refer to the sad experiences of the Exile in Babylonia, although they stand attached to chapters 1–39, which record circumstances in Palestine connected with the prophet Isaiah of the eighth century B. C. Their author is a genius in the depth and breadth of his religious insight. Through him the religious thinking of Israel was brought to a more fully rounded expression. He explained the true significance of Israel's history as a course of divine training. He was the first prophet clearly to describe Jehovah as the one and only God of the universe (Isaiah 40 : 12–26; 44 : 6–20).

There is no God else beside me, a just God and a Saviour. (Isaiah 45 : 21.)

Isaiah proclaimed God's choice of Israel as a servant made ready by him to help redeem the world and to be His witnesses to all mankind.

I will also give thee for a light to the Gentiles, that thou mayest be my salvation unto the end of the earth. (Isaiah 49 : 6.)

This conception of God and of active religion is full of majesty, spirituality, and forcefulness. It is one of the noblest utterances of Judaism. Soon after the Exile, the Jews grew away from the tendency toward idolatry which they had shown before the Exile, despite the early explicit condemnation of it in the Second Commandment of the Decalogue.

9. THE GRADUAL ESTABLISHMENT OF LEGALISTIC JUDAISM (539–400 B. C.)

After the capture of Babylon by Cyrus, in 539 B. C., the Jews were permitted to return to their old home in Palestine. Only a few accepted the privilege. Henceforth the vast mass of Jews lived outside of their homeland. Instead of continuing as farmers, they became a race of business people. They spread out in all directions as opportunity offered. Yet through their synagogues and rabbis they were kept loyal to Jewish ideals and customs as maintained at Jerusalem. Thus Judaism became influential far beyond the boundaries of Judæa.

Under the urgent appeals of Haggai and Zechariah, and with the leadership of Zerubbabel and Joshua, a second temple was completed at Jerusalem in 516 B. C., and regular worship was renewed, while Jerusalem yet lay in ruins. Nearly a century later, under the leadership of Nehemiah, Jerusalem was refortified, repeopled, and restored to its old distinction in Judaism. Soon after, under Ezra the Scribe, a movement came to a head which had been under way two centuries earlier. King Josiah had led his people to undertake to live more perfectly in accord with the principles of the law of Moses as reformulated in the book of Deuteronomy. His reform, with its centralization of worship at Jerusalem, was distinctly Deuteronomic. Then for two centuries this code guided the religious life of the Jewish people. However, during the Exile and later, possibly because of Ezekiel's influence, a definite attempt was made to reduce all the religious practice of the past into a comprehensive scheme. In Ezra's day this elaborate code of religious law, known as the Priestly Code, had been completed. It is found in the legal portions of Exodus, Leviticus, and Numbers. This code Ezra took with him from Babylonia to Palestine. With Nehemiah's aid he persuaded his people to accept it as the final expression of their active loyalty to Jehovah. Its aim was noble, for it sought to inspire respect for the holiness of God and of His people. But its method was to lay stress upon externals; such as the ceremonial purity of priesthood and people, the scrupulous observance of the prescribed rites and sacrifices, the strict observance of the Sabbath, the avoidance of marriages which would endanger the purity of Jewish blood, and a vast number of details which are significant only for enforcing allegiance to Jehovah. Thus, along with the growing appreciation of the character of God to which Judaism had attained, there also developed an elaborate scheme of religious practices, which overshadowed the spiritual side of religion. This legalistic tendency was carried still further in later rabbinical Judaism.

10. THE RISE OF APOCALYPTICISM
(400 B. C.–100 A. D.)

Along with their moral appeals some of the later prophets of Israel, such as Zephaniah, Ezekiel, and Joel, emphasized the teaching that Jehovah would manifest Himself in sweeping judgments. Despairing of their ability as a people to overcome the power of such dominant nations as Persia, they seemed to look forward to a sudden putting forth of Jehovah's power to clear away the obstacles in Israel's pathway. There followed a long era of thinking, which was curiously different from the prophets' vigorous application of moral principles to actual social sins. The apocalyptic writers, such as Daniel, Enoch, and others, became engrossed with dreams of a coming day. Instead of laying responsiblity upon each individual believer to obey the righteous God, they rested their hopes on the divine initiative and omnipotence. Instead of trying to better the present, they looked entirely toward an idealized future.

This apocalyptic movement, which focussed everybody's thought on an expected deliverance, represented a certain magnificent trust in God and committal to Him. But it paralyzed personal initiative, and took away responsibility. However, one significant result was that, amidst experiences which would have annihilated most people, the faith of the Jews was still maintained.

11. THE CONCEPTION OF THE SUPREME BEING IN JUDAISM

The glory of Judaism has been its development of the conception of God. The process went through various phases. Monotheism was not the gift of Moses. The first commandment in the Decalogue does not deny the existence of "other gods" than Jehovah, but forbids the Hebrews to worship them (Exodus 20 : 3; Deuteronomy 5 : 7). So distinctive a builder of the national life as David felt that banishment from his country meant separation from Jehovah (I Samuel 26 : 19). Up to and including the eighth century, perhaps even nearer to the Babylonian Exile, the Hebrews' loyalty to Jehovah did not prevent them from acknowledging to other peoples a similar right to worship their respective deities.

It was the noble series of Hebrew prophets, from Amos to the Great Unknown Prophet of the Exile, who led the way, step by step, to the truly monotheistic conception of one sole God of the whole world. First, the four prophets of the eighth century, Amos, Hosea, Isaiah, and Micah, presented Jehovah in distinctly moral terms. He is righteous, holy, loving, reasonable, and not merely a potentate demanding submission. Then the prophets of the seventh and sixth centuries before Christ, especially Jeremiah and Ezekiel, emphasized each person's moral responsibility to Jehovah. They declared that righteous individuals, rather than the nation as a mass, form the prime essential for the fulfilling of God's gracious purpose for the world. The first intimation that non-Jews might participate in Jehovah worship occurs in Jeremiah 12 : 15–17. Finally the immortal chapters, Isaiah 40–55, dating probably from the end of the Exile, teach a conception of God which disregards all barriers of race and space and time. The omnipotent, all-seeing, all-righteous Creator, Ruler, and Saviour of the world, calls upon His servants to carry forth this inspiring message through self-sacrifice and suffering.[1]

[1] For a typical account of the development of the idea of God, as well as other great ideas in the Judeo-Christian tradition, as understood by

This world-wide missionary interpretation of the divine plan led up to teachings of Jesus Christ. The Jews as a whole did not live up to the highest visions of their religion. Their religious interests were chiefly in external observance. Perhaps their insistence on forms and ceremonies served as a kind of protecting shell for the valuable kernel of their religion during the dark centuries which followed until the time of Christ. Nevertheless, the conception of ethical monotheism, which has been elaborated gradually out of the hard experiences of life, made the Jews the foremost ethical and religious teachers of their time in the whole world. They prepared the way for Christianity.

12. THE MESSIANIC IDEA

One striking feature of Judaism was its cherished hope of a Messiah, or Anointed One of God, who would accomplish a great consummation. This idea, like that of God, had a varied career.

When the Hebrew prophets of the eighth century unfolded a higher conception of God, they also formulated a certain concrete plan for the working out of the divine purpose which came to be of great importance, especially in the beginning of Christianity. Those early prophets, with all their encouragements for righteousness, taught the coming of judgment which would be sweeping and in large measure destructive. However, they had such confidence in the power and goodness of God that, despite the disobedience of men, they believed God's great purpose would still be accomplished, for some would always be repentant. Isaiah declared that to this "remnant" would be given a deliverer and leader, who would enable them to fulfill the divine purpose with increased success. From that century forward devout worshippers of Jehovah have never failed to look for some divinely appointed leader. Sometimes he is referred to as a coming King (Jeremiah 23 : 5; 30 : 9); sometimes as a good Shepherd (Micah 5 : 2–5;

modern scholarship, see: Harry Emerson Fosdick, *A Guide to the Understanding of the Bible,* New York: Harper and Brothers, 1938.

Ezekiel 34 : 23; 37 : 24); sometimes as a devoted Servant (Isaiah 52 : 13–15; 53 : 1–12; Ezekiel 34 : 24).

At first the great expectation was in the form of a political restoration of the overthrown kingdom of Israel. Later, however, the emphasis came to be laid upon a restorer along with the restoration. There are a few evidences that within the sacred scriptures of Judaism the idea of a glorious material future was spiritualized into the hope of a universal ideal social order. But the elaboration of these great ideas has been taken up more valuably in another religion, Christianity. Within the history of Judaism since the beginning of Christianity there has arisen a series of at least thirty-four Jews, extending to Moses Hayyim Luzatto (died 1747 A. D.), who have presented themselves as the expected Messiah mostly in connection with political ambitions (Hastings, *ERE,* 8 : 581–588). Jesus Christ, more than anyone else born of Jewish parents, has claimed to be, and has been recognized by other persons also as being, the finest fulfilment of the spiritual elements in the Jewish Messianic idea.

13. JUDAISM AS DEVOTION TO THE LAW OF GOD

The Judaism of the fifth century B. C. was an heroic but unsuccessful attempt to standardize righteousness in men. In postexilic Judaism, again the Jews at Jerusalem entered into a solemn covenant

to walk in God's law, which was given by Moses the servant of God, and to observe and do all the commandments of Jehovah our Lord and his ordinances and his statutes. (Nehemiah 10 : 29.)

Later the rabbis found that the total number of commandments represented as proclaimed by Jehovah in the first five books of the Law amounts to 613 (*Jewish Encyclopædia,* 4 : 181–186).

Judaism, like some other religions, has developed two distinct types of devotees: those who are intent chiefly on the scrupulous observance of the rules of religion, and those who are eager for personal fellowship with God the Ruler. The

writers of many of the later Psalms belong, perhaps, in the
latter class, even though they could ring the changes of praise
on the commandments of Jehovah.

Oh, how I love Thy law! (Psalm 119 : 97.)

It was a small circle of such truly devoted souls who prepared
the way for Jesus, and who first recognized in Him the fulfilment of the most devout aspirations of Judaism. Such individual Jews are named in the New Testament: Mary, the
mother of Jesus (Luke 1 : 46–55; 2 : 51); Zacharias and Elisa-
beth, the parents of John the Baptist (Luke 1 : 5–25, 57–79);
Simeon and Anna, worshippers in the temple at Jerusalem
(Luke 2 : 22–38); and John the Baptist, the forerunner of
Jesus (Matthew 3 : 1–11; John 1 : 19–36).

Both types of religion have persisted within Judaism, devotion to the Law of God as chiefly ritualistic, legalistic, and
centering upon their own religious community, and also the
type of devotion to the Law of God as chiefly personal obedience to the righteous Supreme Being. The former was in
direct opposition to Jesus, while from the latter came his early
disciples.

14. JUDAISM IN THE DIASPORA

The scattering of the Jewish people began as early as the
eighth century B. C. when Northern Israel was destroyed by
the Assyrians and great numbers of the people were carried
into captivity. They became the "Lost Tribes of Israel." Most
of them never returned to the homeland but were absorbed
into the various peoples of the Near East. The myths of the
Lost Tribes represent them as having appeared in a score or
more of the most unlikely places in the world, including spots
as far distant one from the other as the Americas and Kashmir. Later came the Babylonian exile from which, of course,
some returned, but so many Jews had scattered through the
Mediterranean world, where Greek was the *lingua franca,* that
sometime between 275 and 150 B. C. the Septuagint Version

of the *Bible* in Greek was prepared for Jews who could no longer read their scriptures in the Hebrew language.

The Jewish people who remained in Palestine lived successively under the rule of the Babylonians, the Persians, the Greeks and the Romans, each of these cultures affecting to some extent the development of their religious faith. They were under Roman rule when Jesus appeared and for some forty years after his death. In the year 70 A. D. the Romans destroyed Jerusalem and the temple, and the Diaspora or dispersion left them without either a national home or a center for their religious faith. Henceforth there was to be no centralized temple worship or sacrificial system. And with this went the disappearance of the priesthood. Thereafter the synagogue became the center of Jewish religious life, and it has so continued until the present. The rabbi, not the priest, became the religious leader and teacher of the people.

The synagogue had arisen probably during the Babylonian exile in answer to the need which the exiles felt when they found themselves in an alien land and unable to carry out the temple worship. Long before the time of Jesus, it had already become the center of religious education for the people, and to a considerable extent also a center for their social life. Worship was corporate rather than individual and it was held at stated times, as it came to be in Christian churches. Indeed, the synagogue was the model which largely determined the form which the Christian church took.

The Talmud

Judaism like Christianity suffered persecution at the hands of the Roman Empire. Jews, like Christians, refused to worship the Roman Emperor which seemed to the Romans a sign of lack of complete loyalty to the Empire. In all other respects they enjoyed religious liberty. Later they were sometimes persecuted by the Christians. But they held to their religious beliefs and perhaps partly because they were forced into the ghettos of the cities and were subjected to common disabilities, they maintained a degree of solidarity which they might not otherwise have felt.

The *Old Testament* had been practically completed before the time of Jesus, though the final recognition of the canon as it now exists did not come until near the end of the first century A. D. Around the sacred law there had developed a large body of commentary, at first oral, by leading scholars and teachers. Then came commentary on the accepted commentaries. Often illustrated by stories and legends this mass of material continued to grow after the dispersion. Much of it was written down to form two collections known as the Mishna and the Gemarra, and finally these were joined to form what today is known as the Jewish *Talmud*. This occurred around the sixth century A. D. It appeared in two different forms known as the Palestinian and the Babylonian which differ in some details. The *Talmud* has ever since been a major basis of the education of the rabbis of Judaism. It is secondary, of course, to the Law and the Prophets and the Writings, which make up the Jewish Bible, but it is the *Talmud* which interprets the meaning of the original scriptures. No rabbi would think himself capable of interpreting the Judaic law without knowing what the Talmudic literature had to say on the matter.

Judaism in the Modern Age

Traditional Judaism was taught and practiced in very much the same way wherever Jews were found until about the time of the French Revolution. With the new impulse to freedom and equality which this upheaval brought about in Europe, the walls of the ghettos began to come down. Jews long shut up in them began to feel the new spirit of the age as they moved out into the currents of the world's life. It had an inevitable effect upon their religious outlook. Men began to be critical of their religious heritage. In Germany first appeared signs of a liberal Judaism; then in America and England reforms began to be evident in some of the synagogues. Reformed Judaism was born. It was essentially true to the prophetic strain in Judaism which never felt that the ancient was beyond re-evaluation. It was not afraid of innovation in religion, so the reformers set themselves to prune away what they came to think of as non-essential, and to emphasize what was timeless and universal in their faith. It brought about changes in their forms of worship, in their practice of the old folk-ways of Judaism, their dietary habits, and in some of their cherished beliefs.

Almost at once, as a defense against innovation, traditional or orthodox Judaism reacted against the reformers by an even more rigid conservatism in clinging to the old ways. Then there came to be a self-conscious orthodoxy determined at all costs to hold on to the ancient heritage unchanged which they felt was threatened.

Then, quite as inevitably, a somewhat middle party arose embracing those who felt that while some reform was necessary, the reformers had gone too far. In America this group took the somewhat misleading name Conservative Judaism, by which they meant "conserving Judaism." Other parties of one kind and another have appeared, but, in America at least, a Jew, if he is a synagogue Jew, is associated with either an orthodox, a conservative or a reformed synagogue, and these groups are organized as are the rabbis of the respective groups into national organizations bearing the names Orthodox, Conservative, Reform.

15. ZIONISM

Ever since the Jews were exiled from their homeland there has been a desire to go back again and repossess it. The return has been talked about and been the subject of united prayer through the centuries. The modern phase of this age-long desire, represented in Zionism, began in the last decade of the nineteenth century with the writings of Theodore Hertzl. Various schemes for securing a Jewish homeland have been put forward. It has even been suggested that a home be found for them in East Africa, in Australia or in South America. But Palestine, hallowed by centuries of national life, the home of the patriarchs, the great kings and Prophets of Israel, was the only place that would be emotionally satisfying. Held by the Turks at the turn of the century, attempts were made to work out satisfactory arrangements with the Sultan for the rebuilding of the Jewish community in Palestine, but nothing came of this. Then England took over the country as a protectorate, and in the Balfour declaration gave a new hope to the Zionist leaders. The Jews of the world poured out vast sums of money to aid in the settlement in Palestine. Large amounts were spent in wells, irrigation schemes, roads, and in financing new immigrants who sought escape from the pogroms of European countries.

Schools were built, finally a university, and every effort was made to make of Palestine a great Jewish cultural center. The Hebrew language was made once again a living tongue. Scholars began to write and publish in it. Eventually, a whole new literature in Hebrew appeared. Many Jews favored Zionism as a cultural venture. Others thought this did not go far enough. Nothing short of a Jewish nation could do for the Jews what needed to be done. Then came Hitler and the nightmare of the thirties in Europe. There were some sixteen million Jews before that. Almost six million were wiped out in the fearful years of Hitler and the Second World War.

The utter necessity of a Jewish home seemed indicated as a refuge for the Jewish people threatened with destruction. Many Jews who had had only a mild interest in cultural Zionism became ardent political Zionists. The result of this was eventually terrorism, war, and the emergence in 1948 of the national state of Israel. But nationhood was purchased at the price of incurring the bitter enmity of the entire Arab world, and Israel lives precariously surrounded by hostile Arabs who would destroy her but for the support of the Western powers. But Israel is no theocratic Jewish state. Freedom of religious faith is guaranteed to all citizens, and while many Jews hold fast to the traditional faith, and only orthodox synagogues are found in the city of Jerusalem, there are many Jews who have no religious faith at all. No attempt has been made to pass any laws concerning the practice of religion. The attempt to do so would, it is feared, destroy the unity which is so much required as the new state faces its Arab foes.

The total Jewish population of the world is now about twelve million, of whom over six million live in the Americas. The largest number, nearly five and a half million, live in the United States. About a million and a half are to be found in Israel.

The foremost exponents of Judaism, certainly during the creative period of its history covered by its sacred scriptures, have been zealous for the Law of God. In their reverence for its sacredness they have "built a fence around the Law." Liberal Jews at present tend to emphasize only the moral laws of Jehovah as contained in their scriptures. In its rabbinical phase Judaism has stressed the external exactions of that law, rather than the moral responsibilities and opportunities of devotion to the one God of righteousness. Even when thus rabbinized, Judaism has not lost educative power over its own adherents. However, Judaism as a whole has lost the active world-serving missionary purpose which stands proclaimed by its own noblest exponents. The distinctive and inclusive command of Judaism, "Be ye holy, for I Jehovah your God am holy" is explicit in its scriptures. This command has been taken bodily over into Christianity. In the New Testament (Matthew 5 : 45; I Peter 1 : 16–17) it has been cited almost verbatim, but with characteristic Christian reinterpretation in relation to the Fatherhood of God.

The practical point at which orthodox and liberal Jews differ among themselves, as also from the Christians and the Mohammedans who subsequently derived their monotheism from Judaism, is the specific manner in which they seek to be holy in obedience to the one God of the whole world.

16. ELEMENTS OF STRENGTH IN JUDAISM

Its conception of the one supreme holy God.
Its insistence upon His moral government of the world.

The ethical conception of sin against God as taught by the prophets of Israel.

The emphasis by the Prophets of Israel on the religious duty of man to man.

The direct relationship between God and man as taught by the Prophets and in some of the Psalms.

Its emphasis on the joy of obeying God's law.

Its conception of worship.

Its belief in a high spiritual destiny for God's people.

Its interest in the welfare of its people.

Its emphasis on the purity of domestic life.

Its care for the religious education of its youth.

Its steadfastness and cohesiveness under affliction.

Its hopefulness for a better future.

17. ELEMENTS OF WEAKNESS IN JUDAISM

Its general exclusiveness.

Its undue emphasis on God's preference for the people of Israel.

Its insistence upon a past law which allows little expansion or progress.

The tendency to relapse from the lofty prophetical conception of sin as ethical to the conception of sin as chiefly ceremonial.

The tendency toward excessive legalism and formalism.

The abandonment of effort for the conversion of the world.

X

ZOROASTRIANISM

The Religion of Struggle
along with a Good but Limited God
against the Evil Forces Inherent in the World

1. INTRODUCTION: AMONG THE WORLD'S LIVING RELIGIONS

Of all the living non-biblical systems of religion the one which has had the closest connection with the Bible is Zoroastrianism. It is also known as the religion of the Parsis, whose original home was in Pars in Persia.

(1) Zoroastrianism's Historic Connection with the Bible

This religion is not mentioned by name in the *Bible*, but kings of Persia, who were Zoroastrians, are mentioned in eight books of the *Old Testament* (in II Chronicles 36 : 22–23; Ezra 1 : 1; 8 : 1; Nehemiah 2 : 1; Esther 1 : 3; 10 : 2; Isaiah 44 : 28; 45 : 1; Daniel 9 : 1; 10 : 1; 11 : 1; Haggai 1 : 1; Zechariah 1 : 1). The first book in the *New Testament* reports that the very first persons who came to see the new-born Jesus were certain wise men from the East, Magi, who may be identified as priests of Zoroastrianism (Matthew 2 : 1).

Of all the outside religions connected with the *Bible*, whether European or African or Asiatic, Zoroastrianism is the only one which has remained alive to the present time. Zoroastrians are the only individuals of other religions who not only are not condemned in the *Bible*, but who receive a distinct commendation. The Zoroastrian king Cyrus is addressed by Jehovah as "His Messiah" (Isaiah 45 : 1). Thus the Hebrew designation "Messiah" is used in the *Old Testament* as descriptive of a Zoroastrian several hundred years before it became in the *New Testament* a technical designation for Jesus (John 1 : 41), though more frequently in its Greek translation "Christ" (Matthew 2 : 4; 16 : 16, etc.). Indeed, the Zoroastrian king Cyrus is also referred to by Jehovah with another important title, "my shepherd" (Isaiah 44 : 28), which in another book of the *Old Testament* is used with reference to the Lord God Himself (Psalm 23 : 1).

(2) *Zoroastrianism's Doctrinal Influence upon the Bible*

Of all the other nine extra-Biblical living religions, Zoroastrianism is the only one from which a definite religious belief has been borrowed and included in the *Bible*. Consistently throughout the *Old Testament* down to and including the Isaiah of the Exile, the ultimate source of everything, including evil, is represented as the God Jehovah. But a distinct change took place after the Exile. A comparison of two parallel accounts of a certain experience of King David will show that a postexilic document (I Chronicles 21 : 1) substitutes "Satan" for "Jehovah" in the pre-exilic account (II Samuel 24 : 1). Thus Satan is not an original feature of the *Bible*, but was introduced from Zoroastrianism.

Perhaps certain other innovations besides the idea of a Satan were adopted from Zoroastrianism by the Hebrews after they had come into direct contact with that religion in the Babylonian Exile: for example, the ideas of an elaborate angelology and demonology, of a great Saviour or Deliverer to come, of a final resurrection and divine Judgment, and a definitely picturable future life. Certainly Jesus' word "Paradise" (Greek, *paradeisos*, Luke 23 : 43) was, at least etymologically, derived from Persian origin (Avestan, *pairidaeza*).

(3) *The First Attempt at a Universal Religion, Now Abandoned*

Prior to the emergence of a world-wide outlook and aim in the course of biblical history, Zoroaster was the first among the founders of the world's living religions who taught a religion which should be voluntarily and universally adopted.

A form of confession of the Zoroastrian faith, which stands in the earliest of its canonical scriptures, and which is still repeated as part of the daily liturgy of its worship, asserts the belief that Zoroastrianism is permanently superior over all the religions of the world.

Yea, I praise the Faith of Mazda, the holy creed which is the most imposing, best and most beautiful of all religions which exist and of all that shall in future come to knowledge.—Ahura's Faith, the Zoroastrian creed. (*SBE*, 31 : 250.)

Yet for at least the last 400 years Zoroastrians have lost their founder's vision and purpose, and have been maintaining a religion which is as narrowly hereditary as any in the whole world. Indeed, numerically the adherents of Zoroastrianism, while including some brilliantly able and noble souls, now constitutes the smallest community among the eleven organized historic religions of the world. They number slightly less than 150,000, most of them being located in India. These are descendants of unyielding devotees of their faith, who escaped from the sword of Arab conquerors devastating Persia in the seventh century A. D. It is estimated that there are some thirty thousand adherents still in Iran, where they are known as Gabars.

2. THE LIFE OF ZOROASTER (660–583 B. C.)

His followers have always revered Zoroaster as the most adorable personage in history. But there has been much uncertainty and variety of opinion concerning the actuality and date of his existence—whether 6000 B. C., or 1400 B. C., or 1000 B. C., or the seventh century B. C.[1]

(1) *Alleged Supernatural Preliminaries*

Later Zoroastrian documents report many marvellous items in connection with the beginning of Zoroaster's life. Prophecies

---

[1] The problems of historicity have been treated in a comprehensive critical study entitled *Zoroaster, the Prophet of Ancient Iran* (1901), by Professor A. V. Williams Jackson, who places the latest possible and most probable dates of Zoroaster at 660–583 B. C., though some scholars still incline to an earlier period.

of this great Saviour had been made 3,000 years beforehand, and also 300 years beforehand (*SBE*, 5 : 21; 47 : 31–34, 135–138). The Glory of God (Ahura Mazda) was transmitted to "that girl who became the mother of Zoroaster" (*SBE*, 47 : 17–18). It "came down from the endless light, and mingled with the mother of Zoroaster," who was fifteen years old at the time (*SBE*, 47 : 138–139). Marvels connected with this very unusual young unmarried woman were inexplicable to her family, except as a piece of witchcraft (*SBE*, 47 : 18–20). The Latin writer Pliny Secundus (A. D. 23–79) in his *Natural History* (7 : 15) records an item which is referred to five times in the Zoroastrian scriptures.

At birth he laughed outright. (*SBE*, 47 : 35, 41, 123, 142, 143.)

The infant's life was miraculously preserved many times (*SBE*, 4 : 224–225; 47 : 35–40).

(2) *Life up to His "Call"* (Age 1–30)

As a young boy, Zoroaster was unusually wise in conversation.

A great wonder became manifest owing to the powerful intellect, cautiousness and practice of Zoroaster, when the other children were excessively terrified at their own silliness of speech, and the sagacity of his reply at that childish age. (*SBE*, 47 : 43, 45.)

When he became fifteen years of age, he selected the sacred girdle as a symbol of his devotion to a life of religion (*SBE*, 47 : 151). He was very kind and helpful to the poor, and also to animals (*SBE*, 47 : 153).

"When he became twenty years old, without the consent of his father and mother he wandered forth, and departed from their house," and gave himself to religion. (*SBE*, 47 : 152–153.)

"When his father sought a wife for him, Zoroaster argued," contrary to custom, desiring first to see and approve of her. (*SBE*, 47 : 153.)

A turning-point came at the age of thirty, when Zoroaster felt himself called into the presence of Ahura Mazda, to be purified and appointed to the work of a prophet (*SBE*, 37 :

31, 127; 47 : 14–15, 154–159). The very first passage in the whole *Avesta* represents dramatically the divine call and appointment as coming through "the wail of the kine," *i. e.*, through the concrete social need of his agricultural community, who were being hard pressed by invading Turanians (*SBE*, 31 : 3). The deity Ahura Mazda is represented as having selected Zoroaster on account of his pre-eminent responsiveness and fitness.

This man is found for me here, who alone has hearkened to our enunciations. (*SBE*, 31 : 10–11.)

Yet the kine protested that in him they would be receiving a lord who is a powerless, feeble, pusillanimous man. (*SBE*, 31 : 11.)

(3) *Visions of a World-Wide Religion; Unsuccessful Preaching* (*Age* 30–42)

During the next ten years he had seven further "conferences" with Ahura Mazda (*SBE*, 37 : 32). He was firmly convinced of his own selection and his appointment by the deity.

I was ordained by Thee at the first. All others I look upon with hatred of spirit. (Yasna, 44 : 11; Moulton, *EZ*, 368.) [1]

Zoroaster avowed the purpose of preaching a universal progressive religion and of converting even the wicked.

This do Thou tell us, Mazda, that we may know even with the tongue of thine own mouth, that I may convert all living men. (Yasna, 31 : 3; Moulton, *EZ*, 352.)
Through this word of promise on our tongue will we turn the robber horde unto the Greatest. (Yasna, 28 : 5; Moulton, *EZ*, 345.)
And may we be such as bring on this great renovation, and make this world progressive. (*SBE*, 31 : 33–34.)

He gave himself as a complete self-sacrifice to God.

[1] Some passages in the Yasna are quoted from the translation in Moulton, *Early Zoroastrianism*, which is cited henceforth as Moulton, *EZ*. Otherwise the translations are taken from the *Sacred Books of the East*. The page references to vol. IV of the *SBE* are to the second edition of 1895, not to the first edition of 1880.

As an offering, Zoroaster brings the life of his own body, the choiceness of good thought, action and speech unto Mazda. (Yasna, 33 : 14; Moulton, *EZ*, 360.)

He condemned the filthy, deceiving intoxicant (Moulton, *EZ*, 379).

He preached the religion of an all-seeing God (Moulton, *EZ*, 371). He was a vehement preacher of the truths first revealed to him divinely, and a denouncer of his opponents.

Those of you who put not into practice this word as I think and utter it,—to them shall be woe at the end of life. (Moulton, *EZ*, 370.)

One time in winter he was refused shelter in a certain house, even for his "two steeds shivering with cold" (Moulton, *EZ*, 386). He was tempted by the lying evil spirit to renounce the religion of Mazda, and to obtain temporal sovereignty; but the insidious attack was repelled by prayer and worship (*SBE*, 4 : 210–212). He became discouraged. He was rejected both by his own peers and by the nobles. He pleaded with God for friendly support.

To what land shall I flee? How am I to please Thee, Mazda Ahura? I am without success! Few cattle are mine! I have but few folk! I cry unto Thee. See Thou to it, Ahura, granting me support as friend gives to friend! Teach me by the Right the acquisition of Good Thought! (Yasna, 46 : 1–2; Moulton, *EZ*, 372.)

He wondered whether he would receive God's promises.

This I ask: tell me truly, Ahura, whether I shall indeed, O Right, earn that reward, even ten mares with a stallion and a camel, which was promised to me, O Mazda, as well as through Thee the future gift of welfare and immortality. (Yasna, 44 : 18; Moulton, *EZ*, 369.)

Only one poor convert was made in ten years of preaching (*SBE*, 47 : 163–164). But the last words in the Gathas express trust in the righteous God (Yasna, 53 : 9; Moulton, *EZ*, 389–390).

I have faith that Thou wilt thyself fulfil this for me. (Yasna, 46 : 3; Moulton, *EZ*, 373.)

(4) *Success at the Court of Persia; Vigorous Promulgation of the Faith* (Age 42–57)

Another turning-point in the life and character of Zoroaster came with the conversion of the king, Vistaspa (Yasna, 28 : 7; 46 : 14; 51 : 16; 53 : 2; also *SBE*, 47 : 50, 67, 72). Also the king's brother, son, a counsellor, and the grand vizier were converted.

Several of the realm, who were noble, conspicuous, and well-acting, beheld visibly the will and desirability of Ahura Mazda and the archangels and the progressive religion. (*SBE*, 47 : 125.)

The names of eighty-nine early converts along with the king are recorded (*SBE*, 23 : 203–211). Zoroaster married the daughter of the king's counsellor (Jackson, *Zoroaster*, 76).

And Zoroaster the righteous had three wives, all three of whom survived him.

By Zoroaster were begotten three sons and three daughters. Two of the sons, named Auvartad-Nar and Khursed-Chihar, were from a privileged wife.

Khursed-Chihar was a warrior, commander of the army of a son of Vistaspa. (*SBE*, 5 : 142, 143, note 1.)

A daughter of Zoroaster was married to the grand vizier (Dinkard, 9 : 45. 4; *SBE*, 37. 299, n. 4). Her bridal hymn forms a chapter in the part of the sacred scriptures which was written by Zoroaster (Yasna, 53). The king himself became a "gallant, mighty-speared" propagator of the new faith (*SBE*, 23 : 204–205; Jackson, *Zoroaster*, 81).

The king accepted it, and made it current in the world. (*SBE*, 37 : 442.)

Royal sons accepted the religion as a yoke, while they even wandered to Arum [Asia Minor] and the Hindus, outside the realm, in propagating the religion. (*SBE*, 24 : 171.)

(5) *"Holy Wars," Final Twenty Years* (Age 57–77)

A policy of violence may be found advocated in the sacred scriptures; only once, however, by the founder, but more often in the later documents.

Hew ye them all with the halberd. (Yasna, 31 : 18; *SBE*, 31 : 50.)
The faith that wields the feeling halberd. (Yasna, 12 : 9; *SBE*, 31 : 250.)
Him of the daring spear, devoted to the Lord. (Yasna, 57 : 1; *SBE*, 31 : 297.)

Materials are lacking for determining the extent to which Zoroastrianism in this period associated itself with a policy of militaristic nationalism. The records are explicit that the king, Vistaspa, and his brother invoked divine aid, and won victory over eight powerful unbelieving foes (*SBE*, 23 : 79, 117, 306). Zoroaster gave religious support to the king in refusing tribute to an invading neighbor king; more than 100,000 Persian soldiers were engaged in the fighting (Jackson, *Zoroaster*, 103–119).

In the wars of the religion the Iranians were saved. (*SBE*, 5 : 40.)

The death of Zoroaster is not mentioned in the *Avesta*. But it is repeatedly reported in extracanonical documents as having occurred when he was seventy-seven years old, at the hands of attacking Turanians, probably at the storming of the city of Balkh.

3. THE VENERATION OF ZOROASTER

The founder of Zoroastrianism has done more to turn men's thoughts to a vigorous good God than has any other person born in Persia. Undoubtedly, Zoroaster has been the most venerated figure in the whole history of his native land.

(1) *The Character of Zoroaster*

In the earliest autobiographical portion of the sacred scriptures he is represented as an earnest humble man, who became discouraged and tempted, but who felt an impelling call of God to preach the religion of the one "Wise Lord" for the salvation of his own people and even of the whole world. Yet even in his early evangelistic zeal there are indications of an animosity which was bitterly personal.

Others I look on with hatred of spirit. (Moulton, *EZ*, 368.)
Upon a certain opponent, Bendva, he prays for "ruin" (Yasna
49 : 1; Moulton, *EZ*, 380) or "death." (*SBE*, 31 : 162.)
Whoso seeks to kill me is a son of the Lie's creation. (Yasna 51 : 10;
Moulton, *EZ*, 385; *SBE*, 31 : 182.)

But after a certain delayed success with conversions in the
court of Persia, Zoroaster turned to a policy of military propaganda in the interests of his nation and his religion, and conducted warfare against neighboring nations.

(2) *The Later Veneration of Zoroaster*

The later documents of Zoroastrianism represent him as
morally superlative, the acme of humanity, supernaturally
originated, deserving of religious worship along with the deity
Ahura Mazda and other cosmic beings (*SBE*, 31 : 255, 325,
327).

"Head of the two-footed race"; "the wisest of all beings in the perfection of his holiness"; "the only one who can daunt evil." (*SBE*,
23 : 190, 229, 275.)
"The chieftainship of all things was from Zoroaster"; "the completely good, the righteous Zoroaster." (*SBE*, 5 : 88; 18 : 90.)
Incomparable among mankind through his desire for righteousness,
and his understanding the means of defeating the destroyer, and
teaching creatures. (*SBE*, 37 : 241.)
A heavenly radiance "came down from the endless light" to the
grandmother of Zoroaster for his birth from a radiantly wonderful
virgin mother. (*SBE*, 47 : 18–20, 138–139.)
He was pre-existent, 3,000 years before his physical birth, and
during the interval he remained with the archangels "equal to the
archangels." (*SBE*, 47 : 21, 22, 122.)

4. THE SACRED SCRIPTURES OF ZOROASTRIANISM

The inclusive name is *Avesta*, which perhaps means "knowledge," thus being parallel with the *Veda* of Hinduism. The
language is Avestan, cognate with Sanskrit. The extant remnants of a more extensive original *Avesta* are arranged in five
main groups.

The Yasna, meaning worship or sacrifice, is the earliest and most important section. Embedded within the Yasna are seventeen Gathas (Psalms), which form the only part of the *Avesta* attributable to Zoroaster himself. The Visperad, meaning invocations to "All the Lords," is a minor liturgical work, which is used along with the Yasna in worship. The Vendidad (Law against the Demons) is a priestly code of ceremonial laws, which contains also some cosmological, historical, and eschatological material.

The foregoing three constitute the larger and more important part of the whole *Avesta*. They are used interspersed in ritual, and are reserved exclusively for the priests. The Yashts (Worship Hymns) is an anthology of religious poetry, containing invocations to twenty-one angels and heroes of Zoroastrianism. The Khorda-Avesta (Little Avesta) is a devotional handbook of litanies and prayers for common use by all Zoroastrians. An extensive and important later religious literature has also been produced.

5. THE HISTORY OF ZOROASTRIANISM

The external history of this religion has been closely connected with the history of its native land, except during the last period.

(1) *National Revival and Expansion*, 100 *Years* (583–480 *B. C.*)

Persia was immediately reanimated by the new religion. Its armies conquered the powerful western neighbor, Babylonia (539 B. C.), developed the great empire which Darius ruled, and pushed onward into Europe until stopped at the battle of Salamis.

(2) *Struggle with Greece*, 150 *Years* (480–330 *B. C.*)

The Greek writers were deeply impressed by the religion of their combatants from Asia. Herodotus visited and described Persia. Plato was prevented from fulfilling his desire to go to Persia and study Zoroastrianism by the Græco-Persian Wars, which ended with Alexander's complete victory.

(3) *Subjugation and Relapse,* 550 *Years* (330 *B. C.*— 226 *A. D.*)

Persia came under the rule of foreigners, at first Alexander's Greek successors, and then the Parthians. Zoroastrianism in this period showed a marked tendency to sun-worship and polytheism connected with the religion of Mithra.

(4) *Independence,* 400 *Years* (226–651 *A. D.*)

Ardeshir I, an ardent devotee of Zoroastrianism, re-established Persia's independence, conquered neighboring Armenia, and founded the Sassanian dynasty. His rock reliefs picture the Zoroastrian deity as handing to him the ring of sovereignty.

(5) *Eviction from Persia, and Quiescence,* 1300 *Years* (*from* 651 *A. D.*)

The Arabs, another small nation electrified by a new religion, Islam, conquered Persia, and drove out or converted most of the Zoroastrians. The modern Parsis are scattered in successful business all over the world, but the majority of them are in the Bombay Presidency. They have furnished some of the most public-spirited citizens in all India. In philanthropic gifts they hold the highest per-capita record of any religious community in the world.

6. THE CONCEPTION OF THE SUPREME BEING, AHURA MAZDA

Zoroastrianism teaches that there is one deity, to be worshipped supremely—the power of light, life, truth, goodness. His special name is Ahura Mazda (Wise Lord, or Lord of Wisdom). This compound designation became abbreviated in later Zoroastrianism to Auharmazd, or Ormazd. The first verse in the whole *Avesta* is an adoration of the deity.

Ahura Mazda, the creator, radiant, glorious, greatest and best, most beautiful, most firm, wisest, most perfect, the most bounteous Spirit! (*SBE,* 31 : 195–196.)

This deity appears to have been only one among several objects of worship in Persia. Zoroaster's special work was to emphasize and ethicize this belief, even as Amos and other contemporary prophets in Israel did with the conception of Jehovah.

Zoroaster asked Ahura Mazda: "O Thou, all-knowing Ahura Mazda! Thou art never asleep, never intoxicated! Vohu Manah (Good Thought) gets defiled. The Dævas (Demons) defile him." (*SBE*, 4 : 215–216.)

Some noble characteristics are attributed to Ahura Mazda in the Gathas, which is the portion of the *Avesta* composed by Zoroaster:

Creator: (Yasna, 31 : 7, 11; 44 : 7; 50 : 11; 51 : 7.)
All-seeing: (Yasna, 31 : 13; 44 : 2.)
All-knowing: (Yasna, 31 : 13; 45 : 3; 48 : 2–3.)
Most mighty, greatest: (Yasna, 28 : 5; 33 : 11; 45 : 6.)
Friendly: (Yasna, 31 : 21; 44 : 2; 46 : 2.)
Father of Justice or Right, Asha: (Yasna, 44 : 3; 47 : 2.)
Father of Good Mind, Vohu Manah: (Yasna, 31 : 8; 45 : 4.)
Beneficent, *hudae:* (Yasna, 45 : 6; 48 : 3.)
Bountiful, *spenta:* [1] (Yasna, 43 : 4, 5, 7, 9, 11, 13, 15; 44 : 2; 45 : 5; 46 : 9; 48 : 3; 51 : 10.)
Most bountiful spirit, *spenishta mainyu:* (Yasna 30 : 5.)

The first Yasht contains a list of twenty names of Ahura Mazda revealed unto Zoroaster.

Recite thou these My names every day and every night. (*SBE*, 23 : 26.)

A longer list of fifty-four names contains the following:

I am the Keeper, Health-Bestower, Priest, Most-Priestly-of-Priests, Prosperity-Producer, King-Who-Rules-at-His-Will, Liberal-King, He-Who-Deceives-Not, He-Who-Is-Not-Deceived, Energetic-One, Holiness, Great-One, Good-Sovereign, Wisest-of-the-Wise. (*SBE*, 23 : 27–28.)

---

[1] The phrase "Holy Spirit," which Moulton uses for rendering the original words *spenta mainyu,* probably connotes to most English readers more than was intended by Zoroaster.

Later liturgical books contain a list of 101 honorific names of
Ahura Mazda.

7. THE DEVIL, ANGRA MAINYU

Condemnation of the evil and impurity in the world was a
fundamental feature in the teaching of the founder and in all
subsequent Zoroastrianism. "Deceit," personalized as Druj
(the Lie-demon), and all deceivers and liars as constituting his
brood, are vituperated as least sixty-six times in the Gathas.
The particular name "Angra Mainyu," as designating the
supreme hostile spirit, occurs only once in the teaching of
Zoroaster. But that passage states explicitly that from the
beginning of existence there have been two inherently incom-
patible, antagonistic spirits in the world (Yasna, 45 : 2). In all
the later Zoroastrian documents "Angra Mainyu," which is also
abbreviated into "Ahriman," occurs as frequently as does the
phrase "Ahura Mazda."

The Greeks as early as Aristotle were familiar with the Persian appellation, Areimanios, which the Latins adopted as Arimanius.
(Hastings, *ERE*, 1 : 237.)

An aboriginal and distinctive feature of Zoroastrianism
among all the religions of the world is this doctrine of a fundamental cosmological dualism of a good God and a wicked
devil fighting against one another. These two cosmic powers
are co-equal from the beginning of time, and they will continue
to limit each other until the end of the world.

8. RETINUES OF ACCOMPANYING SPIRITS

Zoroaster did not altogether disentangle his belief in the
Wise Lord to whom supreme allegiance is due, from his inherited belief in a number of other spirits. Some of these were
nature deities in contemporary religion, and some were
dreaded evil spirits. The first chapter in the first book of the
Avesta directs that worship be accorded first to Ahura Mazda,
and then to a long, unsystematic list of objects; for example,

to sun, moon, and stars; to fire, wind, waters, and mountains; to the spirits of departed saints, and

to all the holy creatures of Spenta Mainyu, male and female. (*SBE*, 31 : 195–203.)

(1) *An Array of Good Spirits*

A spirit which is always associated with Ahura Mazda, yet at least poetically distinguished from the deity, is designated in the Gathas five times as "Bountiful Spirit" (*spenta mainyu*), and eight times as "Most Bountiful Spirit" (*spenishta mainyu*).

There is a group of "Bountiful Immortals," Amesha Spentas, later abbreviated to Amshapands. These are frequently referred to in the Gathas individually, though only once all in the same verse (Yasna, 47 : 1).

Vohu Manah: Good Mind, Thought, Disposition.
Asha: Right, Righteousness, Order, Justice.
Kshathra: Power, Dominion, Kingdom.
Armaiti: Piety, Love.
Haurvatat: Wholeness, Weal, Health.
Ameretat: Immortality, Eternal Life.

Originally these were common nouns, denoting religious characteristics. Perhaps they were treated poetically as messengers, functionaries, or attributes of Ahura Mazda. In the history of Zoroastrianism they have become technical theological terms for personalized beings, connected with Ahura Mazda, yet distinguished from the deity. They have also been designated as archangels.

Yazatas, or angels, are minor sacred beings in Zoroastrianism. The Fravarshis are heavenly counterparts, or guardian angels, of human beings.

(2) *An Array of Evil Spirits*

Systematically opposed to Ahura Mazda and his good spirits are Angra Mainyu, and "numberless myriads" of demons (*SBE*, 23 : 49). Among them are Hunger, Thirst, Wrath, Arrogance, Greed, False Speech, Drought, Winter, Harlot. The general name for these evil spirits is "Dæva," which in the later Persian language became "Diu," which, in turn, became the origin of the English word "devil." The third main group of documents in the *Avesta* is occupied with purifications prescribed against the baneful influence of the innumerable noxious beings.

9. CEREMONIAL PURITY, WORSHIP, AND PRAYER

The Zoroastrians have been referred to commonly, but inexactly, as "fire-worshippers." They themselves heartily repudiate this characterization. They regard fire, especially the sun, as a symbol of a deity of light, purity, and grateful warmth. However, the maintenance of an undying sacred fire in connection with formal worship has been an important feature of Zoroastrianism through a period which is several centuries longer than the entire history of Christianity.

It is necessary to maintain the fireplace properly, and to keep watch that the fire shall not die out, and that nothing polluted and impure shall attain to the fire. And it is necessary to make a menstruous woman avoid being within three steps of it. Sad-Dar, 11 : 1. (*SBE*, 24 : 270.)

Various ceremonial purifications are prescribed in the sacred scriptures.

Hair-cuttings and nail-parings should be properly disposed of. Vendidad, 17 : 1–11. (*SBE*, 4 : 190–192.)
Whenever a person sneezes, he should offer prescribed prayers. Sad-Dar, 7 : 1–7. (*SBE*, 24 : 265–266.)
Properly cut tooth-picks alone should be used. Sad-Dar, 17 : 1–2. (*SBE*, 24 : 278.)

Various formulas are efficacious

for cleansing from all evil. Vendidad, 3 : 41–42. (*SBE*, 4 : 33–34.)
Purity is for man, next to life, the greatest good. Vendidad, 5 : 21; 10 : 18. (*SBE*, 4 : 56, 141.)

In the open "Towers of Silence" particular care is exercised in the exposing of corpses, in order that they may not touch and contaminate either earth or fire.

A sin for which there is no atonement—the burying of the dead. Vendidad, 1 : 13. (*SBE*, 4 : 7.)

Zoroastrians claim that their code of ceremonial purity, as elaborated in the Vendidad, is the most thoroughgoing, ancient, and still operative program of enlisting religion in conjunction with sanitation for safeguarding the health of the living.

Zoroastrian worship consists chiefly in repeating prescribed prayers, of which there are many, both daily and seasonal (*SBE*, 31 : 367–388). The two most important are referred to by their first words, like "Pater Noster" for the Latin form of the "Lord's Prayer" in Christianity:

"Ahuna-vairo," often abbreviated to "Honover": "The will of the Lord is the law of righteousness." (*SBE*, 4 : 100, 143, 216; 23 : 39.)
"Ashem-vohu": "Holiness is the best of all good." (*SBE*, 4 : 216; 23 : 30, 34.)

A recurring summary of the Zoroastrian Confession of Faith mentions the following items:

I confess myself a worshipper of Mazda, a follower of Zoroaster, one who hates the Dævas (Evil Spirits), and who obeys the law of Ahura. (*SBE*, 31 : 202, 212, 247, 367.)

10. THE ETHICS OF ZOROASTRIANISM

A summary of ceremonial and practical Zoroastrianism might be made in the form of an exhortation, which is to be applied both literally and symbolically: Keep the light burning! The ideal Zoroastrian is pictured by the founder as

a faithful man, well-knowing and bountiful, like Thee, O Mazda. (Yasna, 43 : 3; Moulton, *EZ*, 364.)

Almsgiving helps forward the kingdom of God.

He who relieves the poor, makes Ahura king. (*SBE*, 4 : 210, 251.)

Good treatment is prescribed toward good people, but ill treatment toward the wicked.

Whether one is lord of little or of much, he is to show love to the righteous; but be ill unto the liar. (Yasna, 47 : 4; Moulton, *EZ*, 377; also Yasna, 33 : 2–3; Moulton, *EZ*, 358.)

Violence against adversaries is explicitly prescribed.

Resist them then with weapon. (Yasna, 31 : 18; Moulton, *EZ*, 354; also *SBE*, 31 : 50, 250, 297.)

With enemies fight with equity. With a friend proceed with the approval of friends. (*SBE*, 24 : 12.)

Thrifty husbandry, not asceticism, is the practical application and need of religion.

He who sows most corn, grass and fruit, sows righteousness; he makes the religion of Mazda walk. . . . No one who does not eat, has strength to do the heavy works of holiness. (*SBE*, 4 : 29–31.)

The most highly prized single virtue in Zoroastrianism is purity.

Make thy own self pure, O righteous man! Any one in the world here below can win purity for his own self, namely, when he cleanses his own self with good thoughts, words, and deeds. (*SBE*, 4 : 141.)

The formula from their sacred scriptures which recurs most frequently in conversations with the Parsis, and which is most fairly representative of their ethics, is:

Hu-mata, Hu-uktha, Hu-varshta: good thoughts, good words, good deeds. (*SBE*, 4 : 56, 289, 376; 31 : 250, 282, 285, 390.)

The basis of ethics in Zoroastrianism, as in Judaism, Christianity, and Islam, is religious. Ahura Mazda is the guarantor of the moral order of the universe, and the good is defined in terms of his will. He judges men, rewarding the good, punishing the evil.

11. THE FINAL HOPE IN ZOROASTRIANISM

Zoroastrianism probably first among the living religions taught the ultimate triumph of moral goodness over the moral evils in the world. One of the earliest and most persistent messages of Zoroaster himself was a great dividing future judgment, with punishment for the wicked and reward for the righteous.

Yasna, 30 : 2, 4, 9–11; 31 : 8, 19; 32 : 6, 15; 33 : 3, 5; 43 : 12; 45 : 7; 46 : 12; 48 : 4; 51 : 6; 53 : 7–9.

Immortality was desired or assured at least seventeen times in his seventeen Gathas.

Yasna, 31 : 21; 32 : 5; 33 : 5, 8; 34 : 1, 11; 43 : 2–3; 44 : 17–18; 45 : 5, 7, 10; 47 : 1; 48 : 1; 51 : 7; 53 : 1.

A great revealing bodily resurrection of the dead was intimated by Zoroaster perhaps only once (Yasna, 30 : 7). But the idea recurs frequently and vividly in the later scriptures.

In that assembly a wicked man becomes as conspicuous as a white sheep among those which are black. (*SBE*, 5 : 123.)

The narrow Chinvat bridge is the most frequent and characteristic single detail in the Zoroastrian picture of the process of separating the good souls from the wicked after death.

In the Gathas three times: Yasna, 46 : 10, 11; 51 : 13.
Elsewhere in the Yasna: 19 : 6; 71 : 16.
Also *SBE*, 4 : 156, 218–219; 23 : 12, 20, 339; 24 : 258; 31 : 345.

Other concrete analogies are used in the pictures of the decisive future Judgment.

One's own actions will confront each soul after death in the form of a good or an evil conscience. (Yasna, 31 : 20; 46 : 11; also *SBE*, 23 : 315–321.)
Two angels record each person's good and evil deeds. (*SBE*, 24 : 258.)
The soul will be weighed in a balance. (*SBE*, 24 : 18.)

Heaven is the reward for good thoughts. Sensual features are completely absent.

The glorious heritage of good thought. (Yasna, 53 : 4; also 30 : 4, 10; 31 : 21; 32 : 15; 33 : 3, 5.)

Hell is described as an age-long and lonely misery of punishment for liars (Yasna, 30 : 11; 45 : 7; 46 : 11). Only twice are gruesome details given in the Gathas.

Darkness, foul food, and woful words. (Yasna, 31 : 20; 49 : 11.)

A future savior, Soshyant, is expected.

In the Gathas: Yasna, 45 : 11; 48 : 9.
Elsewhere in the Yasna: 26 : 9; 59 : 28.

Also *SBE*, 4 : 211; 5 : 33; 23 : 220–221, 306–307; 31 : 339; 47 : 156.

Before the end of the world, at intervals of a thousand years each, there will be three saviors: Aushedar, Aushedar-Mah, and Soshyant. Each will be a supernatural descendant from Zoroaster, and born of a virgin mother just as old as was the mother of Zoroaster when he was born.

Though fifteen years old, the damsel has not before that associated with men. Nor afterwards, when she becomes pregnant, has she done so before the time when she gives birth. (*SBE*, 47 : 106, 111, 115.)

At the end of time there will come a final apocalyptic purifying and ceremonial consummation. Zoroaster himself seems to have referred somewhat vaguely to a future divine testing by a glowing fire (Yasna, 43 : 4), and to a purification by molten metal (Yasna, 30 : 7; 32 : 7). But a much later document presents a detailed picture of events after the resurrection of the dead, the final judgment, the separation of the righteous from the wicked, and the sending of the two groups into heaven and hell respectively.

Then all men will pass into that melted metal, and become pure. . . . All men become of one voice, and administer loud praise to Ahura Mazda and the archangels. Ahura Mazda completes his work at that time. . . . Soshyant with his assistants perform a Yazisn ceremony. And they slaughter the ox. . . . From the fat of that ox they prepare Hush, and give it to all men. And all men become immortal for ever and everlasting. (*SBE*, 5 : 126.)

It is believed by many scholars that these eschatological ideas had a profound influence upon late Judaism and Christianity. Certainly a Christian reading the later literature of Zoroastrianism, in which the highly elaborated eschatology of Zoroastrianism appears, finds himself in familiar territory.

Will Zoroastrianism long continue among the living religions of the world? For centuries it has made no attempt to expand. Indeed it refuses to admit new members to the community in India. Future growth, unless this policy is modified, depends upon the birth and survival rate of the Zoroastrian population. Over the last half century the percentage of increase has not kept pace with the general percentage increase of India's population.

Of course the policy could change. There are signs of an awakening interest in reform, particularly in the direction of modernization of the cult pattern, for example, the abandonment of the use of a dead language as the language of cult, similar to the use of Latin in Roman Catholicism. But whether it lives or finally disappears as a separate faith, it has made significant contributions to religions that will live on and become increasingly important in the life of the world.

12. ELEMENTS OF STRENGTH IN ZOROASTRIANISM

Its personal, ethical, helpful Deity.
Its early universal vision for religion.
Its early enthusiastic missionary zeal.
Its clear appreciation of antagonism between good and evil.
Zoroaster's emphasis on personal choice and responsibility.
Its high valuation of individual human personality.
Its emphasis on activity, not on asceticism or indifference.
Its emphasis on a religious life socially valuable.
Its emphasis on man's co-operation with God for common good.
A certain ethical ideal of final judgment.
Its hope of a final triumph of moral goodness.
A devoted founder admirable in so many respects.

13. ELEMENTS OF WEAKNESS IN ZOROASTRIANISM

Its lack of a winsomely inspiring founder.
Few subsequent prophets or missionary leaders.
Its polytheistic tendency through lack of genuine monotheism.
Its total loss of original missionary world-outlook.
Its tendency to formal stereotyped legalistic ceremonialism.
Its scriptural advocacy of the method of force.
Its historic lack of much dynamic, except military.

Its failure to perceive any value in suffering.

Its too easy satisfaction with merely the good, rather than a progressive quest of the best.

Its too easy blaming all evil onto a primeval Devil.

Its inconsistent and insufficient basis for its admirable optimism.

Its too exclusive dependence upon apocalyptic for its final success.

XI

ISLAM, OR MOHAMMEDANISM

The Religion of Submission to the World-Potentate

1. INTRODUCTION: AMONG THE WORLD'S LIVING RELIGIONS

According to a recent Muslim report, Islam now claims more than 400,000,000 adherents. This is less than some estimates of the number of Confucianists and Buddhists. But since neither of these faiths is exclusive in its claims, and since Islam, like Christianity, does require the exclusive loyalty of its followers, Islam now stands next to Christianity and therefore second among the religions of the world in the number of those who may be classed as belonging to one or another of the living religions. And next to Christianity it is the fastest growing in the whole family of religions.

When classified as regards the method of origin, Islam is found to be one of nine which originated from the religious experience and teachings of a great creative founder. The other two, Hinduism and Shinto, have been a spontaneous communal growth. As regards its outlook on the world, Islam is one of three universal religions—along with Buddhism and Christianity. The other eight are hereditary or national. As regards theology, Islam is one of four monotheistic religions —along with Judaism, Sikhism, and Christianity. The other seven are pantheistic, dualistic, or polytheistic. Thus, among eleven living religions in the world Islam is the only one which stands classified along with Christianity as possessing the three important characteristics of being personally founded, universal, and monotheistic.

Chronologically, Islam is the latest among the world's religions—with the exception of Sikhism—whose followers form a relatively small community confined within the land of India.

It is true that other religions have arisen which regard themselves as independent, and have spread outside of the land of their birth, though historically originating within one or another of the greater faiths, but of these, only the Bahai faith has lived on for more than a century. Among the larger historic religions Islam, with its 1,300 years of history, is the only one which originated later than the Christian era. It is the only one now which is a notably active rival of Christianity in more than one continent, though as noted (p. 37) there is an incipient missionary tendency in Hinduism and signs of a renewal of the missionary spirit in Buddhism. (p. 63). It is the only religion which started in conscious opposition to Christianity. Yet it has not contributed a single new germinal idea to the religious thought of the world. The name which the founder himself used for designating this faith expresses exactly the central principle—"Islam," meaning "submission" to God (3 : 17; 3 : 79; 5 : 5; 6 : 125; 39 : 23; 61 : 7).[1] Another word derived from the same Arabic verbal root is the particle, "Muslim," or "Moslem," which is used as a technical term to designate "those who submit" (22 : 77; 33 : 35; 49 : 14).

The religious ideals of a supreme ruler as exercising absolute authority and of a devout religionist as yielding humble submission have naturally tended toward an autocratic form of government. Muslims in the course of their history have set up some notable dominions in various countries. "However," it was correctly stated in earlier editions of this book, "at the present time, nowhere in the world is there a notably successful self-governing national administration which has been started by Muslims. The largest and most flourishing group is in India."

But this is no longer true. In 1947, the nearly 90,000,000

---

[1] The reference numbers in this chapter are to the chapters and verses of the *Koran* as indicated in Rodwell's translation. Unfortunately, the translation by Palmer in the *Sacred Books of the East*, gives numbers only to every fifth verse. The numbering of the verses sometimes differs slightly from the translations by Ali and Fadl (see p. 306).

Muslims of India demanded a separate autonomous state, and so was born the largest Muslim state in the world, Pakistan, independent, but choosing to retain membership in the British Commonwealth of Nations. At present there are over 70,000,000 Muslims in Pakistan, while nearly 40,000,000 remain in Hindu India. In addition, a strong nationalist spirit has developed in such predominantly Muslim nations as the newly formed Indonesia, as well as in the North African states and those in Asia Minor.

A new sense of Muslim solidarity has appeared around the world, though national self-interest on the part of individual countries often enough interferes with a complete unity of spirit and action as Muslims. There is not a little rivalry among Muslim nations and outstanding leaders for leadership of the world of Islam, or Pan-Islam. The discovery of rich oil and mineral deposits in formerly poor and relatively under developed Near Eastern countries has put a new face upon the Near East, and subjected it to new strains, as the dominant powers of the world seek to exploit and control the new wealth which they possess.

This can but affect powerfully the people and therefore also their religious outlook, as greater resources make possible a higher standard of living, more extensive educational opportunities, and a more intimate contact with the outside world and its very different religions and philosophies.

2. THE LIFE OF THE FOUNDER, MOHAMMED (570–632 A. D.)

The sources of information are partly in the *Koran* and partly in several early Arabic *Lives* and traditions.

(1) An Ordinary Arab (Age 1–35)

Mohammed was born in Mecca, which was the most important city in Arabia, and the center of animism and idolatry. Like the other members of the Koreish tribe to which he belonged, he followed the business of shepherding and trading.

He travelled on his mercantile operations to Syria and Palestine, where he mingled with Jews and Christians.

(2) *Seeking Religious Light* (*Age* 35–40)

An incident in the temple at Mecca, whereby he settled a quarrel between three sheikhs, prompted the idea that he might be a great religious leader of his people, who then were sadly distraught by feuds (Muir, *Life of Mohammad*, 27–30). He was dissatisfied with the existing moral and social conditions. He learned something of monotheism from Jews and Christians. The first chapter in the *Koran*, the "Fatihah," which is the model prayer repeated by faithful Muslims thirty-two times each day, "contains perhaps the germ of [his] frequent prayer at this early period" of groping (Muir, *Life*, 38).

(3) *Visions and Unsuccessful Preaching* (*Age* 40–52)

After his marriage to Khadijah, a wealthy woman of Mecca by whom he had been employed, he was able to devote more time to prayer and meditation. He spent many hours alone in a cave some distance from the city and there experienced repeated visions. It was as a result of these experiences that Mohammed felt himself called to go forth and preach a religion of one absolute God, Creator, Potentate, and Judge of the world. Chapter ninety-six in the *Koran* is usually considered as containing his first vision and appointment as a prophet of Allah. For twelve years he continued to have visions. His preaching of monotheism and future judgment and his denunciation of idolatry and infanticide won only slight success either in Mecca or in the neighboring city of Taif.

(4) *The Flight or Migration, Hegira* (*Age* 52)

With one sole companion Mohammed fled for his life away from his native city. Hiding in a cave three miles north of Mecca, he experienced a narrow escape from his pursuers.

God assisted him formerly, when the unbelievers drove him forth, in company with a second only, when they two were in the cave, when the Prophet said to his companion, "Be not distressed! Verily, God is with us!" And God sent down His tranquillity upon him, and strengthened him with hosts ye saw not. (9 : 40.)

That year, 622 A. D., which marks the lowest point in the personal fortunes of Mohammed, and also the beginnings of his remarkable success, has been adopted as the starting-point of the Islamic calendar—in Latin "Anno Hegiræ," regularly abbreviated to "A. H."

(5) *Growing Theocracy at Medina* (*Age* 52–60)

At the most important city in northern Arabia Mohammed set up the rule of Allah, with himself as the immediate dictator upon the basis of the sixfold Pledge of Akaba.

We will not worship any but the one God. We will not steal. Neither will we commit adultery. Nor kill our children. We will not slander in any wise. Nor will we disobey the Prophet in anything that is right. (Muir, *Life*, 118.)

He built a mosque for daily prayers and for the weekly congregation worship every Friday (62 : 9). He drilled his followers in devotions, religious education, and zealous aggressiveness. The ardent prophet of a God of power found his own power and his followers increasing. To his previous preaching propaganda he added an entirely new method of military campaigning. He acknowledged that only the help of Allah enabled him to win against overwhelming foes the battle of Badr (3 : 11; 8 : 41–46), and also the battle of the Ditch (39 : 9–11). Other noticeable changes took place in his policy and in his own manner of life during this period, when he was becoming powerful and independent as a religious and warring leader. The *qiblah*, or "facing" in prayer, which formerly had been toward Jerusalem, he changed toward the Arabian center, Mecca (2 : 142–144). The fast which formerly had been observed on the Jewish Day of Atonement was changed to a new distinctly Mohammedan fast, covering the month of Ramadan, or Ramzan (2 : 179–183). His former policy of general friendliness toward the Jews was changed to persecution and killing. After the death of his first wife, he took unto himself an increasing number of wives, eleven in all.

(6) *Absolute Sovereignty at Mecca* (*Age* 60-62)

Mecca capitulated, and thenceforth Mohammed exercised political sovereignty over all Arabia. He determined to abolish idolatry, and to reduce Judaism and Christianity to a position of dependence (9 : 29-30; Muir, *Life,* 408-409, 453-454). He had sent embassies to Greek, Persian, Egyptian, and Abyssinian kings, demanding their acceptance of his faith. He saw "men entering the religion of Allah by troops" (110 : 2). He died after a short fever in the arms of Aisha, the favorite wife in his harem. His last words were a prayer.

Lord, grant me pardon! Join me to the companionship on high! Eternity in Paradise! Pardon! The blessed companionship on high! (Muir, *Life,* 495.)

3. THE CHARACTER OF MOHAMMED

(1) *Certain Admirable Characteristics*

He was a man of unquestionable religious experience. He was transformed by a compelling personal conviction of an omnipotent God from an ordinary business man into a flaming prophet of religion. Himself a man of prayer, he enjoined his followers also to pray unto the Almighty; and they have been wonderfully faithful in this respect.

Mohammed was a man of utter devotion to the religious ideal as he conceived it. He risked his life repeatedly for his religion. And his followers have continued absolutely confident in the controlling power of God.

My sole help is in God. In Him do I trust, and to Him do I turn me. (11 : 90.)
Trust in Allah. And Allah is sufficient as a protector. (4 : 83; 33 : 3.)
We created man, and We know what his soul whispers; for We are nigher to him than his jugular vein. (50 : 15; *SBE,* 9 : 242-243.)

Mohammed was an attractive leader and an efficient organizer. He succeeded in uniting the various warring Arab tribes on a new religious basis, and his followers have continued to be bound together closely by their religion.

The Prophet is nearer of kin to the believers than themselves. (33 : 6.)

Verily, those who have believed and fled their homes and spent their substance for the cause of God, and they who have taken in the Prophet and been helpful to him, shall be near of kin the one to the other. (8 : 73; Rodwell, 381.)

(2) Certain Reprehensible Characteristics

To persons with a Christian background there are seemingly very contradictory elements in the character of the Prophet. Sometimes he was vindictive. Sometimes he was very kind even to enemies or rivals. He revenged himself upon the Jews in Medina, yet he acted with magnanimity toward his former enemies when he returned in triumph to Mecca.

Mohammed was a domineering, warring autocrat. He prescribed war, and advocated violence toward non-Muslims.

Prescribed for you is fighting. (2 : 212; SBE, 6 : 31.)

Fight them then, that there should be no sedition, and that the religion may be wholly God's. (8 : 40; SBE, 6 : 167.)

Fight those who believe not in God . . . until they pay the tribute by their hands, and be as little ones. (9 : 29; SBE, 6 : 176–177.)

Verily, God loves those who fight in His cause. (61 : 4; SBE, 9 : 281.)

Fight strenuously against the misbelievers and hypocrites, and be stern toward them. (66 : 9; SBE, 9 : 292.)

Yet, he could also say, "There is no compulsion in religion," and in the Traditions it is reported that he once said:

Say not, if people do good to us we will do good to them, and if people oppress you, we will oppress them, but resolve that if people do good to you, you will do good to them, and if they oppress you, oppress them not again. (Stanley Lane-Poole, The Speeches and Table Talk of Mohammed, London: The Macmillan Co., 1905, p. 147.)

And he had great respect for the "Religions of the Book," Judaism and Christianity, which he distinguished from other faiths of "unbelievers."

On no other point is the Prophet more severely condemned by Christians than in his attitude toward women and marriage. Mohammed's behavior with his numerous wives caused trouble more than once (*SBE*, 6 : xxix; 9 : 290–291; Muir, *Life*, 290–291, 426–428). It all seems quite justifiable to his followers, even at the present time (Ali, *Holy Quran*, 199–200, 1090–1092). Certainly, the sacred scriptures of no other religion intimate that the undesirable wives of the founder might be divorced with the prospect of his obtaining more and better wives through the help of God.

It may be that his Lord, if he divorce you, will give him in exchange wives better than you, Muslims, believers, devout, repentant, worshipping, given to fasting,—such as have known men, and virgins too! (66 : 5; *SBE*, 9 : 291.)

He married Zainab, the divorced wife of an adopted son, Zaid; and justified his action by a special dispensation revealed to him from Allah:

that it might not be a crime in the faithful to marry the wives of their adopted sons, when they have settled the affair concerning them. And the behest of God is to be performed. No blame attacheth to the Prophet where God hath given him a permission. (33 : 37–38; Rodwell, 438.)

He had set four as the limit on the number of wives for Muslims (4 : 3). Yet this limit was removed later for him alone by a special dispensation.

O Prophet, We allow thee thy wives whom thou hast dowered, and the slaves whom thy right hand possesseth out of the booty which God hath granted thee, and the daughters of thy uncle, and of thy paternal and maternal aunts who fled with thee to Medina, and any believing woman who has given herself up to the Prophet, if the Prophet desired to wed her—a privilege for thee above the rest of the faithful. (33 : 49; similarly verse 51; Rodwell, 439.)

Yet modern Muslims as well as some objective scholars point out that on the whole Mohammed definitely improved the status of women; that he gave them a degree of economic freedom not yet attained in some Western, so-called Christian lands; that he set a limit to unregulated polygamy which was highly salutary; that he completely did away with the custom of female infanticide, common in the Arabia of his day; and that in his prescription that plural marriage was permissible only on condition that the husband treat his wives with exact equality, he really laid the basis for monogamous marriage.

It is noteworthy that Mohammed has come to be regarded among some Muslim sects as a wholly exemplary character, much as Jesus is to Christians, and considerable literature has appeared in recent years which presents him in this light. (For example, see Iqbal Ali Shah, *Mohammed, the Prophet*, London: Wright and Brown, 1932.)

4. THE VENERATION OF MOHAMMED

The *Koran* contains many passages which express a rather humble estimate of himself. In the early part of his career he presented himself more than a dozen times as simply a mortal man, one of the common folk, who had been sent by God as a warner.

Muhammad is no more than an apostle. (3 : 138.)
A man from amongst yourselves, to warn you, and that ye may fear. (7 : 61.)
I am only the plain-spoken warner. (15 : 89; Rodwell, 116.)
Similarly also 5 : 22; 10 : 2; 17 : 95; 18 : 110; 22 : 48; 25 : 58; 27 : 94; 38 : 3, 65, 70; 46 : 8, 30–32; 51 : 50–51; 67 : 26; 79 : 45.

In two verses he is characterized as "the illiterate Prophet," even though an apostle from Allah (7 : 156, 158). At least five times he is directed to ask for forgiveness from God (4 : 106; 40 : 57; 47 : 21; 48 : 2; 110 : 3). Mohammed explicitly disclaimed miracle-working power, even though he was challenged to give some sign that he really was a prophet and not merely an ordinary man (6 : 109; 17 : 92–98; 21 : 3, 5, 10; 29 : 49).

Yet in a still larger number of verses Mohammed is closely

associated with Allah, so that obedience to the Prophet is part
of submission to God (3:28–29; 4 : 17–18, 62, 82; 9 : 1–16, 66,
72, 75, 81, 91; 24 : 46–62; 33 : 12, 22, 29, 33, 36; 49 : 1, 15; 57 :
7–28).

The later estimate of Mohammed was that he was superhuman. Mirkhond's *Life*, written in the fifteenth century, contains fifty pages of miracles attributed to him.

Muhammad made no claim to pre-existence; and the strictly orthodox Moslems deny his pre-existence, his power of intercession, and
that his person and tomb should be reverenced. But the Sunnis as
well as the Shiahs are accepting traditions that declare his pre-
existence even before the creation of the world in the form of the
"light of Muhammad." . . . The sinlessness of Muhammad is proclaimed, and pronunciation of his name is vested with delivering
power and saving grace. (J. L. Barton, *Christian Approach to
Islam*, 130; similarly, D. B. Macdonald, *Aspects of Islam*, 97–100;
Andrae, *Die Person Muhammed's*, 92–390. Charles S. Braden, *Jesus
Compared*, N.Y., Prentice Hall, 1957. Ch. 10.)

5. SCRIPTURES OF ISLAM, THE *KORAN*

Islam is unique among the religions of the world in that its
sacred scriptures are avowedly the revelation of God to one
man, the founder. The main speaker in the *Koran* is Allah.
Sometimes he is represented as simply speaking to Mohammed,
and sometimes as bidding Mohammed to speak as the mouth-
piece of God.

Yet the historic facts seem to be that Mohammed himself
did not write one word of the Koran as the document has come
down in its present form. About a year after his death, Abu
Bekr, his successor, ordered a compilation of the teachings of
the Prophet, which could be remembered accurately, or which
otherwise had been preserved by devoted disciples. Eleven or
twelve years after the death of Mohammed, on account of the
variations and confusions which had arisen among the reported
sayings of Mohammed, the third caliph, Othman, ordered a
revision to be made, and all existing copies of the previous
compilation to be destroyed. Thus, the present text of the
Koran is not the first edition, but a second edition, which had

been made in order "to stop the people before they should differ regarding their scriptures, as did the Jews and Christians" [1] (Rodwell, *The Koran*, translated from the Arabic, 1; Muir, four-volume *Life*, vol. I, p. xiii).

From the point of view of literary criticism, material from many sources had entered into the mind of Mohammed before he uttered these teachings. Some traditional Arabic beliefs and folk-lore can be recognized in the *Koran*. Some elements may have been originally Zoroastrian, for example, the devil, angels, the judgment-day, the resurrection. There are many references to persons and events of the *Old Testament*. Some rabbinical remnants from the Jewish *Talmud* may be identified. There are many allusions to the *New Testament* evangel, "Injil," and to Christianity, including at least eight references to the Messiah and twenty-five to Jesus Christ. Indeed, there is a curious resemblance between the meaning of the Greek word "Paraclete" and the Arabic word "Ahmed," which is a synonym for "Mohammed," so that the founder of Christianity is represented as predicting, literally, the future founder of Islam (John 14 : 16; 16 : 7, 12–14).

Jesus, the son of Mary, said: "O children of Israel! Verily, I am the apostle of God to you, verifying the law that was before me, and giving you glad tidings of an apostle who shall come after me, whose name shall be Ahmed." (61 : 6; *SBE*, 9 : 281; Rodwell, 405–406.)

The structural arrangement of the *Koran* is in 114 chapters, or "Suras" totalling slightly less than the *New Testament*, and about one-quarter of the size of the *Old Testament*. The first chapter contains a short opening prayer, the famous Fatihah. Thereafter the chapters are arranged simply according to their length. From the longest at the beginning, with 286 verses, they diminish down to the short chapters at the end, the shortest containing only three verses. Modern critical scholars

---

[1] While the text of Muslim scripture is less of a problem than in the case of the other scriptures, the work of recent scholars on it is evidence that even if the tradition be true concerning the destruction of the earlier editions, substantial differences have crept into the text. See Arthur Jeffery: *The Qur'an as Scripture*, New York, 1952.

believe that they have succeeded in identifying the suras, which were "revealed" in the successive periods of Mohammed's life—first at Mecca, then at Medina, and again at Mecca. Rodwell's translation presents the *Koran* in this rearranged chronological order of chapters, which seeks to disclose the process of development in Mohammed's own mind.[1]

Every one of the chapters, except the ninth, begins with a stereotyped formula: "In the name of Allah, the Compassionate, the Merciful"—*Bismi 'llahi 'rrahmani 'rrahim.* Many passages represent that the *Koran* had been revealed by Allah direct to Mohammed, even in the Arabic language and without any discrepancies (4 : 84, 113; 12 : 1–3; 13 : 36–37; 16 : 104–105; 17 : 85–93; 18 : 1; 25 : 7; 38 : 28; 39 : 24, 28, 29; 46 : 6–7; 53 : 4–12). More than a hundred passages in the *Koran* refer to the book, many of them extolling its excellences. The authority of the *Koran* is absolute for Muslims. Their theologians have propounded dogmas of plenary inspiration, verbal infallibility, and self-attesting truth.

Yet none knoweth its interpretation, except Allah. (3 : 5.)

Historically, the *Koran* has been the most influential book in all Arabic literature. Hardly an Arabic book of any importance has been written subsequently without making allusions to, or quoting from, the *Koran*. It is the chief textbook in the modern Islamic university of Al-Azhar at Cairo.

6. THE CONCEPTION OF THE SUPREME BEING, ALLAH

Monotheism is Mohammed's pre-eminent religious message. Yet in referring to himself, Allah always is represented as using the plural number, "We," "Us," and "Our," even as was done by the "Elohim" God in the early part of the *Old Testament* (Genesis 1 : 26), as is still done in the official utterances of some modern monarchs, and also in the literary device of editorial "we." However, the main teaching of the *Koran* is clear —that there exists one sole God, whose name is Allah.

[1] For another and more recent treatment, see Richard Bell, *The Qur'an*, translated with a critical rearrangement of the Surahs, 2 vols., Edinburgh: T. and T. Clark, 1937.

The historical origin of Islamic monotheism was threefold:
partly in Mohammed's own insight into an ultimate unity in
the Supreme Being of the universe, partly in his learning this
great idea directly from Jewish monotheism, and partly in
his conscious reaction against the crude tritheism of the Syrian
Christians whom he met. More than a dozen passages in the
Koran protest against the preposterous proposition that the
one Supreme Being could enter into any sort of sexual relationship with one woman, so that one Son of God would be begotten, or that the sovereign unity would be impaired by being
split into thirds of a so-called divine Trinity (2 : 110; 4 : 169;
5 : 76–77; 6 : 100–102; 10 : 69; 17 : 111; 18 : 3–4; 19 : 36–39,
91–93; 21 : 19–33; 23 : 93; 37 : 151–163; 39 : 2–8; 72 : 3–4).

The *Koran* contains some noble descriptions of the omnipotent and beneficent Creator, which are entirely acceptable to
Jews or to Christians (2 : 27; 6 : 96–100; 14 : 37; 46 : 32; 50 :
37; 55 : 2–12). The finest description of God in the *Koran* is
the famous "Verse of the Throne," or "Verse of Power," which
is frequently inscribed in mosques (2 : 256).

Seven important characteristics of Allah have been analyzed
and classified in orthodox Islamic theology.

Absolutely unitary, the main attribute repeatedly asserted (3 : 1, 4,
16; 6 : 101–102; 16 : 1–3; 21 : 22; 25 : 1–2; 37 : 4–5; 73 : 9; 112 :
1–4);
All-seeing (6 : 59, 103; 18 : 25);
All-hearing (2 : 257; 44 : 5);
All-speaking (18 : 109; 31 : 26);
All-knowing (2 : 27; 6 : 58; 31 : 22; 33 : 54; 58 : 7–8);
All-willing, *i. e.*, inscrutably irresistible (6 : 35; 13 : 33; 16 : 2, 9;
76 : 31; 85 : 16);
All-powerful (2 : 19; 3 : 159; 55 : 16–17).

Ninety-nine names of Allah are repeated with as many
beads on the Islamic rosary. The most frequent, and the only
one used in some thirty of the early chapters of the *Koran*, is
"Lord" (*Rabb*). Other names for Allah which occur in the
Koran are: The One, the Mighty, the Powerful, the King, the

Overcomer, the Avenger, the Dominator, the Slayer, the Provider, the Compassionate, the Merciful, the Forgiving. Allah is also represented as "Loving" (*wadûd*). But the persons whom Allah loves are:

"Those who do good" (2 : 191).
"Those who follow Muhammad" (3 : 28).
"Not the proud or boastful" (4 : 40).
"Those who believe and act aright" (19 : 96).
"Those who fight in His cause" (61 : 4).

Mohammed's main practical message about God was that He would punish the wicked and reward the good people. Allah is frequently lauded as gracious and forgiving toward the persons who submit to His sovereignty. Moral culpability in the character of Allah is repeatedly denied in the *Koran* (2 : 24; 4 : 44; 28 : 14). But more frequently affirmed is the absolute arbitrariness of Allah.

He guides whomsoever He pleases. (2 : 136; 22 : 16; 24 : 35, 45; 28 : 56; 42 : 12; 76 : 31.)

Equally explicit are statements that Allah misleads certain people (13 : 33; 14 : 32; 40 : 35, 36, 74; 61 : 5). Indeed, numerous passages in the *Koran* state explicitly and conjointly that Allah both guides and misguides, both punishes and forgives, according to His own inscrutable, unquestionable good pleasure (3 : 124; 5 : 44; 6 : 39, 125; 13 : 27; 14 : 4; 17 : 99; 18 : 16; 35 : 9; 39 : 24; 74 : 34). On the whole, Allah is represented as a magnificent, opulent, irresistible World-Potentate—an Arab sheikh glorified and magnified to cosmic proportions.

Salvation, according to such a faith, is expressed explicitly in the simple word which Mohammed used for designating this religion, *"islam"* ("submission" to God).

7. THE ESSENTIAL ISLAMIC BELIEFS

Any intelligent Muslim can state with ease and definiteness his six main beliefs as formulated in traditional theology.

(1) Belief in the One God, Allah

The first and foremost item in Islam is monotheism. This is taught repeatedly in the *Koran*, and forms the first half of the Muslim creed.

(2) Belief in Angels

They intercede with Allah for the forgiveness of men (40 : 7–9; 42 : 3). Eight angels support the throne of Allah (69 : 17). Nineteen angels guard hell (74 : 30). Gabriel is the archangel (2 : 91; 16 : 104; 53 : 5, 6; 66 : 4; 81 : 19). He is called "the Holy Spirit" (2 : 81). Jinn, genii, are a group of spirits midway between men and angels; they are both good and evil (11 : 120; 72 : 11). Some of them have "submitted themselves," and thereby have become Muslims (72 : 13–14). One of the jinn (18 : 48) is the devil. He is designated in the *Koran* as "Shaitin," from the Hebrew "Satan," also as "Iblis," from the Greek "Diabolos." This tempter is a very important personage in the *Koran*. He is accompanied by a group of especially rebellious spirits, "Shaiyatin," devils.

(3) Belief in the Koran

Allah has sent down various books (29 : 45; 42 : 14), among them the Hebrew *Torah*, "Taurat," Law, to Moses; the Psalms, "Zabur," to David; the Evangel, "Injil," to Jesus; and lastly the *Koran* to Mohammed.

(4) Belief in the Prophets of Allah

Twenty-eight such are named in the *Koran*. Twenty-two of them are from the *Old Testament*, including Adam, Enoch, Methusaleh, Noah, Abraham, Lot, Ishmael, Isaac, Jacob, Moses, David, Solomon, Elijah, Elisha, and Jonah. There are three from the *New Testament*—Zechariah, John the Baptist, and Jesus. Among the Islamic prophets outside of the *Bible* is Alexander the Great. Mohammed is the last and greatest of the prophets. He has been prepared for, and attested by, all the preceding prophets.

(5) *Belief in Judgment, Paradise, and Hell*

At the end of the world there will be a resurrection of all the dead on "the day of coming forth" (50 : 41).

The trumpet shall be blown; and behold, from their graves unto their Lord shall they slip out. (36 : 51.)

The great judgment-day of Allah and the unity of God are the two messages of Mohammed from the beginning to the end of his preaching. The two earliest "revelations," as now classified in a chronological order of the preachments of Mohammed, contain this message of the judgment-day to come (74 : 8–10; 96 : 8). In at least 852 verses Mohammed, like some of the Hebrew prophets, delivered thunderous warnings of doomsday impending with decisive rewards and punishments. Concrete pictures are presented of the balance scales which will be used to weigh the good and evil deeds of each soul, even to the weight of a grain of mustard seed (7 : 5–8; 21 : 48; 23 : 103–105; 101 : 6–8).

Paradise, with abundant pleasures for the senses, is pictured awaiting the pious believers in Allah. More than a score of passages, almost without exception, refer to gardens and flowing rivers, luxurious food and ease, and varied sensuous pleasures.

Verily, the pious shall be in gardens and pleasure, enjoying what their Lord has given them; for their Lord will save them from the torment of hell. "Eat and drink with good digestion, for that which ye have done," reclining on couches in rows. And We will wed them to large-eyed maids. . . . And We will extend to them fruit and flesh such as they like. (52 : 17–22; *SBE*, 9 : 249.)

In gardens of pleasure, . . . and gold-weft couches. . . . Around them shall go eternal youths, with goblets and ewers and a cup of flowing wine. No headaches shall they feel therefrom, nor shall their wits be dimmed! And fruits such as they deem the best, and flesh of fowl as they desire, and bright and large-eyed maids like hidden pearls, a reward for that which they have done. (56 : 12–23; *SBE*, 9 : 263.)

Hell for the wicked unbelievers is presented repeatedly with vivid gruesome pictures.

In hell shall they broil, and an ill resting-place shall it be. (14 : 34.) Verily, We have prepared for the evil-doers a fire, sheets of which shall encompass them. And if they cry for help, they shall be helped with water like molten brass, which shall roast their faces. (18 : 28; SBE, 9 : 17.)

A sinner—verily for him is hell. He shall not die therein, and he shall not live. (20 : 76; SBE, 9 : 39.)

(6) Belief in the Divine Decrees

Everything is predestined by Allah's appointment, even men's belief and unbelief (16 : 38).

It is not for any soul to die save by God's permission, written down for an appointed time. (3 : 139; SBE, 6 : 63.) Naught shall befall us, save what God has written down for us. (9 : 51; SBE, 6 : 180.) Ye did not slay them, but it was God who slew them. Nor didst thou shoot, when thou didst shoot, but God did shoot. (8 : 17; SBE, 9 : 165.)

8. THE ESSENTIAL ISLAMIC DUTIES

These are called "the Five Pillars of Islam."

(1) Repetition of the Creed

Every Muslim is required to repeat the Confession of Faith, or Watchword, *Kalimah*, every day in the original Arabic.

There is no God but Allah, and Muhammad is the Prophet of Allah. *La ilaha illa 'llahu, Muhammad rasulu 'llah.*

This formula is not to be found in the *Koran* in this form, but its two parts recur frequently, for example, in 47 : 21 and 48 : 29. Simply the repetition of this creed is accepted as a test of conversion to Islam.

(2) Prayer

The *Koran* frequently enjoins the duty of praying. The call to prayer may be heard from the minaret of every mosque five

times every day. The *Koran* requires prayer at three stated
times—daybreak, noon, and night (11 : 116; 17 : 80–81; 20 :
130; 30 : 16–17; 50 : 38–39). It must always be directed toward
the Sacred Mosque at Mecca:

Wherever ye be. (2 : 139.)
"Come not to prayer when ye are drunken, but wait till ye can understand what ye utter; nor when ye are polluted," even by the
touch of a woman. (4 : 46.)

(3) *Almsgiving*

This is a duty explicitly enjoined upon faithful Muslims (2 :
40; 64 : 16; 98 : 4). Conversion to Islam definitely includes the
paying of this impost (9 : 5, 11).

When ye have taken any booty, a fifth part belongeth to Allah and
to the Apostle and to the near of kin and to orphans and to the poor
and to the wayfarer. (8 : 42.)

It came to be expected that the faithful would give "zakat,"
2½ per cent yearly, not of his income, but of his capital. Of
course, during the centuries that Islam was a theocracy, *i. e.*,
at the same time both a religion and a government, this proportion covered not only his benevolent giving, but what
among other peoples is regarded as taxes to support the government. It served not alone to pay the expenses of the religious establishment, the care of the poor, etc., but to support
the army and the other functions of the state.

(4) *Fasting During the Days of the Month of Ramadan*

O believers, a fast is prescribed for you . . . the month of Ramadan. . . . As soon as any of you observeth the moon, let him set
about the fast. . . . Eat and drink until ye can discern a white
thread from a black thread by the daybreak. Then fast strictly till
night. (2 : 179–183; Rodwell, 357.)

There were other fasts, also, though they were not compulsory. Mohammed fasted frequently during the months of
the year, for example, on the tenth day of the month Muhar-
ram, on six days of the month of Shawwal, and on the 13th,

14th, and 15th of each month. In this many loyal Mohammedans follow his example. There is a *Tradition* that the Prophet once said: "Every good act that a man does shall receive from ten to seven hundred rewards, but the rewards of fasting are beyond bounds."

(5) *The Pilgrimage to Mecca (Haj)*

Every Muslim is required once in his lifetime to go to Mecca, to circumambulate the Sacred Mosque, and to kiss the Kaaba Black Stone seven times. This was easily possible as long as Islam was limited to Arabia, or even the Near East. It became literally impossible for millions of Muslims in the Far East or other distant parts of the world. It came to be accepted that in case of inability himself to go, a Muslim might send a substitute, but the low economic status of multitudes of Muslims in faraway lands made this also impossible. It is now the custom for many to contribute the small sums they can to the expense of one who with help may be able to go, and by so doing, they gain merit.

The pilgrimage is to be performed within certain lunar months, and according to certain other details (2 : 185, 193–199).

And proclaim among men the pilgrimage. Let them come on foot and on every slim camel. (22 : 28.)
There is due to God from man a pilgrimage unto the House for whosoever can find his way there. (3 : 91.)

During years in which travel suffers no interference because of international unrest or war, an enormous number of pilgrims arrive afoot, by camel, by automobile, by truck, by steamer at the Red Sea port of Jiddah, or by air, from all over the Muslim world. In a recent year, 200,000 pilgrims were reported.

9. THE HISTORY OF ISLAM

Mohammed died without leaving a son or any appointed "successor." Then for twenty-eight years the leadership was maintained in turn by four valiant personal comrades of the Prophet: Abu Bekr, who ordered the collecting of Mohammed's sayings; Omar, who conquered Syria and Persia; Othman, who ordered a revision of the *Koran* and the insertion of the vowel-points into the consonantal text; and Ali, Mohammed's son-in-law, with whose assassination Islam became permanently divided into sects. Then there arose a series of different caliphates, some of them simultaneous, and warring against each other.

(1) *Political Divisions in Islam*

The Omayyad Caliphate (660–750 A. D.) at Damascus started the method of an hereditary succession, and extended Islam forcefully over all north Africa and Spain. The westward aggression of Islam continued rapidly far into Europe until it was stopped by Charles Martel, at the battle of Tours, or Poitiers, in France in 732 A. D., exactly one hundred years after the death of Mohammed.

The Abbaside Caliphate (750–1258 A. D.) traced itself back to Abul Abbas, an uncle of Mohammed. It included the most famous of all the Muslim caliphs, Harun-al-Raschid, whose capital was at Baghdad.

A Spanish caliphate held sway at Cordova (755–1236 A. D.), and a Moorish caliphate at Granada (1238–1492 A. D.).

The Fatimite Caliphate (910–1171 A. D.) ruled Egypt and north Africa.

The caliphate of the Ottoman Turks began its power in 1299 A. D. It captured Constantinople in 1453 A. D. and Egypt in 1517 A. D. This continued as the chief Muslim power for about 600 years. In 1922 the sultan, at Constantinople, was deposed by the Turkish National Assembly, at Angora.

(2) *Sectarian Divisions in Islam*

Along with the external political separations, there have arisen within Islam certain notably distinct types of religious experience and of theological formulas.

The Sunni sect constitutes the main body of Muslims. They are pre-eminently the traditionalists. They insist upon the Sunna (or Way), which has come down continuously from the founder. The Turkish Muslims are mostly Sunnis.

The Shia sect split off early in the history of Islam. They contend that the first really legitimate "successor" was Ali, who, as being personally in the family of Mohammed, was the one to continue the true succession from Mohammed. Ali and both of his sons, Hasan and Husein, were religious martyrs, and have been venerated by the Shia Muslims. The various subdivisions of Shia Muslims differ among themselves concerning the number of Imams, or divinely appointed leaders, and also concerning the identity of the latest Mahdi, or Guided One. The Shia Muslims are located chiefly in Persia and Africa. Their tendency is toward liberalism, mysticism, even pantheism. They have been much influenced by other systems, especially Zoroastrianism.

A common belief among Shia Muslims is that the twelfth Imam disappeared, but that he will return again, a belief somewhat similar to the Christian belief in the Second Coming of Jesus. This expectation of one to come has given rise to two notable modern movements in Islam, one in Persia, the other in India.

About the middle of the last century, there arose a figure in Persia claiming not to be the expected one, but the forerunner of his appearance. He was known as the Bab, and soon gathered a substantial following. The new movement fell under the suspicion of the Persian government and the Bab was put to death. Not long afterward a member of the Bab's following, a man of some wealth and social standing, proclaimed that he was the expected one. He was accepted by at least a part of the Bab's followers, and his movement came to be known as the Bahai faith. He was called Baha 'Ullah, the "Splendor of God." His teachings and those of his successor, Abdul Baha, are regarded as the revelation of God, and constitute the scriptures of Bahai.

Baha 'Ullah was a prisoner most of his active life, the latter part of it at Akka on the Mediterranean coast, after periods of prison in Baghdad, Constantinople and Adrianople. After the rise of the Young Turks, Abdul Baha, son and successor of Baha 'Ullah was given freedom to travel abroad, and succeeded in establishing the new faith in both Europe and America.

The group no longer considers itself a branch of Islam, but a new world religion. It is now found actively at work over most of the world. It believes that God is one; that He has revealed Himself in all the nine great religions of the world—they do not consider Jainism and Sikhism as separate religions—through successive prophets each to his own age. Jesus was the prophet for his time; Mohammed for his epoch, and Baha 'Ullah is the prophet-revealer for the present age. Estimates of the number of Bahais in the world run as high as five million, which is much greater than that of either the Jains or the Zoroastrians.

The other movement was founded by The Promised Messiah who appeared in India in the latter part of the nineteenth century. As in the case of Bahai, there is in it a degree of syncretism. The Promised Messiah claimed to be not only the returning Imam of the Shiah Muslims, but also an incarnation of the Hindu god Vishnu; the long awaited Jewish Messiah; the Zoroastrian Saoshyant; the Maitreya or Buddha to come; and the returning Christ of the Christians.

The movement took root in Northwest India, one sect of it at Qadian, the other at Lahore. At the time of the partition of India, Qadian was destroyed, and a little later the Qadian sect re-established headquarters at Rabwah, Pakistan, a completely new city founded at a site some miles to the north of Lahore, chosen by revelation by the Successor to the Promised Messiah, the present head of the movement. The sect is known as the Ahmadiyya. It is probably the most missionary-minded group in Islam. Copying the methods of Christian missions, it sends out missionaries to various parts of the world. Its American headquarters is in Washington, D.C., where it has a mosque and carries on an active program of publication and distribution of propaganda literature. It has groups with resident missionaries in a number of the larger cities of the United States.

Islam, like the other great religions, has its mystics. The Muslims call them "Sufis." In the course of time Orders of Sufis grew up around outstanding mystics, very much as in Catholic Christianity, each with its monasteries and resident monks, to which were usually attached a numerous lay brotherhood. Sufism is sometimes thought to have had its origin in Christian mysticism, in Neo-Platonism, or in Hindu mysticism. It has been explained by Muslim mystics themselves as arising directly out of the experience of the Prophet himself, who, it will be recalled, was given to mystic experiences. Indeed it was probably these which caused him to believe that he was called to be a Prophet of God. Sufism has produced a mystic literature that has been unsurpassed in any religion.

The Sufis, so named from their original clothing of *suf*, or coarse wool, exhibit still another religious trait. The idea of the Shias, that the deity could in any approximate way become man, would have been abhorrent to the austere transcendentalism of Mohammed, although he did experience some of the mystics' sense of divine rapture, or of possession by the Divine. However, this new idea of incarnation has been still further developed by the Sufis. They are characterized by the pantheistic tendency that even ordinary men may almost become divine by a process of asceticism and mysticism. The Sufi Muslims have been located mostly in Persia and India. The most famous Sufi was the Persian mystic Jalal-ud-Din Rumi (1207–1273 A. D.). The most famous religionist, revivalist, and author in the whole history of Islam was Al-Ghazali, who died in 1111 A. D.

Sufism is said to have fallen into decay in recent centuries, though some of the Sufi orders continue to exercise not a little influence in the political realm today. (For a brief study of Sufism, see, A. J. Arberry, *Sufism, an Account of the Mystics of Islam*, London: George Allen and Unwin, 1950.)

At the present time among Muslims there exist some seventy-two distinct divisions, sects, or denominations. These exhibit a tendency which is in marked contrast with the warnings in the *Koran* with regard to the heinousness of sects (*firqah*).

Take tight hold of Allah's rope all together. And do not part in sects. (3 : 98.)

Be not like those who parted in sects and disagreed, after there came to them manifest signs. (6 : 160.)

Be steadfast in religion, and not part into sects therein. (42 : 11.)

10. MODERN TENDENCIES IN ISLAM

Islam has not escaped the common fate of all religions in the modern age of science. It has not yet come to terms with science in respect to its Sacred Scriptures. While there has been some tendency to subject the *Koran* and the *Traditions* to critical scrutiny, this has not yet been generally done. The rigid doctrine of inspiration held by orthodox Muslims is bound to produce conflict when this is attempted, just as it has occurred among conservative Christians.

On the political side, the situation has changed notably in the last two decades. The partition of India brought about the formation of Pakistan as an independent state, the largest Muslim group in the world. The rise of Egpyt and its attempt to unify the Muslim world; its defiance of the Western world in the nationalization of the Suez Canal; and the new importance given the whole Near East and North Africa by the discovery of enormous deposits of petroleum and valuable minerals, have stirred the whole Muslim world and at the same time created formidable new problems for the Islamic faith. How can Islam fit into the new world with all the stresses and strains involved? (For a discussion of modern trends in Islam, see H. A. R. Gibb, *Modern Trends in Islam,* Chicago: The University of Chicago Press, 1947.)

11. ELEMENTS OF STRENGTH IN ISLAM

Its theory of one supreme deity, versus idolatry.
Its confidence in a really sovereign world ruler.
Its teaching that God is also merciful and compassionate.

Its principle of utter devotion to the will of God.

Its theory of an unescapable, just judgment-day.

Its insistence upon a continuous life of prayer.

A certain powerful example in its enthusiastic founder.

Its world-wide outlook.

A certain strong historic missionary aggressiveness.

A certain strong unity among believers, despite sects.

12. ELEMENTS OF WEAKNESS IN ISLAM

The arbitrariness of its deity.

Its reliance upon the method of force.

Its excessive appeals to motives of fear and reward.

Its belief in fatalism (*kismet*).

Its excessively sensuous future—Paradise and Hell.

Its low estimate of woman.

Its lack of a great social program for the salvation of the world.

Its inconsistent animism: jinn, devils, Kaaba stone, repetitious prayers.

Certain pathetic weaknesses in the founder's moral character.

Its theory of non-progress; Mohammed the last of the prophets, "The Seal of the prophets" (33 : 40).

· *XII*

CHRISTIANITY

*The Religion of the Love of God and Love of Man
as Revealed in Jesus Christ*

1. INTRODUCTION: AMONG THE WORLD'S LIVING RELIGIONS

Christianity is one of nine religions, started by an historic leader of great spiritual insight, whose teachings have created a permanent following. Only two, Hinduism and Shinto, have had no personal founder.

Christianity is one of four religions which sprang not merely from a remarkable individual, but also from centuries of religious experience under an organized religion. Jainism, Buddhism, and Sikhism are the other religions in this class of off-shoots. But Christianity is unique in that it adopted into its own canon the sacred scriptures of the antecedent religion, while the *Vedas* are contemned in the sacred scriptures of the three religions which sprang from Hinduism.

Christianity is like all the other living religions in the fact that it originated in Asia. Yet Christianity is unique in the fact that its historic development and influence have been mostly in the West. And the peoples of the West have derived their ideals of justice, freedom, opportunity, co-operation, and progress chiefly from the religion Jesus founded.

Finally, Christianity is unique in the fact that its adherents, along with its opponents and much more than its opponents, feel keenly that the ideals of Jesus Christ are still far from being fully realized.

2. ITS SACRED SCRIPTURES

The Christian scriptures are contained in the *Bible*. This book is the primary source of information concerning the founder and the origin of the Christian Church. It is the authoritative compendium of the principles of Christianity. And it is the most valuable literary help for the maintenance of a Christian life.

But the Christian world is not in complete agreement as to just what constitutes the Christian *Bible*. According to Protestants, it comprises the thirty-nine books of the *Old Testament*, which were the canonical scriptures of Judaism, written chiefly in Hebrew during many centuries, together with the twenty-seven books of the *New Testament* in Greek, which were written during the first century of the Christian Church. The distinctively Christian part of the *Bible* is the *New Testament*, which records the life and teachings of the founder, and the thoughts and experiences of his early disciples. On the content of this all Christians agree, but the *Bible* of the Greek and Latin Churches contains fourteen other books appended to the *Old Testament*, known as the *Apocrypha* by Protestants who do not consider them canonical. This same difference had existed among the Jews who held to either the Palestinian canon, or the Alexandrian. The Christian Church had generally followed the Alexandrian Jews prior to the time of Martin Luther, who, in his monumental translation of the *Bible* into German, translated the entire Alexandrian canon, but separated out the books rejected by the Palestinian canon, which have since been called the *Apocrypha* by Protestant Christians. These books are often included in Protestant Bibles, but fitted in as "extra" books between the *Old* and *New Testaments*. They are regarded by some churches as suitable for "edification," but not as a basis for Christian doctrine.

The combination of all these writings into one volume was already in the making before 200 A. D. Copies of the whole *Bible* were made by order of Constantine about 325 A. D.

A study of the Christian scriptures will show that the *Bible* is a collection of writings which are quite diverse, yet of great value as a unit. The diversity is strikingly set forth in the first book of the *New Testament* (Matthew 5 : 17–48), where Jesus distinctly superseded teachings of the *Old Testament* in six specific instances, and yet also said that his purpose was "not to destroy, but to fulfil." The unity is clear when the *Bible* is viewed as the record of a long historical growth in the comprehension of God and of man and of the universe, perfected through the life and teaching of Jesus Christ.

The authority of the *Bible*, Christians believe, is supreme above all other books because it presents most fully the saving truths of religion. Its influence has exceeded that of any other volume ever written in human history. In 1958 it had been translated, in whole or in part, into over 1100 different languages. Its impression upon human civilization has been profound, although falling far short as yet of the full purpose of Jesus Christ. Certainly Christians are convinced that the scriptures of Christianity tower above all other scriptures in influence, in attractiveness, and in effect on character.

3. THE LIFE OF THE FOUNDER, JESUS CHRIST (4 B. C.–29 A. D.)

Our knowledge of the life of Jesus, the founder of Christianity, is derived from four short interpretations, called "Gospels," and from a few other references to him in the *New Testament*. On the basis of this information, relatively so scanty, yet so momentous, more books have been published about Jesus Christ than about any other person who has ever lived.

(1) *His Early Life*

Christian tradition in two of the Gospels (Matthew and Luke) affirms the virginity of his mother, and so his supernatural birth. However, during his lifetime he was recognized as the son of Joseph and Mary. He was born in Bethlehem of Judea, and brought up in Nazareth of Galilee. He was a typical Jewish child. His parents complied in every respect

with characteristic Jewish customs at the time of his birth and
while he was growing up. That he was an extraordinary youth
is the implication of the graphic narrative in the Jewish temple
at Jerusalem (Luke 2 : 41–51). Living a normal life in a
humble family, he drew upon the best available instruction
and experience of his day. His manhood life revealed the
breadth and depth of his culture.

(2) *The Crisis in Which He Became a Leader*

When Jesus was about thirty years old, John the Baptist,
who, according to Luke, was his cousin, conducted on the
banks of the Jordan a moral and religious revival which challenged the hearts of his dejected countrymen. The new
preacher, who may have been a member of, or influenced by,
the Qumran community, concerning which the recently discovered Dead Sea Scrolls have revealed so much new information, proclaimed:

Repent ye, for the Kingdom of Heaven is at hand. (Matthew 3 : 1.)

To this appeal Jesus responded, and joined the reform movement. At the moment of baptism, he received a vivid conviction that God, his loving heavenly Father, was calling him.
He accepted the call, and in retirement he determined that
he would realize the fulness of sonship to God neither through
self-benefiting nor through self-advertising, nor by a lowering
of ideals. He found the signal for his own activity as a leader
when John was cast into prison.

(3) *His Public Ministry*

The common people heard the message of Jesus gladly.
They looked upon him as a prophet, and at first flocked to
hear him. But the trained leaders of the Jewish Law saw in
him a revolutionary, and regarded his teachings as dangerous.
They did not interfere with his ministry at the outset. But
when they saw that their authority would be set aside by the
way in which he was preaching and teaching and acting, they
became his bitter enemies. He then chose twelve disciples,

whom he carefully trained to understand his mission, and to spread it abroad. It is clear, however, that the people as a whole never accepted him as the expected Jewish Messiah; they were looking for one quite different. Even the people of his own home town rejected him, and his own family was slow to accept his claims. The best description of his work was given in later years by one of his most aggressive disciples:

Jesus of Nazareth, how God anointed him with the Holy Spirit and with power, who went about doing good, and healing all that were oppressed of the devil. (Acts 10 : 38.)

He announced as his own in the home synagogue at Nazareth the program of a Hebrew prophet.

The Lord anointed me to preach good tidings to the poor. He hath sent me to proclaim release to the captives and recovering of sight to the blind, to set at liberty them that are bruised, to proclaim the acceptable year of the Lord. (Luke 4 : 18–19; Isaiah 61 : 1–2.)

Eventually the priestly authorities at Jerusalem arrested Jesus. He was condemned to death by the supreme Jewish court, because he had admitted that he was the Christ, the Son of God. The Roman governor, who had to confirm the conviction, found no fault in him, yet permitted his crucifixion. Thus closed a remarkable ministry, the characteristic features of which may be mentioned.

(4) Methods in His Public Ministry

As a teacher both the method and the content of his instruction were remarkable. The First Gospel impressively exhibits him in that capacity by grouping his classified sayings, and thus indicating their range and value. The Sermon on the Mount is an example. It compares the Christian view-point with that of the good Jew, declaring it to be far more searching, more vital, and more godlike. The parables of Jesus furnish an even more striking example of his skill. By these short stories from life, or illustrations from nature, Jesus habitually conveyed profound religious lessons, which went to the very heart of each of his hearers, setting forth, as they did, eternal principles of truth.

As a preacher, Jesus took every opportunity to declare that the rule of God was at hand. But he emphasized it to be a spiritual kingdom in the heart, achieved through righteousness and friendliness. This conception was very different from that which filled the mind of most of his hearers, who therefore thought him a visionary or an iconoclast.

As a healer, Jesus worked many wondrous cures. He healed many sick people, and restored to sanity abnormal personalities who, according to the ideas of the day, were possessed or tormented by evil spirits. These impressive deeds were done regularly from compassion. Sometimes they were accompanied by the explicit command to go and live a better life, as moral character was the higher objective which he had in view. These deeds were "signs" of the power and help of God. Jesus did them not simply to accredit himself, but as the spontaneous expression of his spirit of love.

(5) The Extraordinary Conclusion of His Life

On the apprehension of Jesus by the soldiers, all his disciples forsook him and fled. Apparently some of them gave up all hope, and went home. His tomb was sealed, yet two days later was found empty.

He is not here, but is risen. (Mark 16 : 6.)
Whom God raised up, having loosed the pangs of death; because it was not possible that he should be holden of it. (Acts 2 : 24.)

Even his own disciples found it hard to believe that he had risen, but through personal intercourse they became convinced that he was alive again. His last words were a benediction, with an assurance of his perpetual spiritual presence, and with a command to bear witness of him and of his gospel throughout the world. Then Jesus seemed to his disciples to ascend into heaven; and they were moved to worship.

And it came to pass, while he blessed them, he was parted from them, and was carried up into heaven. And they worshipped him, and returned to Jerusalem with great joy. (Luke 24 : 51–52.)

And they went forth and preached everywhere, the Lord working with them and confirming the word by the signs that followed. (Mark 16 : 20.)

4. THE CHARACTER OF JESUS CHRIST

The most distinctive single feature of Christianity is the character of the founder. That is the chief contribution which Christianity offers to any individual and to the world at large today.

The many-sided character of Jesus Christ is at once luminous, comprehensive, inspiring, commanding. It needs to be studied from many points of view. The most important approach is from the primary data contained in the sacred scriptures of Christianity. One must include also, as in the case of the founders of other religions, his own estimate of himself.

(1) *Evidences of the Humanity of Jesus,* as sharing variously in the experiences of normal human beings, stand on every page of the four Gospels.

The child grew and waxed strong, filled with wisdom; and the grace of God was upon him. (Luke 2 : 40.)
And Jesus advanced in wisdom and stature, and in favor with God and men. (Luke 2 : 52.)

As a child he was eager in conversation, and especially interested in religion (Luke 2 : 46–49). He became wearied with journeying. More than once he is reported as being thirsty. He drank and ate and slept. More than once he wept. He was repeatedly amazed and surprised, sad and troubled. He was limited in knowledge and in power. He enjoyed human companionship, and appreciated personal attentions. He was fond of his country, and lamented over its condition. He appreciated various aspects of nature, such as flowers, grass, birds, and signs of the weather. In six passages in the *New Testament* he is reported as having been tempted. In an agony he prayed, and great drops of sweat fell to the ground. In twenty-six passages he is reported as having prayed to God; and he received response "from heaven, strengthening him" (Luke 22 : 43). There are more than a dozen verses which report him as seeking the will of God. He was consciously subordinate to God as his Father.

The Father is greater than I. (John 14 : 28.)

The designation which he most frequently used for himself was "son of man." This phrase is reported in at least seventy passages, which occur in all of the four Gospels. Its exact and full significance has been variously interpreted by scholars. But by it perhaps Jesus emphasized his own relation to humanity, that he felt himself to be a typical human being, or an ideal human being.

However, the foregoing experiences, which any and every human being might share with Jesus, were combined with other extraordinary aspects of consciousness and purpose. These indicate such a relationship to God that the Christian Church has regularly called him divine.

(2) *Evidences of an Especially Close Relationship with God in Service to Humanity* are also numerous in the records of the life of Jesus. In thirty-seven verses he speaks of himself as sent by God. In more than thirty verses he is represented as consciously fulfilling the *Old Testament*, yet also consciously superseding phases of the antecedent religion. He was a diligent co-worker with God (John 5 : 17–47; 6 : 38–40; 9 : 4). He predicted that "this gospel shall be preached in the whole world" (Matthew 26 : 13; Mark 14 : 9). In giving his life servicefully to men, he presented himself as an example for all his followers (Matthew 20 : 28; Mark 10 : 43).

He presented himself as a savior of men in a variety of intimate relations both with men and with God, for example, as the door of salvation (John 10 : 9), as the good shepherd caring for his sheep with self-sacrificing service (John 10 : 10), as the indispensable vine, of which his disciples are the fruitbearing branches (John 15 : 1–6), as the resurrection and the life (John 11 : 25), as the way, the truth and the life (John 14 : 6), as the bread of life (John 6 : 35, 48), as the life-giving bread of God (John 6 : 33), as an adequate representative of God (Matthew 11 : 27; 26 : 53; John 8 : 16, 19; 12 : 44–45; 13 :

3; 14 : 6, 7, 9), as one with God his Father. He declared that the words which he uttered were more enduring than heaven and earth, and that he himself would be the judge of the world (Matthew 16 : 27; 24 : 35; Mark 8 : 38; 13 : 31; Luke 21 : 33). Accordingly in a dozen places he demanded absolute loyalty to himself. In each of the synoptic Gospels he indicated that he was "Son of God." He challenged any one to convict him of any sin (John 8 : 46).

5. THE VENERATION OF JESUS CHRIST

His followers revere the founder of the Christian religion as being, among all the persons who have ever lived, the most worthy representative of God and also of man. This superlative estimate is, of course, very different from that held by the religious leaders who put him to death, and also from that held by some of his associates. The *New Testament* frankly records the opposing estimates in the historical narratives of his life.

Unfavorable estimates of Jesus were held by some associates. Thus his own fellow townsmen regarded him as an ordinary country carpenter, though rather inexplicable in certain respects; and on one occasion they almost assassinated him (Matthew 13 : 54–57; Mark 6 : 1–3; Luke 4 : 16–30). His own brothers did not believe in him (John 7 : 5). Some of his friends considered him deranged (Mark 3 : 21; John 7 : 20; 10 : 20). The Jewish leaders hated him and repeatedly threatened him with death. His enemies regarded him as a devilish exorcist and the arch-fiend Beelzebub. He could not possibly be a prophet or the expected Messiah, because he came from the disreputable province of Galilee. He was known to be an associate of wicked, worldly people. He was charged with being a seditionist, dangerous to the Roman rule. The Jewish authorities denounced him as positively blasphemous in "making himself equal with God" (John 5 : 18; 10 : 33; 19 : 7).

On the other hand, some favorable estimates of Jesus were held by his associates. He was loved by the poor and sinful, and was especially welcomed in homes and by children. He was a popular preacher and healer, possessing extraordinary authority. He was marvellously wise. He was adjudged fault-less by two Roman authorities. The populace hailed him as a king and also as the expected Jewish Messiah. All the first five books of the *New Testament* report that many persons were led by his deeds to glorify God. Indeed, all four Gospels report that the impression which Jesus made upon observers was that he was "Son of God."

The Christian veneration of Jesus is of a person who possessed a superbly comprehensive character. On the one hand, he is genuinely and admirably human. He shares variously in the normal characteristics of mankind, but in these at their best. Thus, Jesus is esteemed a very wonderful representation of man as he actually is, and also a very wonderful represen-tation of what man will become by the help of divine grace. Jesus is the ideal whom every Christian should imitate.

Have this mind in you, which was also in Christ Jesus. (Philippians 2 : 5.)

On the other hand, Jesus is also genuinely divine. Within the circumstances of time and humanity he shares in the moral character of the eternal God. Thus, Jesus is venerated as a very wonderful representation of God, especially of the pur-pose of God to save mankind.

6. THE HISTORY OF CHRISTIANITY

Jesus taught potent principles of religious belief and life, which have been applied variously in the growth of the Christian Church of today.

(1) *The Early Christian Community* (30–50 A. D.)

The assurance of a resurrected and living Christ trans-formed the dejected followers of the crucified Jesus into out-spoken witnesses. The early Christians continued to worship in the temple at Jerusalem as faithful Jews. But they formed a distinct community, devoted to Jesus as their Lord. The rulers, however, persecuted them severely, and scattered them widely. Yet their numbers continually increased.

(2) The Work of Paul (50–65 A. D.)

By his original Jewish training, by his experience of conversion to Christianity, by his thoughtfulness and activity, Paul was remarkably fitted to be the first Christian leader to realize the fuller significance of Jesus, and actually to make Christianity international. He saw that Jesus, through his conception of God and through his own life, had brought into the world a new life of religious freedom and power. Though some non-Jews had become Christians before Paul's conversion, it was he who became the apostle to the Gentiles and in the First Council of the Church at Jerusalem (Acts 15 : 6–22) won the right of Gentiles to be admitted to the Christian community without the necessity of first becoming circumcised, that is, of becoming Jews. Thus was Christianity freed to become a universal religion. Paul's letters to the churches which he established in Europe and Asia were the earliest writings in the *New Testament*. They have become permanent expressions of Christian thought and practice.

(3) The Completion of the New Testament (65–150 A. D.)

Most important for the entire subsequent history of Christianity was the early literary work done in recording the life of Jesus Christ and the beginnings of the Christian Church, the interpretation of Jesus and practical exhortations for Christian living. These writings came into actual use in the public worship of the Christian community during this period.

(4) Christianity's Struggle for Existence in the Roman Empire (150–325 A. D.)

After its first persecutions from its own parent religion, Christianity encountered and survived persecutions from several of the Roman emperors. The first Roman monarch to be converted to Christianity and formally to receive Christian baptism was Constantine. In 325 A. D., at Nicea, he convened in person the first Council of the entire Christian Church. He made Christianity the official religion of the empire, and adopted the cross as the official Christian symbol.

(5) *Becoming the One Official Religion of All Europe* (325–1054 A. D.)

During this period the Christian Church suffered from some theological and ecclesiastical disputes concerning the metaphysical nature of Christ and also from inadequate practical applications of the Christian life, as in monasticism. Nevertheless, the Christians accomplished during these seven centuries what has never been accomplished on any other continent except in America, and that, too, for Christianity, viz., that practically all the national governments in an entire continent were led to profess a common religion.

But Christianity itself became divided. From time to time small sections of the church broke off from the main stream and went their separate ways. Differences arose both in faith and practice between the East and the West which led, in the eleventh century, to a break which has never been healed. The Eastern Church has since been called popularly the Eastern Orthodox Church; the Western, the Roman Catholic Church.

(6) *The Supremacy of the Pope* (1054–1517 A. D.)

Then, for about five centuries, the outstanding fact was the unsurpassed power of the bishop of Rome, even over some of the governments of western Europe. The mediæval church may be criticized for many shortcomings. But it was the most effective agency for aiding the poor and the weak, and for promoting law, order, and education during this whole period of European history. It was the only agency in the whole world which was striving, however imperfectly, for that ideal which is still unattained, a spiritual unity of all people which is superior to all political or racial groupings, functioning for the promotion of justice, peace, mercy, co-operation, and fraternity.

(7) *The Reformation, and World-Wide Dissemination* (1517—— *A. D.*)

After vigorous, but unavailing, protests by Wycliff, Huss, and other reformers against the extravagant claims and practices of the Roman papacy, a German monk named Martin Luther successfully led "the Protestant Reformation." This was a complex popular movement aiming to secure social, economic, educational, and governmental betterment as well as ecclesiastical and theological reform. Roman Catholicism also underwent a certain corresponding "counter-reformation" and revival. The most important objective fact in the history of Christianity has been its dissemination both by Roman Catholics and by Protestants to all parts of the inhabited world.

To Christianize human life thoroughly is a process partly geographical, but also intellectual, social, industrial, national, and international. It can be accomplished only with mutual appreciation, co-operation, and progress. The Orient and the Occident must work together for this stupendous ideal. The foremost problem and inspiring task of Christianity at the present time is to appreciate and apply the full Christian gospel to every phase of the individual and social life of mankind.

7. THE CONCEPTION OF GOD IN CHRISTIANITY

In every religion the controlling and comprehensive conception is concerning the character of the Supreme Being.

Historically, the Christian belief concerning God started from the highest point that had been reached in Judaism. When Jesus declared "the first and great commandment" in religion, he did not announce some new idea, or even some new formula. He quoted directly from the "Shema" or confession of faith, which was a part of every synagogue worship, and which every pious Jew was supposed to repeat twice daily.

The Lord Our God—the Lord is one. And thou shalt love the Lord thy God with all thy heart and with all thy soul and with all thy might. (Deuteronomy 6 : 4–5.)

(1) *Love of the One God*

God, in Christianity as in Judaism, is the sovereign moral personality of the world. Many verses in the *New Testament* describe his characteristics, *e. g.*, all-seeing and all-knowing, "Lord of heaven and earth," righteous, holy, merciful, a just judge of the world, and a great king.

However, Jesus made a certain new emphasis in Jewish monotheism when he taught that the supreme God is supremely loving, and that the indispensable practical consequence of love to God is unselfish love to one's neighbor. For this purpose he again quoted, verbatim, from the *Old Testament:*

Thou shalt love thy neighbor as thyself. (Leviticus 19 : 18.)

Yet even so Jesus' teaching marks a remarkable advance beyond the religion of the *Old Testament*. Judaism had interpreted the idea of a neighbor as being a member of a certain group. Jesus, in his parable of the Good Samaritan, interpreted neighborliness as the giving of loving help to any human being in need.

(2) *The Kingdom of God*

Both Jews and Christians believe that, despite disbelief and disobedience on the part of men, God's moral rule will at some time in the future be fully established over the whole world. The phrase "The kingdom of God" never occurs once in the *Old Testament*, although it is approximated there in at least seven passages. The phrase, with its variant "kingdom of Heaven," in Matthew, is the most frequently recurring phrase in the four Gospels.

The difference between the two religions is more than verbal. Judaism cherishes the hope that at some indefinite date God, by divine power, will finally establish his rule. Jesus in addition set all his followers to work and pray daily for the consummation by actively doing the will of God, and by carrying the Christian gospel "even unto the uttermost part of the earth."

(3) The Forgiveness of God

The teaching of Jesus concerning the forgiveness of sins constitutes another very important part of Christianity, and also a very significant continuation, yet differentiation, of it from Judaism. Many passages in the *Old Testament* represent Jehovah as a God of wrathful vengeance. Consequently, a Jew was explicitly allowed, and even commanded, to exact retaliation for an injury.

Thine eyes shall not pity. Life shall go for life, eye for eye, tooth for tooth, hand for hand, foot for foot. (Deuteronomy 19 : 21; also, Exodus 21 : 23–25; Leviticus 24 : 17–21.)

The priestly code in the *Old Testament* prescribes elaborate material sacrifices (Leviticus 1–7). Some few passages offer Jehovah's free forgiveness of sins without specifying any conditions. Only a very few passages intimate that God forgives sins upon condition of personal repentance (II Chronicles 7 : 14; Isaiah 55 : 7; Ezekiel 33 : 15–16). Out of these four methods by which Jews had believed that God deals with sins, Jesus chose only the last, which is the highest and hardest. Yet even so he introduced two further notable innovations.

First, Jesus taught that God forgives sins not merely upon condition of personal repentance, but also upon condition of the sinner himself having given forgiveness to all who may have done wrong to him, even his enemies, because God also gives unfailing good treatment to all (Matthew 5 : 23–24, 43–48; 6 : 12–15; Mark 11 : 25–26; Luke 6 : 27–36; 17 : 3–4). This is unparalleled among the religions of the world.

The second marvellous innovation which Jesus introduced into the religious life of Judaism, and even of the world, was his own example. No individual in *Old Testament* history, and no founder among the religions of the world, is reported to have forgiven as Jesus forgave. Under circumstances of undeserved humiliation, while dying upon the cross, Jesus was thoughtful for his enemies and prayed for them:

Father, forgive them; for they know not what they do. (Luke 23 : 34.)

This forgiving attitude has helped to interpret the character of God and Jesus' own filial relation to God's plan for the redemption of the world (John 3 : 16).

(4) The Fatherhood of God

The distinctively Christian conception of God is that he is "the Father of our spirits" (Hebrews 12 : 9).

In the *Old Testament* the distinctive designation for deity is "Jehovah," with emphasis on the attributes of holy aloofness and sovereignty. He is described in a number of places as caring for individuals. And there are twenty-eight passages in the *Old Testament* which, either explicitly or inferentially, teach the specific analogy that God is a Father. Yet even so he is the Father of a group, such as Israel, or the Father of "them that fear him" (Psalms 103 : 13). Never once does the *Old Testament* affirm that Jehovah is the universal Father of all mankind. Only two passages speak of "our" Father, and both of these speak of him as incomprehensibly arbitrary (Isaiah 63 : 16–17; 64 : 8–9). Never once does the *Old Testament* report any individual as actually addressing God in prayer "my Father." Never once did Jesus, or any of the New Testament writers, use the characteristic Jewish term for God. Indeed, when Jesus quoted from a Psalm where the name "Jehovah" occurs ten times, and from a verse which contains that name, he omitted the traditional sacred name, and used instead the simple designation "Father" (Luke 23 : 46; Psalms 31 : 5).

Jesus' characteristic designation for God is reported about 150 times in the four Gospels to be "Father," used in various connections.

"The Father," used in sixty-one verses.
"O Father," in prayer to God—seventeen verses.
"My Father," in fifty verses.

"Your Father," sometimes "your heavenly Father," in eighteen verses.

"Our Father," in the Lord's prayer. (Matthew 6 : 9; Luke 11 : 2.)

Altogether the word "Father" as referring to God occurs about 300 times in the *New Testament*.

Nowhere among the sacred scriptures of the world is there to be found even an approximation to this wide and consistent usage among all writers of the sacred scriptures of Christianity of this simple, vital, intimate, feelingful, personal name, "Father," used along with the more abstract term "God."

(5) Some Emphases in the Christian Conception of God

The distinctively Christian conception of the Fatherhood of God retains selectively the noblest elements in the distinctively Jewish conception of the sovereignty of God. And then it proceeds to supplement them with still better features.

Both conceptions contain some common elements, such as: supreme authority in the group, insistence upon obedience to law, and punishment to wrongdoers.

The different elements may be presented succinctly in a table of parallels, which state the relation between the head and the subordinate members in the two different groups:

A SOVEREIGN	A FATHER ALSO
is superior to his subjects in authority.	is similar to his children in essential personality.
dominates from above.	shares with, and assimilates.
commands obedience.	trains through, and for, co-operation.
rules through law.	controls through influence.
is concerned for the glory of his principles.	loves, serves, forgives, rears persons.
is impartial between persons.	is especially appreciative of persons.
causes wrong-doers to suffer.	himself suffers with wrongdoers, even while punishing "for our profit, that we may be partakers of his holiness." (Hebrews 12 : 10.)

8. CHRISTIANITY'S PROBLEM OF EVIL AND SALVATION, ANALYZED AND DIFFERENTIATED

At least a dozen different kinds of evil may be analyzed. Accordingly there are as many different kinds of good to be desired:

THE KIND OF EVIL	THE SPECIAL DISTRESS	THE CORRESPONDING SALVATION
Physical	Pain, suffering, sickness	Good health
Intellectual	Ignorance	Knowledge
Metaphysical	Limitation on individuality	Wholeness, oneness with the All
Emotional	Sorrow	Peace, serenity
Volitional	Failure	Power, success
Social	Disorder, injustice	Orderly justice
Legal	Crime	Obedience to command, submissiveness
Æsthetic	Ugliness	Beauty
Ceremonial	Impropriety	Propriety, rite
Moral	Wrong	Right
Religious	Sin against deity	Righteousness
Distinctively Christian conception	Selfishness	Love

The breadth and depth of a religion may almost be measured by the keenness of its analysis of evil and by the appropriateness of the salvation which it offers. Thus Jainism is concerned chiefly with physical evil; yet even so, the Jains are not encouraged by their religion to enjoy good health, but rather to practise bodily asceticism. Buddhism is concerned chiefly with emotional evil; yet even so, the Buddhists are not encouraged to live a more abundant personal and social life, but rather to suppress individuality altogether. Jesus alone among the founders of religions declared to his followers that he "came that they may have life, and may have it abundantly" (John 10 : 10).

Among the religions of the world Christianity presents the most remarkable combination of evils to be overcome and also of abundant satisfactions to be secured in a comprehensive, harmonious salvation. Christianity is far from pessimistic; yet it perceives in the world much more of evil which is amenable to positive betterment than does any other religion. Optimistically, Christianity perceives an abundance of resources in the form of responsible and responsive persons, both God and oneself and other people who are available for the overcoming of evil, and for the positive enjoyment of abundant good. An incisive presentation, comparison, and classification of religions may be made according to the answers which they give to five simple, but profound, questions regarding evil and salvation.

These are the five questions:

(1) How extensive is evil?
(2) Who is responsible for evil?
(3) What really is evil?
(4) How may an individual attain salvation?
(5) What is the program for social salvation?

The answers to each question in order by eight religions follow: [1]

(1) *Evil Is Something Virtually to Be Ignored*

Taoism says:

(1) There is very little evil in the world.
(2) No one is to be held responsible. There exists no supreme personal God, nor a personal Devil, nor hardly an impersonal Law. A human being may be a fool and a sufferer, but he is not a sinner.
(3) No need of a theory of evil.
(4) Simply by a quiet following of the impersonal "Way" (Tao) of the world.
(5) No social program of salvation, except "Return to Nature."

[1] These are general statements representing what the writer regards as the main historic teachings of the various faiths as found chiefly in their scriptures. They would not apply strictly to some of the later developed ideas of some of the sects.

(2) *Evil Is Ultimately Unreal (Because Illusory)*

Hinduism says:

(1) No evil really; only a temporary mistaking.
(2) No one responsible: neither the evanescent individual, nor the eternal Brahma; illusion is inherent in existence.
(3) The temporary illusion of apparent individuality, due to ignorance of the divine immanence.
(4) Best by pantheistic knowledge and rapture; also by emotional religious devotion; also by ceremonial works.
(5) No social program of salvation; the caste system is perpetual.

(3) *Evil Is Relatively Unreal (Because Arbitrary)*

Islam says:

(1) Not much evil in the world; mostly among the non-submitters, *i. e.*, the non-Muslims.
(2) An individual human being may be insubordinate; yet strictly it is the omnipotent Allah who does everything, and no kind of responsibility may be charged against the inscrutable Supreme Being by any human individual.
(3) Any lack of submissiveness.
(4) Any individual may surely attain Paradise by submission (*islam*) to the inevitable and by forcible propaganda for Islam.
(5) No social program of salvation, except to make Allah and Islam genuinely dominant—by force, if need be.

(4) *Evil Is Very Real*

Buddhism says:

(1) All existence is evil; "to be" means "to be miserable."
(2) No one is responsible for evil in the world, although the law of Karma does entail suffering upon an individual for his deeds in a previous incarnation.
(3) The inherent insatiability of desire; the miserable consequences of all individuality and of all activity.
(4) By suppressing desire; thereby escape from individuality, activity and the necessity of re-incarnation.
(5) No special program of salvation, except to flee from all society into quietude, preferably into a monastery.

Jainism says:

(1) Half of all existence is evil; matter, as distinct from spirit, is essentially and permanently evil.
(2) No one; the world itself is inherently and statically dualistic.
(3) Simply the encumbrance of a vile material body upon an individual's eternal spirit.
(4) By suppressing the flesh, and thus freeing the individual's spirit.
(5) No social program of salvation; the superior religionist is properly an ascetic.

Zoroastrianism says:

(1) Half of all existence is evil, viz., all darkness, untruth, error and death.
(2) The Devil (Angra Mainyu) alone is ultimately responsible for evil in the world.
(3) Simply the natural opposition between the forces of good and of evil; an active dualism is inherent in the very constitution of the world.
(4) By obedience to the good God (Ahura Mazda); specifically by "good thoughts, good words, good deeds."
(5) No special program of social salvation, though originally Zoroaster enjoined agricultural improvement; let every one make a general good effort, and finally God will be triumphant at the end of the world.

Confucianism says:

(1) Not much evil in the world; man is inherently good.
(2) Superiors are responsible for lack of proper superiority, and inferiors are responsible for lack of proper subordination.
(3) The fundamental evil is social impropriety.
(4) Simply by observing the rules of reciprocal social propriety.
(5) A social program of salvation is simply good propriety, good example, and good government.

Christianity says:

(1) Evil is a terrible and wide-spread fact in human life; man was made potentially good; yet all individuals are liable to evil,

and actually do sin against God, against other persons, and also against their own best self.

(2) God is responsible for the possibility of evil in the world through having given free will unto men; the social organization of man is responsible for the transmission of evil through heredity and variously otherwise; each individual is directly responsible for choosing evil, rather than good.

(3) The fundamental evil is any selfish use of God-given free will; any injury done towards moral personality.

(4) By the individual's loving whole-heartedly, by society's organizing servicefully, and by God's helping graciously.

(5) A social program of salvation is imperative, even for the individual's salvation; every individual and all society must render reciprocal service with God's continual help in fellowship with Jesus Christ.

9. BY WAY OF SUMMARY

Christianity, like all other faiths is the result of the fusion of many diverse elements. It was born in a Jewish environment, founded by Jesus, a Jew. Its earliest followers were Jews who took over bodily the ancient Jewish scriptures as their own. Its greatest apostle was one who united in himself the best of both Jewish and Greek culture, and planted Christianity in the Graeco-Roman world. He made it a Gentile church, and its theological doctrines were wrought out largely in terms of Greek thought, while its organizational features were greatly influenced by the political organization of the Roman Empire.

The rigid monotheism of Judaism was somewhat modified in Christianity by the acceptance of Jesus as divine, and by the felt presence of God as an active force in the lives of individuals and the church, through the Holy Spirit—both manifestations of God and inseparable from Him. The oneness of God they were sure of. This and the other, also, they preserved in the doctrine of the Trinity, one God in three persons, or "hypostases," to use the Greek word; God the Father, Christ the Son, and the Holy Spirit. This has remained the belief of most Christians, Catholic or Protestant, Eastern or Western, until the present time, though always there has been a minority group, known in the modern period as Unitarians, who refused to accept Christ as divine.

Christianity appears today in a great variety of forms, but underneath the variety there is a surprising core of agreed-upon beliefs and practices, whether Catholic or Protestant, liberal or conservative. The chief are these:

1. The oneness of God, though Trinitarians posit a "threeness" in that unity.
2. God is the guarantor of the moral order of the universe, that is, God is moral in character, and concerned about good and evil. Indeed, good is conceived of largely as that which is in accord with the will of God.
3. Sin is an infraction of God's law, or disobedience to his will, and requires forgiveness. Forgiveness is possible under certain conditions.
4. God has revealed himself to man. Both *Old* and *New Testaments* witness to this.
5. God revealed Himself most clearly and completely in Jesus Christ, who was, if only a prophet, as Unitarians believe, nevertheless the greatest revealer of them all. (This would not apply to some of the left-wing humanistic Unitarian groups today.)
6. That man's salvation is bound up in some way with Jesus. There is great difference of opinion as to just how Jesus is to be conceived of as Saviour, whether by his life, his teachings, his example, or by his death and resurrection, or by all together. But to all Christians, Jesus Christ stands at the center of their faith.
7. That the Bible is basic to the Christian faith. Protestants believe that it is the ultimate authority. Catholics believe that the authority lies in the Bible as interpreted by the church. Some consider it inspired verbally in its every word and phrase; others think that while it contains the record of God's revelation to man, there is in it a very human element, including error in some of its details.
8. That God continues to reveal Himself to man, and that man must continually strive to know God's will. Some trust to individual personal communion with God for guidance; others believe that God's continuing revelation is channeled through the church.

9. All believe in a church of some kind, whether as a divine institution, the living body of Christ, or merely a community of
those who seek to know and do God's will.

10. Almost all believe in some sort of sacramental observances
which go back to Jesus, through which the life of the individual and the group is enriched and sustained. This varies all
the way from the High Mass of Roman Catholicism, which
thinks that there are six other sacraments, to the Quaker whose
only sacrament is that of silence. Most Christians observe baptism and the Lord's Supper, the two which are directly trace-
able to Jesus' own institution.

11. All believe in some kind of a future life which is morally conditioned.

12. All believe in the coming one day of the Kingdom of God
which Jesus came preaching. Some think that it will be established here, some place it beyond history. For some it is a
great social ideal to be achieved through human effort with
God's help, in the here and now; to some it is a Kingdom that
will be ushered in by the direct and even catastrophic irrup-
tion of God into human history and the ending of the age.

Christianity has its orthodoxies and its heresies, its liberalism, its modernism, its fundamentalism, and its neo-ortho-
doxies; its sectarianism and its ecumenical movements. It is
forever having to make itself at home in a changing world, and
to find new ways to make its gospel relevant to the changing
scene. The infinite variety that it has assumed is in some measure a result of that effort. It may be assumed that new expressions will continue to appear as long as it continues to
be a force in the life of the world.

10. ELEMENTS OF STRENGTH IN CHRISTIANITY

Its conception of God as a loving, holy Father.

The character and the teachings of its founder, Jesus Christ.

Its conception of a divine Holy Spirit, providing for progress.

Its teaching concerning the Kingdom of God.

Its confidence that even death does not check the constant
development of human life.

Its distinctive scripture.

Its practical responsiveness to relieve suffering.

Its civilizing influence.

Its missionary activity.

11. ELEMENTS OF WEAKNESS IN CHRISTIANITY

The tendency in certain sections of Christendom to relapse from the founder's lofty ideal of personal fellowship with God.

The tendency in certain sections of Christendom to shirk the responsibilities which accompany the privileges belonging to children of God.

The tendency in certain sections of Christendom to overemphasize theology instead of maintaining the founder's emphasis on moral conduct.

The tendency in certain sections of Christendom to be domineering instead of following the founder's teaching and example of humble service.

The tendency in certain quarters of Christendom to divide, because of questions of belief, worship, and organization, instead of fulfilling the founder's ideal of brotherly love and unity.

XIII

A SUMMARY COMPARISON
OF THE LIVING RELIGIONS

1. SOME GENERAL POINTS OF SIMILARITY AND DISSIMILARITY

The religions of the world, all without exception, have some features in common. Yet even at those points Christianity can be differentiated. These common features deserve a special review and examination.

(1) *The Belief in One Supreme Being*

This idea was frankly repudiated by original Jainism and by original Buddhism. But in the later developments of both systems the founder was worshipped.

Judaism up to the Exile believed in one supreme worshipful God, Jehovah, and acknowledged also that other nations might just as properly worship their respective deities. But after the period of the Exile the Jews were consistently monotheistic.

Confucianism teaches the belief in one Supreme Being, designated either personally as "Supreme Ruler," or impersonally as "Heaven." But Confucianism limited the worship of this Being to only one person in China, the emperor, and that, too, only once a year, on the night of the winter solstice, December 22. Popular Confucianism encourages the common people to worship many spirits, both nature spirits and the spirits of deceased ancestors.

Zoroastrianism sets forth one cosmic Power which is supremely worshipful, Ahura Mazda. But this Being is not supremely powerful, because there has always existed an opposing cosmic Power, Angra Mainyu, the arch spirit of evil. Furthermore, Zoroastrianism recognizes many other good spirits, subordinate to Ahura Mazda, yet deserving of worship.

Both Hinduism and Taoism believe in one supreme impersonal cosmic Being, named Brahma and Tao, respectively, to be meditated upon, but not exactly to be worshipped. But in both religions the popular phases have been notoriously polytheistic, characterized by the actual worship of many deities. Genuine monotheism, that is, a definite belief in and a worship of one supreme cosmic Power by all people, can be found in only four religions: postexilic Judaism, Christianity, Islam, and Sikhism.

While these four religions agree as to the oneness of God, yet Christianity is unique as regards the moral character of God. Neither Judaism nor Islam present a deity who in his own character is self-sacrificingly seeking the redemption of the world, and who in human history has been represented by a person of that same moral character. Christianity's doctrine of monotheism has the highest possible moral content—a holy, loving heavenly Father, who actively seeks the welfare, trust, obedience, co-operation, love, and worship of all mankind.

(2) *The Claim of Divine Incarnation*

The idea that deity can become incarnate is found in several religions, but with various settings and applications.

In philosophic Hinduism, ever since the period of the *Upanishads*, every object may be regarded as a temporary manifestation or embodiment or impersonation of the impersonal, non-moral, eternal Brahma, though the high-caste Brahman priests are especially venerated as such.

In popular Hinduism there are several deities, notably Krishna and Rama, who are believed to have taken the form of men. The god Vishnu is believed to have entered upon several incarnations; the list varies from nine to twenty-two, but always includes animals. And it is believed that still another incarnation is to appear. None of these Hindu "Avatars" are represented as morally perfect, nor are they represented as manifestations of one supreme personal cosmic deity.

In Buddhism, despite its explicitly non-theistic basis, Buddha came to be regarded as a kind of incarnation, yet even so only as one of many incarnate "Buddhas," with one still to come.

In Islam, despite its dominant doctrine of the absolute transcendence of Allah, the doctrine of incarnation has manifested itself. The Shiite sect broke away from the other main sect, the Sunnite, on the issue that the fourth caliph, Ali, was a veritable *Imam*, or divine incarnation, and therefore the true successor of the Prophet. But some subsects among the Shiites differ concerning the exact number of still other incarnations, whether seven or twelve, and concerning the identity of the last one.

In Christianity, however, there is a distinctive and central teaching concerning Jesus Christ as a unique incarnation, the Word of God, pre-eminently manifested in a historic person, on the ground that his moral character perfectly represents the character and purpose of the invisible holy God, so far as these characteristics can be compassed within the range of a human life.

(3) *The Claim of a Supernatural Origin of the Founder*

Four non-Christian religions advance a theory of a supernatural birth of the founder. Indeed, there are legends of unusual occurrences in connection with the birth of all the great founders of religion. (See Charles S. Braden, *Jesus Compared,* New York: Prentice Hall, 1957, in which each founder is compared with Jesus.)

Buddha in some later scriptures which abound in the marvellous is represented as a pre-existent heavenly being who, in connection with a prophetic dream of a queen, became her first-born child when she was forty-five years old.

Lao-tze in documents dating a thousand years after his day is represented as having been born a fully matured "Wise Old Boy," or "Wise Old Philosopher," with white hair, who had been carried in his mother's womb for seventy-two years, or for eighty-one years, according to different traditions. (See p. 137. Also *Encyclopædia Britannica*, 11th ed., 16 : 192.)

Mahavira in a Jain document dating 980 years after him is represented as a pre-existent being who, in fulfilment of fourteen wonderful prophetic dreams, was supernaturally placed in his royal mother's womb.

A virgin birth seems to be intimated in the case of Zoroaster. According to a late document his mother was supernaturally "glorified" when she was an unmarried young woman of fifteen. Three future saviors in Zoroastrianism are certainly predicted to be born of a mother who, similarly, is to be a virgin fifteen years old.

In the canonical *New Testament* of Christianity there are varying data concerning a divine, or an ordinary, origin of Jesus. However, Jesus represented himself, and he was recognized by others, as having come from God, whom he called "Father," and with whom he lived constantly in the intimacy and likeness of a son.

(4) *The Claim of Divine Revelation*

Every one of the eleven living religions in the world has made the claim of possessing divinely saving truth, not merely man-made, nor even man-discovered. Moreover, every Christian may recognize certain specific revelations of truth which God has made in each one of the other systems of religion, whereby "He hath not left himself without witness" (Acts 14 : 17) anywhere among the communities in the world. The following may be specified as outstanding revelations of truth:

Hinduism	The immanence of the divine in the world; human society, a divinely ordained structure; union with the divine, the goal of existence.
Jainism	Self-renunciation, the condition of salvation; the ideal of a liberation of the spirit with subjugation of the flesh.
Buddhism	Selfishness as the root of misery; salvation through inner purity and self-discipline.

Sikhism	Religion as discipleship of the One True God, with trust in His Name.
Confucianism	The essential goodness of human nature, as divinely implanted; religion as exercised in proper social relationships.
Taoism	Religion as exercised in humbly following the serene divine "Way."
Shinto	Nature to be recognized as a beautiful divine creation; religion as involving purity and also loyalty to the supreme authority.
Judaism	Superlative satisfaction to be obtained through obedience to a God of righteousness.
Zoroastrianism	Religion as involving active co-operation with a cosmic Power of goodness in a struggle against evil.
Islam	Superlative satisfaction to be obtained through submission to an omnipotent God, who is not only a sovereign, but also a judge and rewarder.

All of the foregoing teachings among the religions of the world may properly be regarded as divine revelations of truth. None of them are lacking in Christianity. But in Christianity they are included, harmonized, and supplemented by a higher revelation; that the Supreme Power in the world is a perfect Person; that He may best be conceived of and lived with as a Father-God; that He has been adequately presented by His Son Jesus Christ; and that the supreme satisfaction of every human being consists in loving obedience to Him and in loving service to brother man.

(5) The Claim of an Inspired Scripture

None of the twelve dead religions possessed anything which might be called a canon of sacred scriptures. But all of the eleven living religions do possess definite sets of documents which are regarded as conveying unique divine truths which need to be known for salvation: [1]

[1] For a relatively brief introduction to the several scriptures of these religions, their sources, authorship, general nature and content, and the role they have played in their respective cultures, see Charles S. Braden, *The Scriptures of Mankind.* New York: The Macmillan Co., 1952.

Hinduism	*Vedas*, books of "Knowledge."
Jainism	*Angas*, "Bodies" of knowledge.
Buddhism	*Tripitaka*, "Three Baskets" of teachings.
Sikhism	*Granth*, pre-eminently "The Book."
Confucianism	*The Five Classics* and *The Four Books*.
Taoism	*Tao-Teh-King*, "The Canon of Reason and Virtue.
Shinto	*Ko-ji-ki*, "The Records of Ancient Matters," and *Nihon-gi*, "The Chronicles of Japan."
Judaism	"The Law," "The Prophets," and "The Sacred Writings."
Zoroastrianism	*Avesta*, "The Knowledge."
Islam	*Koran*, "The Reading," or "The Recital."
Christianity	*Bible*, pre-eminently "The Book."

For two among these sacred scriptures, the *Rig Veda* and the *Koran*, a theory of verbal inspiration and literal infallibility has been propounded as high as that set forth by some Christian theologians for the authority of the *Bible*. For all of them claims have been made as pre-eminent above the rest of literature.

In Zoroastrianism: "One marvel is the Avesta itself, which according to all the best reports of the world is a compendium of all the supremest statements of wisdom." (Dinkard, 7 : 5. 11; *SBE*, 47 : 76.)
In Shinto: "There is none among all the writings in the world so noble and important as this classic." (*Nihon-gi*, translation by Aston, vol. I, p. xix, foot-note 1.)

In Christianity the claim for unique inspiration of its sacred scriptures is propounded along with a practical test of its value. The *Bible* is offered to all people as pre-eminently inspired by God, because the *Bible*, through the knowledge which it gives of God and of man, does actually give the superlative inspiration for a holy religious life.

(6) *The Report of Miracles Wrought*

All of the eleven living religions report, usually in connection with the life of their founders, some wonderful events of great religious significance. For example:

Buddha:

Crossed the river Ganges instantly without a boat. (*SBE*, 11 : 21; 17 : 104.)

Appearing and disappearing inexplicably. (*SBE*, 11 : 48–49; 13 : 104–107.)

Healed a sick woman simply by a look. (*SBE*, 17 : 83–84.)

Converted an unbeliever by preaching and by miracle. (*SBE*, 10 : 2. 12–14.)

Converted multitudes by his many miracles. (*SBE*, 13 : 122–134; 17 : 3–5; 19 : 221–226.)

Fed 500 disciples without previous supplies. (*Jataka Story*, 78.)

Zoroaster:

Performed no miracles in the earliest documents, the *Gathas*. But many prodigies are reported later, *e. g.*, in connection with his birth. (*SBE*, 47 : 17–34, 139–143.)

His infancy. (*SBE*, 47 : 35–46, 144–148.)

His "curing of diseases, counteraction of wolves and other noxious creatures, liberating of rain, confining of hail, spiders, locusts, and other terrors." (*SBE*, 47 : 76.)

Mohammed:

Repeatedly disclaimed miracle-working power, though challenged. (*Koran* 6 : 109; 10 : 21; 17 : 92–98; 21 : 5–10; 29 : 49.)

Yet later is reported as having wrought many miracles. (Fifty pages in Mirkhond's mediæval *Life*.)

While many of the reported miracles in the *Bible* may be paralleled from the sacred scriptures of other religions, no other historic person in the world has ever been reported to have arisen shortly after his death and burial, and to have continued his customary influence upon his disciples as in the case of Jesus.

(7) *The Principle of the "Golden Rule"*

This teaching concerning the proper method of dealing with other people has been approximated as a summary rule of right conduct in eight different systems of religion and philosophy:

Hinduism:

"Do naught to others which, if done to thee,
Would cause thee pain: this is the sum of duty."

(Mahabharata, 5 : 1517; as translated in Monier-Williams, *Indian Wisdom*, 446.)

Buddhism:

In five ways should a clansman minister to his friends and familiars, . . . by treating them as he treats himself. (*Sigalovada Sutta*, 31; *Sacred Books of the Buddhists*, 4 : 182.)

Is there a deed, Rahula, thou dost wish to do? Then bethink thee thus: "Is this deed conducive to my own harm, or to others' harm, or to that of both?" Then is this a bad deed, entailing suffering. Such a deed must thou surely not do. (*Majjhima Nikaya*, 1 : 415; as translated in Mrs. Rhys Davids, *Buddhism*, 125.)

Confucianism:

The "Silver Rule" of Confucius is to be found in six different places among the sacred scriptures of this religion, but uniformly in the negative form:

The Master replied: ". . . What you do not want done to yourself, do not do unto others." (*Analects*, 15 : 23; also 5 : 11; 12 : 2; *Great Learning*, 10 : 2; *Doctrine of the Mean*, 13 : 3; *Li Ki*, 28 : 1. 32; in *SBE*, 28 : 305.)

Taoism:

Recompense injury with kindness. (*SBE*, 39 : 106.)

To those who are good to me, I am good; and to those who are not good to me, I am also good. And thus all get to be good. To those who are sincere with me, I am sincere; and to those who are not sincere with me, I am also sincere. And thus all get to be sincere. (*SBE*, 39 : 91.)

Zoroastrianism:

Whatever thou dost not approve for thyself, do not approve for any one else. When thou hast acted in this manner, thou art righteous. (*SBE*, 24 : 330.)

That nature only is good when it shall not do unto another whatever is not good for its own self. (*SBE*, 18 : 271.)

When a good man is beaten through malice, the effort of every one . . . should continue just as though it happened to himself. (*SBE*, 37: 51.)

Judaism:

Take heed to thyself, my child, in all thy works; and be discreet in all thy behavior. And what thou thyself hatest, do to no man. (*Tobit*, 4 : 14–15.)
Whatsoever thou wouldest that men should not do unto thee, do not do that to them. (Babylonian Shabbath, 31a.)

Greek Philosophy:

Do not do to others what you would not wish to suffer yourself. (Isocrates, *Nicocles, or the Cyprians*, 61; E. S. Forster, *Isocrates' Cyprian Orations*, 149.)
Treat your friends as you would want them to treat you. (Aristotle, as reported in Diogenes Laertius, *Lives and Opinions of Eminent Philosophers*, 5 : 21; Bohn Library translation, 188.)
Do not do what any one is vexed to suffer. (Philo's dictum as reported in Eusebius, *Præparatio Evangelica*, 8. 7. 6.)

Christianity:

All things therefore whatsoever ye would that men should do unto you, even so do ye also unto them. (Matthew 7 : 12.)
As ye would that men should do to you, do ye also to them likewise. (Luke 6 : 31.)

In comparing the teachings of these eight systems, which bid a person apply to his conduct of other people the simple test whether he would like such treatment accorded to him, it will be perceived that Lao-tze and Jesus Christ are the only two founders of religions, or teachers of general wisdom, who stated the principle of the "Golden Rule" positively and universally, *i. e.*, not negatively as a warning to abstain from misbehavior, nor limitedly as a counsel to observe reciprocity within the circle of friends and good men. Yet even so, Christianity is different because Lao-tze is not reported as having done anything positive during eighty years of life besides giving his beautiful good advice; indeed, he actually withdrew from difficulty rather than face evil and organize some positive reform.

Furthermore, at just this point of comparing the founders of religions or great original teachers of philosophic wisdom, where the principle of the "Golden Rule" has been approximated, it will be perceived that Jesus is unique in two remarkable ways. Jesus was the only one who himself applied that principle with consistent self-sacrifice, even toward enemies. And Jesus was the only one who based this universal rule of human conduct upon the character and universal conduct of the Supreme Person Himself:

I say unto you: "Love your enemies, and pray for them that persecute you, that ye may be sons of your Father who is in heaven; for he maketh his sun to rise on the evil and the good, and sendeth rain on the just and the unjust." (Matthew 5 : 44–45.)

(8) The Recognition of an Especially Sacred Community

Every religion in the world teaches that there is, or should be, some particular group of people regarded as peculiarly sacred.

The two most individualistic religions, viz., Jainism and Buddhism, have organized their holy ascetics into a monkish order ("Sangha," or congregation); but women are regarded as inherently inferior.

Hinduism teaches that its whole hereditary caste system is a sacred institution as compared with the rest of the world, and that as compared among themselves the upper castes are successively the more holy.

Islam cuts clean across the common ideas of hereditary status, of social superiorities, and even of international exclusiveness by its insistence upon absolute submission before the one omnipotent world potentate, Allah, and upon active joining in his cause.

They who believe and have bled and have fought . . . these shall be next of kin to each other. (Koran, 8 : 73.)

However, Mohammed taught that the infidels, who do not literally "submit themselves," and thus technically join the great sacred community of devoted "Muslims," deserve only to be exterminated.[1]

Christianity teaches that all human society should be made sacred in moral character, and that every individual and every nation should be brought lovingly into a comprehensive brotherhood of humanity under the universal Father-God.

(9) *The Hope of a Universal Religion*

The eleven living religions of the world fall into several groups when tested as to the extent of their hopes in the world.

The idea of becoming universal does not occur in the sacred scriptures of two religions, viz., Sikhism and Taoism. And it seems never to have arisen in their whole history.

The idea of becoming a universal religion does not occur in the sacred scriptures of three other religions, viz., the chief national religions of India, China, and Japan, although within recent years, particularly since the outbreak of the First World War, there have arisen a few reformers who are advocating a world-wide sweep for Hinduism, Confucianism, and Shinto respectively.

In the case of three religions, Jainism, Judaism, and Zoroastrianism, the hope of their becoming universal stands clearly expressed in their sacred scriptures; but it has been definitely dropped in their later history.

In the case of three other religions, Buddhism, Christianity, and Islam, the plan of becoming universal stands clearly commanded in their sacred scriptures, and was acted upon by the founder himself, and has been followed up actively in their later history, so that they have actually become international through missionary effort.

Buddhism as a whole has until quite recently been relatively

---

[1] While it is true that verses can be cited from the *Koran* to support such a statement, modern Muslims cite others which reflect a much more tolerant attitude toward those who do not follow the Prophet.

quiescent, though now once again it is becoming missionary-minded. Islam remains as the most formidable rival to Christianity as a universal religion. Even so, Islam excludes half of its own adult adherents, the women, from full participation in the privileges and responsibilities of their professed religion.

Christianity alone among the religions of the world teaches a basis broad enough for a genuinely universal religion, namely, that all human beings are children of a common Father-God. And Christianity teaches also a practical, constructive program for attaining unto universality: all Christians should engage in loving self-sacrifice, in winsome religious testimony, and in varied systematic service unto all the world. This is a stupendous hope, which requires the fullest co-operation of all Christians.

(10) *The Hopes and Fears of a Future Life*

All the religions of the world have the teaching that the spiritual life of the human individual continues beyond physical death. However, the various religions differ widely concerning the details in their picture of the future life, and even concerning the desirability of a future life.

Hinduism and Buddhism teach that the present life is so sadly marred by illusion and suffering that it really is not worth continuing; although the future life is thus for most people a dread necessity, yet by various proper processes a person's evanescent miserable individuality may finally be extirpated altogether.

Jainism teaches that immortality is inherently unavoidable, with ultimate residence in either heaven or in hell.

All four of the religions which originated in India teach the doctrine of transmigration—that by power of the inexorable impersonal law of Karma a person's soul becomes reincarnate after death in some other earthly body, according to his conduct in this present life.

Confucianism regards religion as consisting chiefly of proper ethical conduct, yet offers for the future only a ghostly kind of existence, without hope of heaven, without fear of hell, without consequences of any kind resulting from a person's present manner of living.

Zoroastrianism and Islam teach an inescapable picturesque judgment scene, when appropriate rewards and punishments will be administered. Islam glowingly pictures a paradise which shall contain abundant sensual delights for the pious, and a hell with perpetual agonies of physical torments for the unsubmissive unbeliever. Zoroastrianism reduces the sensual features of heaven and hell to a minimum, and finally manages to eliminate all evil, but by means of an apocalyptic ceremonial.

Taoism in its popular form stresses strongly the idea of a future life, with appropriate rewards and punishments in its several heavens and hells.

In Shinto there is a belief in a continuing life after this, but it is little emphasized. Some of the Sectarian Shinto sects give it greater importance than others. It is not without significance that perhaps the best book in English on Shinto does not include in the index the terms "heaven," "hell," "future-life," "after-life" or "life after death."

Christianity contains a considerable variety of eschatological beliefs within the *Bible,* and also in its subsequent history. However, Christianity has taught uniformly that there will be a sure and just judgment for all mankind, when the good people will enter into the increasing joy of closer fellowship with God, and when the wicked will suffer the terrible consequences of the separation from God, which they have already chosen. "God is not mocked. Whatsoever a man soweth, that shall he also reap" (Galatians 6 : 7). Jesus clearly offered to his followers the glorious hope of a progressive spiritual life, but only upon the condition of a person's present loving attitude toward personalities. The alternative consequences have been variously formulated. One of the influential formulas on this problem has been a sentence from Paul: "The wages of sin is death, but the gift of God is eternal life" (Romans 6 : 23).

2. THE RADICAL DISSIMILARITIES OF CHRISTIANITY

The foregoing comparison of the religions of the world has indicated ten specific points where there exist similarities between Christianity and other religions. Yet at each of these ten points certain dissimilarities seem to a Christian to indicate the superiority of Christianity.

There are three features of Christianity which cannot be paralleled anywhere among the religions of the world. In a comparison with all the religions of the world these three distinctive features of Christianity will be recognized as being those which Christians themselves throughout their history have regarded as essential.

(1) *The Character of God as a Loving Heavenly Father*

The idea that God is a "Father" is fairly simple, and it has been thought of in three other religions besides Christianity.

Zoroaster, in describing two of the six archangels, speaks of Ahura Mazda as the Father of Justice or Right, and also as the Father of Good Mind (Yasna, 44 : 3; 47 : 2, and Yasna, 31 : 8; 45 : 4, respectively). But Zoroastrianism never suggests that human beings might regard God as their Father.

In the sacred scriptures of Judaism there are twenty-eight passages where Jehovah is alluded to as a Father, but always as the Father of the people of Israel, or of "them that fear him" (Psalms 103 : 13); only once in its canonical scriptures does Judaism suggest universal fatherhood of Jehovah, even after Judaism had conceived of Jehovah in universal terms (Malachi 2 : 10).

In the earliest document of Hinduism the most important among the almost fourscore deities, Indra, is supplicated in various ways, even as being a "father (*pitar*), most fatherly of fathers" (*Rig Veda*, 4 : 17. 17). Yet that same Hindu deity is also represented elsewhere in that same document as being a drunken braggart, who boasts of his utter indifference to his human worshippers:

"Not as a mote within the eye
Count the five tribes of men to me!
Have I not drunk of soma juice!"   (*Rig Veda*, 10 : 119. 5.)
Griffith, *Hymns of the Rig Veda, Translated*, 2. 563.

And the same Hindu deity, Indra, is represented later in
the most philosophical of all the canonical scriptures of Hinduism as boasting of numerous specific deeds of treacherous
destructiveness which he did with impunity, and as assuring
his followers that they also will be uninjured by any deed
which they may do:

I slew the . . . son of Tvashtri. I delivered the Arunmukhas, ascetics, to the wild dogs. Transgressing many compacts, I transfixed the
people of Prahlada, . . . the Paulomas, . . . the Kalanjakas. Of
me, such a one as I was then, not a single hair was injured. So he
who understands me—by no deed of his is his world injured.
(*Kaushitaki Upanishad*, 3 : 1; translation, Hume, *TPU*, 320–321.)

The more lofty idea of deity as being a "Heaven-Father,"
is found in one notable instance among the eleven living religions of the world. One of the two deities of the sky in early
Hindu nature-worship, is designated six times in the *Rig Veda*
with the title "Dyaus-Pitar," which means precisely "Heaven-
Father." This Hindu deity belongs emphatically to the male
sex. He is generally coupled with another deity, who is his
counterpart, a female deity named "Prithivi-Matar" (meaning
"Earth-Mother"). Linguistically, the names of these two
deities occur in Sanskrit as a compound noun in the dual
number for designating the two parents of mankind. Thus, the
exact application of the Hindu idea of heaven as being a
"Father" is along the line of sexual paternity. However, so
minor is this particular deity in the Hindu pantheon, that
among the 1,028 hymns of the *Rig Veda*, there is not a single
hymn addressed to him alone. Indeed, subsequently the person of the heaven god, Dyaus, disappeared entirely from
Sanskrit literature, and even the gender of the noun became
changed into feminine as a common noun, designating simply
"day."

World-wide comparison shows that the very simple analogy

for God as being a "Father" has been used among the non-Christian religions only with a very limited application or with a very limited content. The noble moral idea that God is a loving, spiritual Father of all mankind, has been developed nowhere among sacred scriptures except in Christianity.

The *New Testament* is the only document among the canonical religious scriptures of the world which teaches that the Supreme Deity is a universal heavenly Father. One essential and unique feature of Christianity is the teaching that God is the wise, holy, serviceable Sovereign of the whole world, who in his love and righteousness experiences suffering for the sins of his human children, and who patiently and successfully is helping to redeem men from their sins into the likeness of his own perfect character.

(2) *The Character of the Founder as Son of God and Brother of All Men*

The nine founders among the eleven living religions in the world had characters which attracted many devoted followers during their own lifetime, and still larger numbers during the centuries of subsequent history. They were humble in certain respects, yet they were also confident of a great religious mission. Two of the nine, Mahavira and Buddha, were men so strongminded and self-reliant that, according to the records, they displayed no need of any divine help, though they both taught the inexorable cosmic law of Karma. They are not reported as having possessed any consciousness of a supreme personal deity. Yet they have been strangely deified by their followers. Indeed, they themselves have been worshipped, even with multitudinous idols.

All of the nine founders of religion, with the exception of Jesus Christ, are reported in their respective sacred scriptures as having passed through a preliminary period of uncertainty, or of searching for religious light. Confucius, late in life, confessed his own sense of shortcomings and his desire for further improvement in knowledge and character. All the founders of the non-Christian religions evinced inconsistencies in their personal character; some of them altered their practical policies under change of circumstances.

Jesus Christ alone is reported as having had a consistent God-consciousness, a consistent character himself, and a consistent program for his religion. The most remarkable and valuable aspect of the personality of Jesus Christ is the comprehensiveness and universal availability of his character, as well as its own loftiness, consistency, and sinlessness.

Jesus Christ seems to have grown up even as every human being should grow. The record is explicit that "he advanced in wisdom and in stature, and in favor with God and man" (Luke 2 : 52). Christians believe that he was thus thoroughly normal, yet also that he is ideally typical. He is the unique, yet the exemplary, combination of being clearly a son of man and also pre-eminently the Son of God. He grew in the flesh, yet he participated consciously in the Eternal, and he has made the superlative manifestation of God to the world. He is Elder Brother of all men, foremost as the pioneer of their faith, and the Captain of their salvation. He is unequalled by any other person who has ever lived upon earth, yet he possesses the qualities of personality which all persons should possess. Indeed, by the fellowship of his grace they will attain unto the perfection of his character.

(3) *The Work of a Divine Universal Holy Spirit*

Along with the character of God and the character of the Founder there is a third item in the characteristic Christian belief and in the characteristic Christian experience. All three items were taught by the Founder, as recorded in the sacred scriptures of Christianity. They form the main points in the summary formula of the Christian faith, which is used in admitting new members. They have been regarded as essentials of Christianity from its beginnings as a separate religion. And now by a comparison with all the other living religions in the world they are seen to be the markedly distinctive features of Christianity, even while the other religions have made certain approximations to these three essential and radically unique features of Christianity.

Zoroastrianism teaches that its deity, Ahura Mazda, though limited, is "a bountiful spirit," or else works through an agency which may be designated as "Bountiful Spirit" (Spenta Mainyu). But in either interpretation of the exact meaning of the crucial words in the Avestan document, Zoroastrianism teaches that the good Spirit is not really supreme, because from the beginning of time there exists a coequal evil spirit.

Confucianism teaches that the nature of man is aboriginally or divinely good; but Confucianism does not teach that in the efforts of man for complete goodness there is any help from God available for every person.

Judaism came the closest to Christianity in respect of the doctrine of the Spirit of God, but that doctrine occupies a very subordinate position in its sacred scripture, and has been practically neglected in the actual religious life of Judaism.

Christianity is the only religion which teaches as a doctrine of great practical as well as scriptural importance that there is at work in the world a divine universal Holy Spirit, indwelling, teaching, suggesting, reprimanding, inspiring, transforming, available for every individual who will open his heart to this divine inner influence. Jesus himself taught what every true Christian experiences—that there is a powerful divine agency active in the world, seeking to apply the principles of Jesus, and leading on to a fuller appreciation of truth.

3. AN EPITOME OF CHRISTIANITY AND OF THE WORLD'S RELIGIOUS ASPIRATIONS

These three essential and distinctive features of Christianity may be stated systematically in relation to God, the chief essential of all religion, as follows:

(a) In God there is something eternal. That aspect of God which perpetually is the creator and loving ruler of human life may best be known as "Father."

(b) In God there is something historic. That aspect of God

which has come most fully into the compass of a human life, in the gracious character of Jesus Christ, may best be known as his "Son."

(c) In God there is something progressive. That aspect of God which like a continual companion is leading human life forward may best be known as "Holy Spirit."

These three features of Christianity, on the one hand, are highly theoretical; they involve momentous theological implications. On the other hand, they are thoroughly practical; they may be understood and tested in experience. Together they constitute a comprehensive summary of what Christianity itself really is. But Christians also believe that these three Christian beliefs represent exactly the finest aspirations among the religions of the world; accordingly, together they constitute a prophetic fulfilment of the religious history of the world.

A compact statement of the essence of Christianity, and also of the blessing which Christianity seeks to give unto the world, has been formulated in the New Testament in the well-known benediction: "The grace of the Lord Jesus Christ and the love of God and the communion of the Holy Spirit be with you all" (II Corinthians 13 : 14).

BIBLIOGRAPHY

BIBLIOGRAPHY

I. GENERAL

In the nature of the case, the bibliography here offered is a very limited one. A much more inclusive, but still highly selected bibliography covering all the religions of the world, both past and present will be found in Section D of *A Guide To Historical Literature* to be published by The American Historical Association in 1959, and likely to be found in most reference libraries.

Sources and Encyclopedias

Sacred Books of the East, edited by MAX MÜLLER, 50 vols. (Oxford, 1879–1910.) Invaluable as a collection of sources. But contains only seven religions: Islam and Taoism, complete; Confucianism and Zoroastrianism, in large part; Jainism, in small part; Hinduism, 21 vols.; Buddhism, 10 vols.

Sacred Books and Early Literature of the East, edited by CHARLES F. HORNE, New York: Parke and Lipscomb, 1917. 14 vols. Less complete and lacking in notes and scholarly introductions such as found in *SBE*, but excellent for general reading in the sources.

Several anthologies containing at least some of the source writings from the major religious groups are available. Among them:

The Bible of the World, edited by ROBERT O. BALLOU, New York: Viking Press, 1939. A shorter selection is called *The Pocket Bible of the World*.

The Bibles of Mankind, edited by MIRZA AHMAD SOHRAB and topically arranged, New York: Universal Publishing Co., 1939.

BROWNE, LEWIS, *The World's Great Scriptures*, New York: The Macmillan Co., 1946.

HUME, ROBERT E., *The Treasure-House of the World's Religions*, arranged topically, New York: Charles Scribner's Sons, 1932.

BOUQUET, A. C., *Sacred Books of the World*, London: Penguin Books, paper bound.

FERM, VERGILIUS, *Encyclopedia of Religion*, New York: The Philosophical Library, 1945.

HASTINGS, J., *Encyclopædia of Religion and Ethics*. 13 vols. (Scribners and T. & T. Clark, 1913–1922.) Valuable for treatment of special topics.

Encyclopedia of Religion and Ethics, edited by SHAILER MATHEWS and G. B. SMITH, New York: The Macmillan Co., 1921.

General

Books dealing with some one or more aspects of all or several of the religions of the world

1. Archæology

    FINEGAN, JACK, *Archeology of the World's Religions*, Princeton: Princeton University Press, 1952.

2. Christianity and the Other Religions of the World

    KRAEMER, HENDRIK, *Religion and the Christian Faith*, Philadelphia: Westminster Press, 1957. A conservative view.

    TOYNBEE, ARNOLD, *Christianity Among the Religions of the World*, New York: Charles Scribner's Sons, 1957. A liberal view.

3. The Founders

    BRADEN, CHARLES S., *Jesus Compared, A Comparative Study of Jesus and Other Great Founders of Religion*, New York: Prentice Hall, Inc., 1957.

    BURROWS, MILLAR, *Founders of Great Religions*, New York: Charles Scribner's Sons, 1931.

4. The Future Life

    SNEATH, E. HERSHEY, *Religion and the Future Life*, New York: Fleming H. Revell, 1922.

5. The Gods

    HAYDON, EUSTACE A., *Biography of the Gods*, New York: The Macmillan Co., 1941.

6. The Idea of Salvation

    BRADEN, CHARLES S., *Man's Quest for Salvation*, Chicago: Willett, Clark and Co., 1941.

7. The Modern Trends

    BRADEN, CHARLES S., *Modern Tendencies in World Religions*, New York: The Macmillan Co., 1933.

    —— *War, Communism and World Religions*, New York: Harper and Brothers, 1953.

    HAYDON, EUSTACE A., *Modern Trends in World Religions*, Chicago: University of Chicago Press, 1934.

    WIDGERY, ALBAN G., *Living Religions and Modern Thought*, New York: Round Table Press, 1936.

8. The Scriptures
BRADEN, CHARLES S., *The Scriptures of Mankind*, New York: The Macmillan Co., 1952. An introduction to the various scriptures with bibliographies indicating translations into English and where found.

9. General:
HOCKING, W. E., *Living Religions and a World Faith*, New York: The Macmillan Co., 1940.

Some widely used texts

ATKINS, GAIUS GLENN, and BRADEN, CHARLES S., *Procession of the Gods*, New York: 3rd rev. ed., Harper and Brothers, 1948.

BRADEN, CHARLES S., *The World's Religions*, New York and Nashville: Abingdon-Cokesbury, rev. ed., 1954. Elementary.

ARCHER, JOHN C., *Faiths Men Live By*, New York: Ronald Press, rev. ed., 1958.

MOORE, GEORGE FOOT, *History of Religions*, 2 vols., New York: Charles Scribner's Sons, 1920, 1932. Scholarly and thorough. Still valuable.

MURPHY, JOHN, *Origins and History of Religions*, Manchester: University of Manchester Press, 1947.

NOSS, JOHN B., *Man's Religions*, rev. ed., New York: The Macmillan Co., 1956.

SOPER, E. D., *Religions of Mankind*, 3rd rev. ed., New York: Abingdon Press, 1951.

HUTCHINSON, JOHN ALEXANDER, and MARTIN, JAMES ALFRED, JR., *Ways of Faith*, New York: Ronald Press, 1953.

BURTT, EDWIN A., *Man Seeks the Divine*, New York: Harper and Brothers, 1956.

JURJI, EDWARD J. (editor), *The Great Religions of the World*, Princeton: Princeton University Press, 1946.

II. TRANSLATIONS OF THE SACRED SCRIPTURES OF HINDUISM

Rig Veda: GRIFFITH, R. T. H. *Hymns of the Rig Veda*. 2 vols. (Benares, 1896.)

Atharva Veda: WHITNEY and LANMAN. 2 vols. in "Harvard Oriental Series." (1905.)

Satapatha Brahmana: EGGELING, J. 5 vols., *SBE,* 12, 26, 41, 43, 44. (1882–1900.)

Aitareya and Kaushitaki Brahmanas: KEITH, A. B., in "Harvard Oriental Series." (1920.)

Upanishads: MAX MÜLLER, twelve in *SBE,* vols. 1 and 15. (1879–1884.)

HUME, R. E., *The Thirteen Principal Upanishads.* (Oxford, 1921.)

S. RADHAKRISHNAN, *The Upanishads,* edited with introduction, text, translation and notes, New York: Harper and Brothers, 1953.

Laws of Manu: BUHLER, G. *SBE,* vol. 25. (1886.)

Bhagavad Gita: BARNETT, L. D., in *Temple Classics.*

ARNOLD, SIR EDWIN, *The Song Celestial,* in "Harvard Classics."

DAVIES, J., in "Trübner's Oriental Series."

There have been many English translations of the *Bhagavad Gita.* Among the more recent are: Franklin Edgerton, *The Bhagavad Gita,* 2 vols., Cambridge: Harvard University Press, 1946. This includes the Edwin Arnold Translation; also: S. Radhakrishnan, *The Bhagavad Gita,* with Sanskrit text and notes, New York: Harper and Brothers, 1948.

Epics: DUTT, R. C., *The Ramayana and the Mahabharata, Condensed into English Verse,* a free paraphrase of selections, "Everyman's Library."

Not all the sacred scriptures of Hinduism have been translated into English. In the translated portions the number of pages amounts to some twenty thousand or more. Representative selections from the whole range of their sacred literature will be found in the anthologies mentioned in sect. I and in:

LIN YUTANG, *The Wisdom of China and India,* New York: Random House, 1942.

MAC NICOL, NICOL (editor), *Hindu Scripture,* London: J. M. Dent and Co., Everyman's edition, 1938.

A Source Book in Indian Philosophy, edited by S. RADHAKRISHNAN and CHARLES A. MOORE, Princeton: Princeton Press, 1957. Contains selections particularly relating to philosophic Hinduism.

FARQUHAR, J. N. *An Outline of the Religious Literature of India,* London: Oxford University Press, 1920. Lists all the sacred writings of Hindus, Buddhists, Jains and Sikhs, and the translations in existence at the time of its publication.

HINDUISM

An excellent bibliography on Hinduism in general, and a valuable set of selections from the philosophic writings of India, illustrating the thought of philosophic Hinduism, is to be found in *A Source Book in Indian Philosophy*, edited by s. RADHAKRISHNAN and CHARLES A. MOORE, Princeton: Princeton University Press, 1957.

DAS GUPTA, s. n., *Hindu Mysticism*, Chicago: Open Court, 1927, a brief survey of Hinduism by a distinguished Indian philosopher.

FARQUHAR, J. N., *A Primer of Hinduism*, London: Oxford University Press, 1912.

———— *The Crown of Hinduism*, London: Oxford University Press, 1913.

GRISWOLD, H. D., *The Religion of the Rig Veda*, London: Oxford University Press, 1923.

HOPKINS, E. W., *The Religions of India*, Chicago: Ginn and Co., 1898.

———— *The Ethics of India*, New Haven: Yale University Press, 1924.

MAC NICOL, NICOL, *Living Religions of India*, London: Student Christian Movement Press, 1934.

MORGAN, KENNETH W. (editor), *The Religion of the Hindus*, New York: Ronald Press, 1953. The various chapters are written by distinguished Indian scholars. Includes also a representative selection of portions of the Hindu Scriptures.

PRATT, JAMES B., *India and Its Faiths*, New York: Houghton Mifflin, 1915.

SARMA, D. S., *The Hindu Renaissance*, Madras, 1946. An account of some of the major reforms within Hinduism as reflected in the work of several outstanding Hindus of the nineteenth and twentieth centuries, by a distinguished Indian scholar and teacher.

WHITEHEAD, HENRY, *The Village Gods of Southern India*, London: Oxford University Press, 1916. Discusses religion at the village level in India.

III. SACRED SCRIPTURES OF JAINISM

Out of the 33, or 44, or 81 canonical documents there are translations of only 4 in two volumes of the *Sacred Books of the East*: SBE, 22: *Acharanga Sutra and Kalpa Sutra*.

SBE, 45: *Uttaradhyayana Sutra and Sutrakritanga Sutra.*

HOERNLE, R., *Uvasagadaso, Text and Translation.* 2 vols. (Calcutta, Bibliotheca Indica, 1888–1890.)

BARNETT, L. D., *Antagadadaso and Anuttaravovaiyadasao.* (London, Oriental Translation Fund, 1907.)

JAINISM

STEVENSON, MRS. S. *The Heart of Jainism.* (Oxford, 1915.)

STEVENSON, MRS. S. *Notes on Modern Jainism with Special Reference to the Svetambara, Digambara and Sthanakvasi Sects.* (Oxford, 1910.)

BUHLER, J. G. *On the Indian Sect of the Jains.* (London, Luzac, 1903.)

JAINI, J. *Outlines of Jainism.* (Cambridge, 1916.)

HASTINGS. *ERE,* articles "Ajivakas" and "Jainism."

IV. SACRED SCRIPTURES OF BUDDHISM

Portions of the *Tripitaka* have been translated in five volumes in the *SBE;* in fourteen volumes of the *Sacred Books of the Buddhists,* and in twenty-four volumes of the "Pali Text Society Translation Series."

Dhamma-pada: WAGISWARA, W. D. C. and K. J. SAUNDERS, *The Buddha's Way of Virtue.* (Dutton, 1912.) "Wisdom of the East Series." Important non-canonical documents in five volumes of the *SBE,* 19, 21, 35, 36, 49.

Extensive selections from canonical and non-canonical documents in H. C. WARREN, *Buddhism in Translations,* 1909, 1923, in "Harvard Oriental Series."

Brief selections from canonical and non-canonical documents, in K. J. SAUNDERS, *Heart of Buddhism.* (Oxford, 1915.)

LIN YUTANG, editor, *The Wisdom of India and China,* New York: Random House, 1942. Contains a good selection of material from the Buddhist scriptures.

CARUS, PAUL, *The Gospel of Buddhism,* Chicago: Open Court, 1921.

HAMILTON, CLARENCE H., *Buddhism, A Religion of Infinite Compassion,* New York: The Liberal Arts Press, 1952. Representative selection from Buddhist scriptures.

WOODWARD, F. L., *Some Sayings of the Buddha,* according to the Pali Canon, London: Oxford University Press, 1925.

A complete listing of the books of the Pali Canon is to be found in EDWARD J. THOMAS, *The Life of Buddha as Legend and History,* New York: Barnes and Noble, 1952.

FARQUHAR, J. N., *An Outline of the Religious Literature of India* lists most of the Buddhist scriptures and indicates translations available to date of publication.

The entire list of translations of both the *Sacred Books of the Buddhists,* and the Pali Text Society down to 1956 will be found in *A Source Book in Indian Philosophy,* edited by S. RADHAKRISHNAN and CHARLES A. MOORE, Princeton: Princeton University Press, 1957, pp. 658–659.

BUDDHISM

COOMARASWAMY, ANANDA, *Buddha and the Gospel of Buddhism,* New York: G. P. Putnam's Sons, 1916.

CONZE, EDWARD, *Buddhism, Its Essence and Development,* New York: The Philosophical Library, 1954.

ELIOT, SIR CHARLES, *Hinduism and Buddhism,* 3 vols., London, Routledge and Kegan Paul, 1954. Earlier edition, E. Arnold and Co., 1921.

MONIER-WILLIAMS, SIR MONIER. *Buddhism in Its Connection with Brahmanism and Hinduism, and in Its Contrast with Christianity.* (Murray, 1889.)

MORGAN, KENNETH W. (editor), *The Path of the Buddha,* New York: Ronald Press, 1956. Similar to the book on Hinduism, the various chapters written by distinguished Buddhist leaders and scholars.

PRATT, J. B., *The Pilgrimage of Buddhism,* New York: The Macmillan Co., 1927.

RHYS-DAVIDS, T. W., *Buddhism, Being a Sketch of the Life and Teachings of Gautama, the Buddha.* 1st ed., 1877; rev. ed., 1914. (London, Society for Propagating Christian Knowledge.)

THOMAS ED. J., *The Life of Buddha as Legend and History,* New York: Barnes and Noble, 1952.
———— *History of Buddhist Thought,* London: Kegan, Paul, Trench and Co., 1933. Good bibliography.

SAUNDERS, KENNETH, J. *Gotama Buddha, A Biography based on the Canonical Books of the Theravadin,* New York: The Association Press, 1920.

SAUNDERS, KENNETH, J. *Buddhism and Buddhists of Southern Asia,*
New York: The Macmillan Co., 1923.

V. SACRED SCRIPTURES OF SIKHISM

Granth, "The Book," or *Granth Sahib,* "The Lord Book."

TRUMPP, ERNST. *The Adi Granth, or Holy Scriptures of the Sikhs.*
(Trübner, 1877.)

MACAULIFFE, M. A. Translations scattered through six volumes of
The Sikh Religion: Its Gurus, Sacred Writings, and Authors. (Oxford, 1909.)

SIKHISM

FIELD, DOROTHY. *The Religion of the Sikhs.* ("Wisdom of the East
Series," 1914.)

HASTINGS, *ERE.* Articles: "Granth," 6 : 389–390; "Nanak," 9 : 181–
184; "Sikhs," 11 : 507–511.

THAPAR, SEWARAM SINGH. *A Critical Study of the Life and Teachings
of Sri Guru Nanak Dev, the Founder of Sikhism.* (Rawalpindi,
1904.)

COURT, HENRY. *History of the Sikhs: or Translation of the Sikkhan
de Raj di Vikhia.* (Lahore, 1888.)

ARCHER, JOHN CLARK. *The Sikhs.* (Princeton University Press, 1946.)

SINGH, KUSHWANT, *The Sikhs,* London: George Allen and Unwin,
1953. Useful for the more modern movements and recent history of
the Sikhs.

VI. SACRED SCRIPTURES
OF CONFUCIANISM

Mostly in LEGGE, J. *The Chinese Classics: Text, Trans., Notes.* 8
vols. (Trübner and Oxford.)

The Five Classics

Shu King, Book of History.

SBE, 3 : 31–272.

LEGGE, *Chinese Classics: Text, Trans.* 2 vols.

OLD, W. G. (Theosophical Society, 1904.)

Shi King, Book of Poetry.

LEGGE. *She King.* (Trübner, 1876.)

JENNINGS, W., in Sir John Lubbock's *Hundred Books*. (London, Routledge, 1891.)

ALLEN, C. F. R. (Trübner, 1891.)

Selections in *SBE*, 3 : 273–446.

I King, Book of Changes, or Divination.

SBE, 16 : 1–442.

Li Ki, Book of Rites.

SBE, vols. 27 and 28.

Chun Chiu, Spring and Autumn.

LEGGE, *Chinese Classics: Text, Trans.* 2 vols.

The Four Books

Lun Yu, Analects of Confucius.

Not translated in *SBE*.

LEGGE, *Chinese Classics: Text, Trans.* (1861.)

LEGGE, *Life and Teachings of Confucius.* (1875.)

LEGGE, *Chinese Classics.* (Alden, 1885.)

SOOTHILL, W. E. (Shanghai, Mission Press, 1910.)

JENNINGS, W., in Sir John Lubbock's *Hundred Books*. (London, Routledge, 1895.)

LYALL, L. A. (Longmans, 1909.)

KU HUNG-MING. (Shanghai, Kelly & Walsh, 1898.)

WALEY, ARTHUR, *The Analects of Confucius,* New York: The Macmillan Co., 1939.

Ta Hsio, Great Learning.

LEGGE, *Chinese Classics*, vol. 1.

As *Li Ki*, chap. 39; *SBE*, 28 : 411–424.

Chung Yung, Doctrine of the Mean.

LEGGE, *Chinese Classics*, vol. 1.

KU HUNG-MING, *The Conduct of Life,* in "Wisdom of the East Series." (Murray, 1912.)

As *Li Ki*, chap. 28; *SBE*, 300–329.

Mencius.

LEGGE, *Chinese Classics*, vol. 1.

LEGGE, *Life and Works of Mencius.* (1875.)

FABER, *Mind of Mencius.* (Boston, Mifflin, 1882.)

A Sixth "Classic" sometimes recognized

Hsiao King, Book of Filial Piety.

SBE, 3. 465–488.

CHEN, *Book of Filial Duty* in "Wisdom of East."

CONFUCIANISM

Most books on Chinese religions deal with Taoism also, and some with Buddhism as well. Older books are:

GILES, H. A. *Confucianism and Its Rivals.* (1915.)

LEGGE. *The Religions of China.* (Scribners, 1882.)

SOOTHILL, W. E. *The Three Religions of China.* (1913.)

DOUGLAS, R. K. *Confucianism and Taoism.* (1911.)

Among the more recent books are:

CREEL, H. G., *The Birth of China,* New York: The John Day Co. 1937.

—— *Confucius, The Man and the Myth,* The John Day Co., 1949.

HUGHES, E. R., *The Religion of China,* London: Hutchinson House, 1950.

LIN YUTANG, *The Wisdom of Confucius,* New York: The Modern Library, 1938.

SHRYOCK, JOHN K., *Origin and Development of the State Cult of Confucius,* New York: The Century Co., 1932.

WEBER, MAX, *The Religion of China,* translated from the German by Hans Gerth, Glencoe, Ill.: The Free Press, 1951.

WING-TSIT CHAN, *Religious Trends in Modern China,* New York: Columbia University Press, 1953.

WEI, FRANCIS C. M., *The Spirit of Chinese Culture,* New York: Charles Scribner's Sons, 1947.

YANG, Y. C., *China's Religious Heritage,* New York: Abingdon, 1943.

VII. TRANSLATIONS OF THE SACRED SCRIPTURES OF TAOISM

The *Tao Teh King* has been translated many times into English. Among the older translations are:

SBE, 39 : 47–124.

CARUS. *Lao-tze's Tao-Teh-King, Chinese-English.* (Chicago, Open Court, 1898.) A new abridged edition, *The Canon of Reason and Virtue, Being Lao-tze's Tao-Teh-King,* 1913.

GODDARD and BOREL. *Lao-tzu's Tao and Wu-Wei.* (New York, Brentano, 1919, pp. 11–53.)

PARKER, E. H. *China and Religion,* pp. 271–301. (New York, Dutton, 1905.) Also in *Studies in Chinese Religion,* pp. 96–131.

Among the more recent translations are:

CHU TA-KAO, *The Tao-Teh-King,* in *The Bible of the World,* edited by Robert O. Ballou, New York: The Viking Press, 1939.

LIN YUTANG, *The Book of Tao,* in *Wisdom of China and India,* New York: Random House, 1942. Also in *The Wisdom of Laotse,* The Modern Library.

WALEY, ARTHUR, *The Way and its Power,* London: George Allen and Unwin, 1934.

The "Tai-Shang Kan-Ying Pien"

SBE, 40 : 235–246, *Tractate of Actions and Their Retributions.*

CARUS and SUZUKI. *Treatise on Response and Retribution.* (Chicago, Open Court, 1906.)

DOUGLAS. *Confucianism and Taouism,* pp. 257–271.

WEBSTER, JAMES. *Book of Rewards and Punishments.* (Shanghai, Mission Press.)

WIEGER, L. *Moral Tenets and Customs in China,* pp. 245–259. (Ho-Kien, China, 1913.)

Kwang-Tze, the Most Important Subsidiary Work

SBE, 39 : 127–392; 40 : 1–232.

GILES, H. A. *Chuang Tzu.* (London, Quaritch, 1889.)

GILES, L. *Musings of a Chinese Mystic* in "Wisdom of the East Series." (London, Murray, 1911.)

TAOISM

See chapters in various books.

DOUGLAS. *Confucianism and Taouism,* pp. 173–287.

LEGGE, J. *The Religions of China,* pp. 157–236.

DE GROOT. *Religion of the Chinese,* pp. 132–162.

SOOTHILL, W. E. *The Three Religions of China.* (1913.)

See other books listed under Confucianism, most of which deal also with Taoism. To these should be added:

DORÉ, ENRI, *Researches into Chinese Superstitions,* 10 vols. Shanghai, 1914–1933.

VIII. SACRED SCRIPTURES OF SHINTO

Ko-ji-ki. "Records of Ancient Matters."

CHAMBERLAIN, B. H. In *Transactions of the Asiatic Society of Japan.* (Tokyo, Supplement to vol. 10, 1882; reprinted 1906 and 1920.)

Nihon-gi. "Chronicles of Japan."

ASTON, W. G. In *Transactions and Proceedings of the Japan Society.* (London, Trübner, 1896.)

Yengi-shiki. "Institutes of the Period of Yengi."

Selections from the Nori-to: articles, "Ancient Japanese Rituals," in *Transactions of the Asiatic Society of Japan;* SATOW, vol. 7 (1879), pp. 95–126, 393–434; vol. 9 (1881), pp. 183–211; FLORENZ, vol. 27 (1899), pp. 1–112.

Manyo-shiu. "Collection of Ten-Thousand Leaves." Selections by Aston, W. G., in *History of Japanese Literature,* pp. 36–48; Chamberlain, B. H., in *Classical Poetry of the Japanese* (Trübner, 1880); in *Library of the World's Best Literature,* vol. 14, pp. 8157–8161; in *The World's Great Classics: Oriental Literature, Japanese,* vol. 2, pp. 223–267 (New York, Colonial Press, 1899.)

SHINTO

ASTON, W. G. *Shinto, the Way of the Gods.* (Longmans, 1905.) Abridged into the following book.

—— *Shinto, the Ancient Religion of Japan.* ("Religions Ancient and Modern Series," 1910.)

HOLTOM, D. C. *The National Faith of Japan: A Study in Modern Shinto.* (London, Kegan Paul, 1938.)

HOLTOM, D. C. *Modern Japan and Shinto Nationalism: A Study of Present Trends in Japanese Religions.* (Chicago, University of Chicago Press, 1943.) A volume in the Haskell (Oberlin) Lectures in Comparative Religion.

HOLTOM, D. C. "The Political Philosophy of Modern Shinto: A Study of the State Religion of Japan," in *Transactions of the Asiatic Society of Japan*, vol. XLIX (1922), part 2, pp. 1–325.

KATO, GENCHI. *A Study of Shinto, The Religion of the Japanese Nation.* (Tokyo, Meiji Japan Society, 1926.)

Religions in Japan, Compiled and edited by General Headquarters, SCAP, Tokyo, 1948. Includes various SCAP directives concerning religion during the Occupation and much useful information in respect to the various Buddhist and Shinto sects.

IX. SACRED SCRIPTURES OF JUDAISM

(Easily accessible as the *Old Testament* of Christianity)

The Holy Scriptures according to the Massoretic Text: A New Translation. By a committee of Jewish scholars. (Philadelphia, Jewish Publication Society, 1917.)

KENT, C. F. *The Student's Old Testament*, 5 vols. (Scribners, 1904–1914.)

MOFFATT, J. *The Old Testament: A New Translation*, 2 vols. (Hodder & Stoughton, 1924; or Doran, 1924–1925.)

The Complete Bible, An American Translation. The Old Testament translated by J. M. Powis Smith and a group of scholars. Chicago: The University of Chicago Press, 1939.

The "Talmud"

The Babylonian Talmud, Translated with notes, glossary and index. Edited by Rabbi I. Epstein, 35 vols., London: Soncino Press, 1935–48. Index Vol., 1952.

There are several books containing selections from the *Talmud,* among them:

COHEN, A. *Everyman's Talmud,* London: J. M. Dent and Sons, 1934.

Talmudic Anthology, selected and edited by Louis I. Newman and Samuel Spitz, New York: Berman House, 1945.

See also anthologies in Sect. I.

JUDAISM

KOHLER, K. *Jewish Theology, Systematically and Historically Considered.* (Macmillan, 1918.)

ABRAHAMS, ISRAEL. *Some Permanent Values in Judaism* (Oxford, 1924.)

MOORE, G. F. *Judaism*, 3 vols. (Cambridge, Massachusetts, Harvard University Press. 1930.)

SNAITH, N. H. *The Distinctive Ideas of the Old Testament*. (London, Epworth Press. 1945.)

OESTERLY, W. O. E. and ROBINSON, T. H. *Hebrew Religion, Its Origin and Development*. London: S.P.C.K., 2nd rev. ed., 1937.

BARON, SALO W., *A Social and Religious History of the Jews*, 3 vols., New York: Columbia University Press, 1952–.

MONTEFIORE, CLAUDE G., *The Old Testament and After*, London: The Macmillan Co., 1923. From the viewpoint of a liberal Jewish scholar.

The Jewish Encyclopedia, 12 vols., New York and London: Funk and Wagnalls, 1901–1906. Authoritative as of 1906.

The Universal Jewish Encyclopedia, edited by Isaac Lanman, 10 vols., New York: 1939–1943. More popular than the older encyclopedia.

X. SACRED SCRIPTURES OF ZOROASTRIANISM

I. Yasna, "Worship" or "Sacrifice"

MILLS, L. H. *Sacred Books of the East*, 31 : 1–332.

BLEECK, A. H. *Avesta: The Religious Books of the Parsees, from Spiegel's German Translation*. (Hertford, Austin, 1884.) Vol. II, pp. 26–141.

GATHAS, Psalms of Zoroaster Himself. (Constitute seventeen chapters of the Yasna.)

MOULTON, J. H. *Early Zoroastrianism*, pp. 344–390. (Williams & Norgate, 1913.)

GUTHRIE, K. S. *The Hymns of Zoroaster*. (Brooklyn, Comparative Literature Press, 1914.) Transliterated text, translation, dictionary, and concordance.

MILLS, L. H. *SBE*, 31 : 1–194.

MILLS, L. H. *The Gathas of Zoroaster in Metre and Rhythm*. (Oxford, 1900.)

II. Visparad, Invocations to "All the Lords"

MILLS, L. H. *SBE*, 31 : 333–364.

BLEECK, A. H. *Spiegel's Avesta*, 2 : 5–24.

III. Vendidad, "Law against the Demons"

DARMSTETER, J. *SBE*, 4 : 1–240.

BLEEK, A. H. *Spiegel's Avesta*, 1 : 1–156.

The foregoing three main divisions constitute the larger and more important part of the *Avesta*, reserved for priests.

IV. Yasts, "Worship Hymns"

DARMSTETER, J. *SBE*, 23 : 21–345.

BLEECK, A. H. *Spiegel's Avesta*, 3 : 21–135.

V. Khorda Avesta, "Little Avesta"

BLEECK, A. H. *Spiegel's Avesta*, 3 : 1–192.

ZOROASTRIANISM

JACKSON, A. V. W. *Zoroaster, the Prophet of Ancient Iran.* (Macmillan, 1901.)

MOULTON, J. H. *Early Zoroastrianism.* (Williams & Norgate, 1913.)

——— *Early Religious Poetry of Persia.* (Cambridge, 1911.)

——— *The Treasure of the Magi, a Study of Modern Zoroastrianism.* (Oxford, 1917.)

HAUG, M. *Essays on the Sacred Language, Writings and Religion of the Parsis.* (Trübner, 1878.)

DHALLA, M. N. *Zoroastrian Theology from the Earliest Times to the Present Time.* (New York, 1914.)

GUTHRIE, K. S. *The Life of Zoroaster in the Words of His Own Hymns.* (Brooklyn, Comparative Literature Press, 1914.)

DAWSON, MILES M., *The Ethical Religion of Zoroaster*, New York: The Macmillan Co., 1931.

HENNING, W. B., *Zoroaster, Politician or Witch Doctor*, London: Oxford University Press, 1950.

HERZFELD, ERNST, *Zoroaster and His World*, 2 vols., Princeton: Princeton University Press, 1947.

XI. SACRED SCRIPTURES OF ISLAM, OR MOHAMMEDANISM

RODWELL, J. M. *The Koran*, in "Everyman's Library." Rearranges the chapters in probable chronological order. Probably the handiest translation.

PALMER, E. H. *The Quran. SBE,* vols. 6 and 9. Verse divisions not indicated, except every fifth.

ALI, MUHAMMAD. "The Holy Quran, Arabic Text, Translation, Notes." (*Islamic Review,* Woking, England, 1917.) Notable reinterpretations by a liberally educated, devout Muslim.

FADL, MIRZA ABUL. *The Quran, Arabic Text and English Translation.* (Allahabad, 1911, 2 vols.)

SALE, GEORGE. Many editions since its first appearance in 1734; valuable commentary.

The Meaning of the Glorious Koran, translated by Marmaduke Pickthall, an English-speaking Muslim. Now available in paperback edition.

There are also various sectarian Muslim translations, e. g., *The Holy Qur'an,* Arabic Text and English Translation by Maulawi Sher'Ali, and published under the auspices of the Head of the Ahmadiyya Movement in Islam, at Rabwah, West Pakistan: Oriental and Religious Publishing Co., 1955. Contains a lengthy introduction by the Head of the Movement.

Selections from the "Koran"

STANTON, H. U. W., in "Texts for Students Series" (London, Society for Promoting Christian Knowledge. Also New York, Macmillan, 1922.)

WOLLASTON, A. N. *The Religion of the Koran,* in "Wisdom of the East Series." (1911.)

Selections from the Traditions

LANE-POOLE, S. *Speeches and Table-Talk of the Prophet Mohammed,* in "Golden Treasury Series." (London, 1882.)

MUHAMMAD ALI, *A Manual of Hadith,* Lahore: Ahmadiyya Anjuman isha-at-i-Islam, 1945.

ISLAM, OR MOHAMMEDANISM

HUGHES, T. P. *Dictionary of Islam.* (London, Allen, 1885.)

The Encyclopedia of Islam, 4 vols., with Supplement, Leiden: 1913–1938. New edition now in process, 1954–.

The Shorter Encyclopedia of Islam, edited by Gibb and Kraemers, Leiden, 1954.

There are many biographies of the Prophet, in English and other European languages, some scholarly, some popular, or semi-popular. An older, much used one is:

MUIR, SIR WILLIAM, *The Life of Mohammed,* 1 vol., Edinburgh: Grant, 1912.

A quite recent study is:

WATT, MONTGOMERY, *Mohammed at Mecca,* Oxford: Clarendon Press, 1953.
———— *Mohammed at Medina,* Oxford: Clarendon Press, 1956.

Two by Muslims are:

BENGALEE, M. R., *Life of Mohammed,* Chicago: Moslem Sunrise Press, 1941.

IKBAL ALI SHAH, *Mohammed the Prophet,* London: Wright and Brown, 1932.

Others who have written of the Prophet are: Washington Irving, Thomas Carlyle, Tor Andrae, Emile Dermenghem, R. V. C. Bodley, R. F. Dibble, and so forth.

ALI, AMEER, *The Spirit of Islam,* London: Christophers, 1922.

ARNOLD, T. W., *The Preaching of Islam,* Oxford: The Clarendon Press, 1913.

CRAGG, KENNETH, *The Call of the Minaret,* New York: Oxford University Press, 1956. Largely contemporary study, and in relation to Christianity.

DONALDSON, DWIGHT M., *The Shi'ite Religion,* London: Luzac and Co., 1933.
———— *Studies in Moslem Ethics,* London, 1953.

GIBB, H. A. R., *Modern Trends in Islam,* Chicago: University of Chicago Press, 1947.

HURGRONJE, C. S., *Mohammedanism,* New York: G. P. Putnam, 1916.

LEVY, R., *The Social Structure of Islam,* Cambridge: Cambridge University Press, 1957. A new one-volume edition of the former *Sociology of Islam,* 2 vols.

NICHOLSON, R. A., *Studies in Islamic Mysticism,* Cambridge: University Press, 1921. See also various books by A. J. Arberry on Sufis and Sufism.

STANTON, H. U. W., *The Teaching of the Qur'an,* New York: The Macmillan Co., 1919.

ZWEMER, SAMUEL M., *Across the World of Islam,* New York: The Macmillan Co., 1926. Out of date in respect to many aspects of the Muslim world, but valuable in showing the world-wide extent of Islam.

XII. SACRED SCRIPTURES OF CHRISTIANITY

Translations of the *Bible* most used by Protestants:

King James, or Authorized Version. (1611)

English Revised Version. (1885)

American Revised Version. (1901)

Revised Standard Version of the Bible, by thirty-one scholars appointed by the International Council of Religious Education. (New York. Nelson; *New Testament,* 1946, *Old Testament,* 1952)

Translation of the *Bible* used in the Roman Catholic Church:

DOUAY BIBLE, translated from Latin translation, the Vulgate; *Old Testament,* first published at Douay, 1609; *New Testament* at Rheims, 1582.

Some other modern translations of the *Bible* from among more than a score such already published:

KENT, C. F. *The Historical Bible,* 6 vols. (New York and London, Scribners, 1908–1916.)

MOFFATT, JAMES. *The Holy Bible: A New Translation,* 3 vols. (New York and London, Harper, 1913–1925.)

SMITH, J. M. P., and GOODSPEED, E. J. *The Complete Bible: An American Translation.* (University of Chicago, 1939.)

KNOX, MONSIGNOR RONALD A., *The Holy Bible,* London: Burns and Oates, 1955. A translation from the Latin Vulgate in the light of Hebrew and Greek originals. Authorized by the hierarchy of England and Wales and the hierarchy of Scotland. Roman Catholic.

Some selections from the *Bible* from among more than a score such already published:

KENT, C. F., and others. *The Shorter Bible.* (New York and London, Scribners, 1918.)

NAIRNE, ALEXANDER, editor. *The Cambridge Shorter Bible.* (Cambridge, England, University Press, 1928.)

GOODSPEED, E. J. and SMITH, J. M. P. *The Short Bible.* (University of Chicago Press, 1933.)

HAMMOND, MRS. EMILY. *The Golden Treasury of the Bible.* (New York, Bible Society, 1940.)

The Bible Designed to be Read as Living Literature, edited by E. S. BATES, New York; Simon and Schuster, 1936.

The Dartmouth Bible, edited by ROY B. CHAMBERLAIN and HERMAN FELDMAN, New York: Houghton Mifflin Co., 1950. Both eliminate duplicate material. The latter combines the four gospels into one continuous narrative, and includes useful introductions and notes.

Some modern translations of the *New Testament:*

WEYMOUTH, R. F. *The New Testament in Modern Speech.* (Boston, Pilgrim Press, and London, Clarke, 1904.)

MOFFATT, JAMES. *The New Testament: A New Translation.* (London, Hodder & Stoughton, and New York, Doran, 1913 and frequently.)

GOODSPEED, E. J. *The New Testament: An American Translation.* (University of Chicago Press, 1923.)

MONTGOMERY, MRS. HELEN. *Centenary Translation of the New Testament.* (Chicago, American Baptist Publication Society, 1924.)

New Testament, The Revised Standard Version, by nine scholars, appointed by the International Council of Religious Education. (New York, Nelson. Published 1946.)

Two new Catholic translations are:

KNOX, MONSIGNOR RONALD A., *The New Testament,* New York: Sheed and Ward, 1944.

The Rheims New Testament, revised by Roman Catholic scholars under the patronage of the Confraternity of Christian Doctrine, Paterson, N.J.: St Anthony Guild Press, 1947.

J. B. Phillips has translated the Pauline letters under the title *Letters to Young Churches,* New York: The Macmillan Co., 1948, and *The Gospels Translated into Modern English,* New York, The Macmillan Co., 1953, a rather free rendering in vernacular English. Also the book of Acts as *The Young Church in Action,* New York: The Macmillan Co., 1955; and *The Book of Revelation,* New York: The Macmillan Co., 1957. These four titles now combined in one volume under title, *The New Testament in Modern English,* New York, The Macmillan Co., 1958.

CHRISTIANITY

Concerning Jesus

An endless stream of books about Jesus continues to appear, written from every possible point of view, scholarly, critical, devotional, popular, conservative, liberal, radical, Jewish, Protestant, Catholic, some stressing his humanity, some his divinity. A few typical books are:

BACON, BENJAMIN W., *Jesus, Son of God,* New York: Henry Holt Co., 1930.

BAILLIE, JOHN, *The Place of Jesus Christ in Modern Christianity,* Charles Scribner's Sons, New York, 1929.

BRANSCOMB, HARVIE, *The Teachings of Jesus,* Nashville: Cokesbury Press, 1931.

CASE, SHIRLEY J., *Jesus, A New Biography,* Chicago: The University of Chicago Press, 1933. Extreme liberal.

GOODSPEED, EDGAR J., *A Life of Jesus,* New York: Harper and Brothers, 1950.

GUIGNEBERT, CHARLES A., *Jesus,* London: Kegan Paul, Trench and Trübner, 1935.

KLAUSNER, JOSEPH, *Jesus of Nazareth,* New York: The Macmillan Co., 1929. By a great Jewish scholar.

PAPINI, GIOVANNI, *The Life of Christ,* translated by Dorothy Canfield Fisher, New York: Harcourt, 1923. A popular life by a Roman Catholic.

SCOTT, ERNEST J., *The Ethical Teachings of Jesus,* New York: The Macmillan Co., 1929.

The History of the Church

ANGUS, S., *The Mystery Religions and Christianity,* New York: Charles Scribner's Sons, 1925.

BEVAN, E. R., *Christianity,* London: Home University Library of Modern Knowledge, Butterworth, 1932.

CRAIG, CLARENCE TUCKER, *The Beginning of Christianity,* Nashville: Abingdon-Cokesbury Press, 1943.

GOGUEL, MAURICE, *The Birth of Christianity,* London: George Allen and Unwin, 1950.

LATOURETTE, KENNETH S., *A History of Christianity,* New York: Harper and Brothers, 1953. Extensive bibliographies on every period.

MC SORLEY, JOSEPH, *An Outline of Church History by Centuries,* London: Herder, 1948. By a Roman Catholic scholar.

SWEET, WILLIAM W., *The Story of Religion in America,* New York: Harper and Brothers, rev. ed., 1950. Extensive bibliographies.

BRADEN, CHARLES S., *These Also Believe,* New York: The Macmillan Co., 1949. A study of minority religious groups in America.

CLARK, ELMER T., *The Small Sects of America*, New York: Abingdon Press, rev. ed., 1949. Brief description of some 200 sects.

ELLIS, JOHN TRACY, *American Catholicism*, Chicago: The University of Chicago Press, 1955. By a Catholic scholar.

Extensive bibliographies of every aspect of the development of the Christian Church will be found in *A Bibliographical Guide to the History of Christianity*, by S. J. Case, *et al.*, Chicago: The University of Chicago Press, 1931, and the most recent edition of *A Guide to Historical Literature*, published by the American Historical Association, New York, Section of the History of Religion. In these will be found books on general church history, the history of Christian thought, Christian art, music, the liturgy, literature, philosophy, ethics, biography, mysticism, and so forth, as well as an account of the church in various areas, its missionary outreach, and the modern movements toward church unity.

QUESTIONS

QUESTIONS

What other approaches to the study of religion would be profitable besides the nine which are mentioned in the first chapter of this book?

Which religions are located now chiefly in the land of their origin?

Which religions have spread notably beyond the land of their origin?

Which religions started with a conscious dependence upon, and continuation of, a previous religion? In what respects? With what results?

Which religions started in direct opposition to other religions? In what respects? With what results?

Which religion was most eclectic, consciously attempting to adjust itself to pre-existent religions? In what respects? With what results?

Which five religions started as a conscious attempt to improve upon a previous religion? In each case what did they retain? What did they change?

Which religions during the course of their subsequent history have been influenced perceptibly by religions other than those from which they branched off? In what respects?

Which religions during the course of their subsequent history have intermingled with other religions, and yet not been influenced thereby? Why not? With what results?

In which religions has there been a perceptible relapse from the ideals of the founder? In what respects?

In which religions has there been a perceptible advance upon the ideals of the founder? In what respects?

In which religions has there been conscious attempt at self-reformation? By whom? In what respects?

What advantages and what disadvantages have accrued to the religions in which sects have arisen?

What beliefs taught in the *Old Testament* are retained unchanged in Christianity? Which are rejected entirely? Which are modified, and how? What is there in the modern application of Christianity which is not taught specifically either in the *Old Testament* or in the *New*?

What verses in the *Bible* might be paralleled from other sacred scriptures?

What religious truths could a Christian learn from other religions which are not expressed or implied in Christianity?

What customary religious satisfactions would be lost to a member of each of the four Hindu castes who becomes a Christian? What new religious satisfactions would he gain?

What traditional advantages to the Japanese nation as a whole and to any section of it would be lost by the adoption of Christianity? What new advantages would be gained?

Which religion, when a person changes from it to Christianity, would require him to make the most changes in his religious beliefs and manner of life? Which religion would require the least change? What is the basis for your answer?

Which of his inherited religious beliefs would a Confucianist need to relinquish when he becomes a Christian? Which ones would he retain? What new ones would he acquire?

Answer the same three questions in the case of each of the other non-Christian religions.

What personal experiences in the life of Jesus Christ are paralleled in the lives of other founders of religions?

In what fundamental respects has the character of Jesus Christ been surpassed by any of the other founders of a religion in the previous twelve centuries, or in the subsequent fifteen centuries?

In what fundamental respects might the character of the founders of religions other than Christianity be improved upon?

In which religions does the conception of the Supreme Being contribute to a rich and helpful personal life? In what ways?

From a sociological point of view, which religions possess a concept of the human individual and of human society that promotes social progress? What is the basis for your answer?

Which religions would serve as a practical basis for a political democracy? Which religions would be inconsistent with democracy? Why do you think so?

Which essential elements in the various religions have produced perceptible results in the civilization of the different countries? In what respects?

How can a personally founded religion remain true to the principles of the founder, and yet keep abreast of changing conditions?

Which fundamental religious beliefs help to maintain a static type of civilization?

Which religions are likely to die? For what reasons?

What vital elements in any religion serve to keep it virile?

What are the elements which will enable a religion to become fully universal?

On what possible basis could another new religion be started?

INDEX

INDEX

Abbasid Caliphate, 239

Abhidhamma Pitaka, a Buddhist Scripture, 78

Abraham, Hebrew Patriarch, 180
and Islam, 234

Abu Bekr, Mohammed's Successor, 229, 239

Agamas, Jain Scriptures, 49

Ahimsa, Non-Injury, in Jainism, 52
in Hinduism, 52

Ahmadiyya, Islamic Sect, 241-242

Ahura Mazda (Ormazd), Supreme Being in Zoroastrianism, 201-207, 209-212, 265, 270, 283, 287

Aisha, a Wife of Mohammed, 225

Akalis, a Sikh Sect, 107

Al-Azhar, Islamic University in Cairo, 231

Al-Ghazali, Islamic Theologian, 242

Alexander the Great, 208-209, 234

Ali, Translator of *Koran*, 227

Ali, Son-in-law of Mohammed, 239-240, 272

Allah, Supreme Being in Islam, 223-225, 227, 229, 231-234, 236, 264, 272, 279
in Sikhism, 101

Almsgiving in Islam, 237

Ama-Terasu (*see* Sun-Goddess in Shinto)

Ameretat, a Good Spirit in Zoroastrianism, 212

Ames, Prof. Edward S., 7

Amesha Spentas, "Bountiful Immortals" in Zoroastrianism, 212

Amitabha, a Buddha, 71

Amos, Hebrew Prophet, 182-184, 189, 210

Analects, a Confucian Scripture, 120, 122-123, 126, 135, 277

Ancestor-Worship, in Confucianism, 126-127
in Taoism, 149

Andrae, 229

Angas, Jain Scriptures, 49-50, 83, 275

Angelology, in Islam, 230, 234
in Judaism, 200
in Zoroastrianism, 200, 208, 212, 216-217

Angra Mainyu (Ahriman), Devil in Zoroastrianism, 211, 265, 270

Animism, in Hinduism, 33
in Islam, 244
in Shinto, 176

Apocalypticism, in Judaism, 188
in Zoroastrianism, 217, 219, 282

Apocrypha, 246

Arberry, A. J., 242

Ardeshir I, Zoroastrian Monarch, 209

Arhat, "Blessed One" in Jainism, 47

Arjuna, a Hindu Knight, 30

Arnold, Sir Edwin, 29

Arnold, Matthew, 7

Arya Samaj, Hindu Reform Sect, 37, 62, 99

Asceticism, in Buddhism, 65, 82, 84, 279
in Hinduism, 82, 84, 93
in Islam, 242
in Jainism, 46-47, 51-52, 54, 58, 60, 82, 84, 265, 279
in Zoroastrianism, 218

Asha, a Good Spirit in Zoroastrianism, 204, 210, 212

Ashteroth, Semitic Goddesses, 181

Asoka, Buddhist Monarch, 55, 64, 80-81

Asramas, Four Stages in Hinduism, 29

Assyria, Dead Religion of, 13

Aston, W. G., 156-157, 159, 164-167, 169